Praise for *Employment Law (in Plain English)*®

"In *Employment Law (in Plain English)* Leonard and his coauthors apply their decades of experience practicing law along with Leonard's background in teaching to help the reader grasp often difficult, yet important, concepts in law. After reading this book, you will walk away with a clearer understanding of the laws in which we operate and live with every day."

—Doug Holt, CEO at the Biocybernaut Institute

"Leonard DuBoff and his coauthors have written a book which addresses a wide range of employment-related issues in a style easily accessible to employers, attorneys, and layman alike. As a practicing Administrative Law Judge, his work assists me in understanding all matters presented in each hearing by each participant, employer, judge, and claimant, and I deem it essential in aiding me to promulgate fair and just decisions."

—Courtney Paine Snider, State Appellate Administrative Law Judge

"*Employment Law (in Plain English)* couldn't be more valuable to small businesses needing to focus on product to stay competitive. Leonard DuBoff's Law Group has been a reliable resource for my company for decades. Their advice is practical, knowledgeable, and incredibly useful."

—Aimee Sunseri, Winemaker for New Clairvaux Vineyard and Nichelini Family Winery

"With Leonard DuBoff, and his coauthors, you get more than an attorney's knowledge. They reveal the education of a lifetime. In reading *Employment Law (In Plain English)*, you will have the greatest resource for any employer or employee. Think you already know employment law? Well, that is your first mistake. This book should be in every employer and employee's library."

—Nancy Stecher, business owner and employer since 2001

Employment Law

(in Plain English)®

Employment Law

(in Plain English)®

Leonard D. DuBoff, Christopher Perea, Kenneth A. Perea, *and* **Lauren Barnes**

Attorneys-at-Law

ALLWORTH PRESS
NEW YORK

25 24 23 22 21 5 4 3 2 1

Published by Allworth Press, an imprint of Skyhorse Publishing, Inc. 307 West 36th Street, 11th Floor, New York, NY 10018. Allworth Press® is a registered trademark of Skyhorse Publishing, Inc.®, a Delaware corporation.

www.allworth.com

Cover design by Mary Belibasakis

Library of Congress Cataloging-in-Publication Data is available on file.

Print ISBN: 978-1-62153-767-0
eBook ISBN: 978-1-62153-768-7

Printed in the United States of America

To my mother, Millicent, and my father, Rubin, who provided me with the gift of life and the desire to use that gift effectively. To my mother-in-law, Cumi Elena Crawford, for her faith, trust, and inspiration, and to my wife, Mary Ann, for her enduring love and continuing support.

—Leonard D. DuBoff

To my loving parents, Kenneth and Parletta, for their unending support and love on my journey through life. To my partner in crime, Lauren Barnes, for her trust, inspiration, and the constant reminder that "legalese" is not, in fact, plain English.

—Christopher Perea

To my mom and dad, Dot and Ed, and my father- and mother-in- law, Harold and Lois, members of the Greatest Generation, of whom I am eternally grateful and proud; to my wife, Parletta, whose love and strength make all things possible; and to our son, Chris, whose love, intelligence, and goodwill bring joy into our lives every day, this book is lovingly dedicated.

—Kenneth A. Perea

To my father, Bill Barnes, for supporting me and encouraging me to accomplish whatever I set my mind to, regardless of the challenges faced. To my partner, Chris Perea, for his constant love and encouragement, as well as for the many debates and brainstorming sessions on the finer points of the law.

—Lauren Barnes

Contents

Acknowledgments

In order to assemble the vast quantity of statutes, cases, articles, and books that are available in this field, it was necessary to enlist the aid of numerous friends and colleagues. Their help is greatly appreciated, and some deserve special recognition. I would, therefore, like to express my sincere thanks to my collaborator, Kenneth A. Perea, a prominent employment law arbitrator, for his extraordinary help with this book. He has sacrificed many evenings and weekends to bring this project to fruition.

We would also like to express our extreme gratitude to Lauren Barnes, Esq. and Christopher Perea, Esq., for the time they spent in reviewing the manuscript for this book, providing recommendations, and assisting us with writing numerous sections of this book. They too have sacrificed numerous days, nights, and weekends working on the manuscript.

I am also grateful for the skill that my college English professor Anne Louthan provided me at Hofstra University many years ago, which enabled me to write books such as this in plain English.

We are indebted to Tad Crawford of Skyhorse Publishing and his staff especially our two editors, Chamois Holschuh and Caroline Russomanno, for their help in publishing this volume. Thanks also to my paralegal Francesca Hurd for all of her assistance and numerous recommendations.

Christopher would like to thank his mother, Parletta, for reminding him that even great writers sometimes need help when it comes to spelling and punctuation. Christopher would also like to thank his coauthor Leonard DuBoff for the opportunity to work on and learn from this project.

Ken Perea acknowledges with gratitude and appreciation his colleague, Leonard D. DuBoff, whose legal insight, enhanced by many years of both teaching and practicing law, boundless energy, enthusiasm for each given day, and sharp intellect are both inspirational and a guiding light to all who have had the privilege of contributing to his book. While many fine lawyers may practice law and serve their clients well, counsel DuBoff, in the highest traditions of the legal profession, explains the law in plain and understandable language so that ordinary people may consult these pages, seek his wisdom, and preventatively avoid entanglement in the legal system.

Lauren would like to thank her father, Bill Barnes, and her brother, Connor Barnes, for not only supporting her throughout life, but also for challenging her to articulate her points clearly and to think critically. She would also like to thank her legal research and writing professor, Edward Harri, for the countless hours spent mentoring her to become not only a better writer, but also a better lawyer and person.

We are very grateful for the blurbs written by Aimee Sunseri, one of the most prominent winemakers in California while serving as winemaker for New Claivaux Vineyard and Nichelini Family Winery. We are also grateful for the endorsement from Courtney Paine, a respected State Appellate Administrate Law Judge who specializes in employment law cases. She is kind enough to acknowledge that she will rely on this book for many of her important decisions. We are also extremely pleased for the very complimentary blurb written by Doug Holt, CEO of Biocybernaut Institute. Mr. Holt's recognition of this book, given his prominence and the prominence of his international company, is truly flattering. The Biocybernaut US office is in Sedona, Arizona, and the company also has offices in Canada and Germany. Finally, we are also indebted to Nancy Stetcher for recommending this book to both Employers and Employees. Ms. Stetcher has operated one of the country's leading childcare centers in several locations in Oregon..

I am grateful for the support of my children and grandchildren. My son, Robert, and his wife, Sabrina Hunter, have been very helpful with technology issues, and my daughter, Colleen, has been extremely creative with her graphic design skills. Her husband, Rudy, a lawyer with The DuBoff Law Group, PC, has been very helpful with research. I am also grateful to my grandson, Brian, and his wife, Megan, for their personal assistance, and to the newest member of my family, my granddaughter, Athena, for her cheerfulness. I am also thankful for the love and support of my other grandchildren Taliek, Grant, and Tony. My brother, Michael Duboff, Esq., a New York attorney, was also helpful in gathering information for this book.

My late sister, Candise DuBoff Jones, JD, Northwestern School of Law, Lewis & Clark College, 1977; my late father, Rubin R. DuBoff; and my late mother, Millicent Barbara DuBoff, all provided me with the inspiration to create works such as this.

I valued my mother-in-law Cumi Elena Crawford's faith, trust, and inspiration, which helped me create this project. Also, the love, kindness, and encouragement of my grandfather Isidore and my grandmother Rose helped lay the foundation for my writing. Finally, I would like to express my sincere gratitude and acknowledge the contribution to this project by my partner in law and in life, Mary Ann Crawford DuBoff. Without her, *Employment Law (in Plain English)* would never have become a reality.

—Leonard D. DuBoff, Portland, Oregon

Introduction

Throughout my professional career as a law professor, and now as a practicing attorney, I have realized the importance of pre-problem counseling. This is especially true in the field of employment law, where many of the issues are complex and not usually understood by the individuals involved.

Employers and employees are often depicted as opposing teams in a tug-of-war. Nothing could be further from the truth. The individuals who are employed and those who employ them are allies, engaged in a mutually beneficial relationship. While there is a common interest shared by employers and employees, the legal issues encountered by each group are unique.

Our goal is to sensitize employers and employees to the law so that risky courses of conduct can be avoided and problems can be spotted at an early enough stage so as to minimize their ultimate impact on the success of the employment relationship.

Although there are a number of books available for employers and employees, there have been, until now, none in plain English. This book is intended to fill that void and provide a readable source of information.

My coauthor Kenneth A. Perea has been an employment arbitrator for more than thirty-one years, and before that he was an employment attorney. His extensive knowledge, experience, and skill in this field are unsurpassed. He has provided much of the information contained in this book, based on the thousands of cases he has handled in this field.

Christopher E. Perea has coauthored another book in this series and he too is a practicing attorney working on cases in this field. Christopher's skill and experience have contributed greatly to the quality of the material in this book.

This book begins by providing you with an analysis of the advertising process. It discusses what you should look for if you are searching for a job and what you should consider if you are advertising for employees. The book is intended to cover both employers' and employees' issues so that you will be able to understand both sides of every item discussed.

The book then follows the employment process from initial interview through hiring, including the numerous issues that may occur in the workplace. It discusses the many laws and cases that have defined the rights and obligations of both employers and employees.

It is intended to provide with you as much information as possible on all of the issues discussed, and it ends by considering unions and collective bargaining. This book also addresses the COVID-19 problem and some of the issues that employers must consider before reopening during the pandemic.

My coauthors and I have tried to present the most up-to-date analysis of the myriad of legal issues that employers and employees encounter in their day-to-day activities. This book is not intended to serve as a substitute for hiring an attorney; rather, it is designed to make you aware of the issues and options available in a host of common employment situations and to provide you with sufficient knowledge to enable you to communicate effectively with your attorney.

We sincerely hope that *Employment Law (in Plain English)*® continues the tradition established by the other books in this series of providing an accurate, up-to-date, and readable text for an important segment of the business community.

—Leonard D. DuBoff
Portland, Oregon, May 2020

CHAPTER 1

Advertising

A host of different issues arise in the context of advertising. When preparing an advertising program, it is essential for you to take care not to violate the rights of other businesses or individuals. Care should be taken to work with an attorney skilled in employment law in order to be assured of having an effective program that will enable you to advertise employment opportunities without exposing your business to potential liability. A poorly drafted employment advertisement is likely to result in problems for the advertiser. This chapter covers several important legal considerations that may arise when advertising for employment opportunities, whether the ad is for an individual to replace an employee or for a newly created position. We will provide information for both employers who prepare the ads and for individuals whom the ads are attempting to attract.

GOVERNMENT REGULATIONS

To begin with, a business may always tout the qualities of its products or services, but those representations must be true. If there are any misrepresentations contained in ads or promotions, the state or federal government may file a lawsuit to redress this wrong.

Most states have consumer protection laws that, among other things, impose fines and other legal sanctions on businesses that engage in misleading advertising. The state attorney general can cause an offending advertisement to be withdrawn and may even require corrective advertising. Similarly, the Federal Trade Commission (FTC) is involved in policing businesses that are engaged in interstate commerce. If your business activity extends beyond your state boundaries and either touches or affects another state, then the Federal Trade Commission has jurisdiction over your company. This is also true if you advertise over the web. Indeed, advertising online may subject your advertising to regulation throughout the world, and the laws of other countries may be quite different than those in the United States.

PUBLICITY AND PRIVACY

A company may use a celebrity to endorse its product, provided the celebrity consents to the endorsement. If not, the company may be liable to the celebrity for violating their right of publicity. This right is granted by the majority of states in the United States to those who commercially exploit their names, voices, or images, such as actors or singers. The use of a look-alike for commercial purposes may also be actionable. Thus, when manufacturers used look-alikes for Jackie Onassis, Woody Allen, and the rap group the Fat Boys, liability was imposed.

People who have not achieved notoriety because of their commercial activities may have a right of privacy and, thus, may have a claim if their names or likenesses are used in an advertisement without their permission. This applies even to employees. They must grant permission for their names, voices, or likenesses to be used for advertising purposes.

If an individual's photograph is not the focal point of the ad, but rather is merely an incidental part, such as a head in a crowd or a member of an audience, then an individual's permission may not be essential for the photograph to be used commercially.

Even though you may not be required to have permission from an individual before using their photograph, it is a good idea to get a signed photo release whenever possible. The release should be worded in such a way as to give your business permission to use the name and likeness or, where relevant, the person's voice, for any and all purposes, including advertising your business. This will protect you if, for example, the individual ultimately becomes popular and you wish to use the photos you obtained at an earlier date before the individual became a celebrity.

UNAUTHORIZED USE OF TRADEMARK

An advertiser may be permitted to use the name or logo of another business in its ad as long as there is no likelihood that the average viewer would believe that the ad was sponsored by the company whose name or logo you are using. For example, it would be permissible for you to have an ad for a baseball team contain a photo of individuals incidentally holding a distinctively shaped Coca-Cola bottle, as long as it is clear from the advertisement that the soft drink manufacturer is not sponsoring the ad. Similarly, an individual in your ad may be shown wearing Nike running shoes so long as it is clear that Nike is not involved in the ad.

UNAUTHORIZED USE OF COPYRIGHTED MATERIAL

An advertiser may not use copyrighted work of another without obtaining permission from the owner for that use, unless the use is a "fair use" under the copyright law. To begin with you should determine whether the item you wish to use in the ad is protected by copyright. Copyrighted material includes photos, pictures of all kinds, literature, music, phrases, animation, and every form of pictorial, graphic, and sculptural works.

IN PLAIN ENGLISH

The copyright law states that in order to determine whether a use would be considered a "fair use" it is necessary to consider at least the following four factors:

1. The nature of the use, that is whether the use is going to create something new.
2. The nature of the work, that is whether the work was intended to be copied. For example, quotes from a book of quotable quotes.
3. The extent of copying, that is whether all of the work is copied or only a small portion is used.
4. The effect the copying will have on a copyright owner's market—that is, will your use of the copy deprive the copyright owner of a sale?

In order to be protected by copyright, the item must also be original, creative, and not merely functional. Generally, material that is protected by copyright is identified by the word copyright, its abbreviation, or the symbol ©. Unfortunately, this is no longer a requirement under US law and it is not required by the laws of many other countries throughout the world. For this reason, it is not always clear whether the work is protected by copyright and, under the American copyright statute. If an individual relies on good faith on the fact that no copyright notice appears on a work, then that individual's use of that work without obtaining appropriate permission is defined as an innocent infringement. Innocent infringers may be permitted to continue using the work without permission and if liable for damages would be required to pay no more than $200. It is very likely that an innocent infringer would not wind up in litigation because the cost of a copyright lawsuit would likely exceed the amount the copyright owner could recover.

IN PLAIN ENGLISH

The term "liable for damages" means that if a lawsuit is filed, and it is ultimately completed by a trial, that a party to that lawsuit may be awarded some money, referred to as damages. In addition, if permitted by law, or contract, then the winner of the lawsuit may also be awarded reimbursement of the amount spent on attorney's fees. In the United States, the winner of a lawsuit is only permitted to recover the attorneys' fees incurred if the law involved in the lawsuit states that attorneys' fees are available or if the contract in dispute states that attorneys' fees are available.

If you desire to use material that might be protected by copyright, you should either obtain written permission to use that item from the copyright owner or the owner's representative. If you are not able to obtain permission, then you should consult an attorney in order to determine whether there is a possibility that your use would be considered "fair use."

One of the most complex areas of copyright law involves music. If you intend to use music in your ad then you should definitely consult your attorney before using music or lyrics from a song.

USE OF THE NAMES OR IMAGES OF PEOPLE IN ADVERTISEMENTS

If you desire to use the name or image of an individual in your ad, then you should obtain written permission from the individual for such use. Every individual has the right to protect the individual's name and likeness for the individual's entire life. Of course, if the individual's name is a common name such as Jones or Smith, then the individual would not be entitled to prevent the use of that name unless the individual can prove that the name used actually identifies that person.

If the individual is famous, such as an actor, sports figure, or politician, then the individual's name and likeness are protected for the individual's life and, in most states, for a significant period after the individual dies. Because the use of names and likenesses in advertisements can be complex, and because the rules in the United States differ from the rules in other countries, if your advertisement is online you should definitely consult with an experienced attorney before using any names or likenesses in your advertisements.

GEOGRAPHIC LOCATIONS

Geographic locations may also be used in advertisements without obtaining the owner's consent. It would be permissible for a company to advertise its product by having someone stand in front of a famous building, such as the Empire State Building or the Sears Tower, now known as the Willis Tower. Similarly, an automobile advertisement may show its vehicle streaking through a metropolitan area and passing several famous businesses.

This is so because items of utility are not copyrightable. Buildings, parks, and other landmarks may incidentally be used in advertising programs without the owner's permission. (However, it was held that a building that was architecturally unique, identifiable, and famous could enjoy the protection of the trade dress laws when it was prominently featured on a poster.)

ADVERTISING FOR NEWLY CREATED POSITIONS

If the position you are advertising to fill is newly created, then you should define the job to be performed to the best of your abilities and the requirements you believe are important for an individual to have in order to perform that job.

The ad should be as clear and unambiguous as possible. If special licensing requirements are necessary—for example if you are advertising for a medical doctor, accountant, lawyer, or professional engineer—then you should state that requirement in the ad, because you would not want to waste your time and that of applicants in reviewing applications from unqualified individuals.

Rarely, if ever, should an ad contain the salary being offered, because that is something that should be discussed at the initial interview. You should also specify whether the position in full-time or part-time.

If there are any other special requirements that you believe are necessary for the newly created position, then those requirements should be spelled out in the ad as well. If you do not feel comfortable preparing an ad, then there are companies that specialize in creating advertisements, though they generally charge a significant fee for their services. You can find such companies with a Google search.

ADVERTISING FOR REPLACEMENT OF EXISTING EMPLOYEES

An ad for replacement of an existing employee is very similar to an ad for a newly created position. Though in this situation you should have a better understanding of the work to be performed and the qualifications necessary to do that job. It should therefore be easier to prepare this ad, because you will likely know the type of person who can do the job and you should be able to prepare this ad a lot faster. You may also have a copy of the ad you or your business used when advertising for the person you are trying to replace. If so, you can merely update that advertisement.

WHERE TO ADVERTISE

Historically, businesses advertised for positions in newspapers and magazines. The newspaper ads were customarily in local newspapers so that individuals residing near the business would be attracted by those ads. In addition, advertising in professional publications would also attract applications from individuals in the desired profession.

Word of mouth in a particular location or profession has always been a method by which individuals could learn about an available position. This form of advertising will always be available, because individuals will always spread the word that a job in a particular field or with a particular business is available.

Today, virtually everything occurs online, and advertising for a job opening is no exception. The fact that advertising online is inexpensive, easy to accomplish, and available worldwide makes it the ideal way to advertise.

Virtually every business has its own website, and placing an ad on that website is an excellent starting point for finding an employee. Your business's website should have a section devoted to job availability so that individuals who are interested in working for your business will be able to periodically check that section in order to determine when a position is available.

In addition to having the advertisement on your businesses website, you may also wish to have it appear on other sites so that the ad reaches a greater number of possible applicants. Most local newspapers and professional journals have an online presence. Of course, there will likely be a charge for using those sites, so you should determine which of them will best serve your business's needs in order to obtain the maximum exposure for your ad while keeping costs down. Because there are a huge number of possible sites for your ad, you should determine which ones will provide you with the best opportunity to obtain the applicants you are interested in interviewing, while spending the least amount of money on the advertisements.

WORKING WITH EMPLOYMENT AGENCIES AND HEADHUNTERS

If your business is not equipped to advertise for new employees on its own, or if it urgently needs those employees, then it can work with an employment agency. In addition, employment agencies generally screen potential employees so that your business will not have to spend the time and devote resources to that portion of the interview process.

There is a cost involved in working with employment agencies. If, however, the agency advertises for the position, screens prospective applicants, and merely provides your business with a group of qualified applicants, the cost may be lower than what your business would spend conducting the same procedure.

Agencies frequently guarantee that if the applicant they provide is hired and within a prescribed period of time that individual is not working out, then the agency will provide a replacement free of charge or for a reduced rate. If you plan to work with an employment agency, you should negotiate the terms of the arrangement first. In this way you will know the cost, the probationary period, and whether the agency will replace the employee without charge or for a reduced charge.

If you have an ongoing relationship with an employment agency, then it is likely to be able to respond to your company's requests more rapidly than if you merely contact an agency for the first time. Frequently employment agencies make cold calls on companies in order to determine whether the business is looking for new employees. It is a good idea to establish a relationship with an employment agency even before your company actually needs to work with it. In this way, your company can negotiate an acceptable arrangement while it is not under time pressure.

In addition to employment agencies, there are "headhunters." These individuals are usually employed for the purpose of finding professionals such as doctors, lawyers, engineers, technicians, accountants, and the like. The headhunter will generally contact the desired professional and determine whether that professional would be interested in finding a new position. If the professional is willing to consider a new opportunity, then the headhunter will interview the professional to find out what is desired regarding salary, title, location, benefits, and any special needs that professional may have. The headhunter will then search for a position that comes closest to meeting those requirements. The headhunter may be paid by the professional or the business that hires that professional.

If you are approached by a headhunter, then you should determine who will be paying for the headhunter's service. If you are the professional who is approached by the headhunter, then you would certainly want to have your new employer pay the headhunter's fees. If, on the other hand, you are the prospective employer, then you should decide whether paying the headhunter's fee is acceptable or whether you would prefer to have those fees paid by the prospective employee or divided between the employer and employee. No matter which arrangement you prefer, you should determine it before making any commitment and you should have the arrangement confirmed in writing. The writing should also contain other terms such as whether the headhunter will be required to find a new position for the professional if the one selected does not work out. If this is agreed to, then the period within which the replacement position will be provided should be specified.

Employers who work with headhunters should also consider requiring the headhunter to guarantee that if the professional does not work out within a prescribed period of time, then the headhunter will either provide a replacement professional or refund all or a significant part of the fee paid.

By doing an online search for employment agencies, you will be able to find the best employment agencies in your location. If you are interested in finding headhunters, a Google search can provide you with a number of them and additional information about the process of working with them as well.

POTENTIAL EMPLOYEE CONSIDERATIONS

Individuals who are interested in working for a company may research the company online before the interview in order to determine the company's reputation, mission statement, overall atmosphere, number of other employees, and whether the company has experienced any positive or negative situations. It is a good idea to research a business before applying for a position and before an interview. In this way, you will be able to determine whether that business is one that you would be comfortable working for. By checking out the business before an interview, you will be able to know a great deal about the business, and you will be prepared to ask the interviewer appropriate questions so that you can find out whether the position is likely to work for you.

Because prospective employees may very well check online, it is important for companies to have websites that showcase the business as effectively as possible.

CONCLUSION

The benefits of advertising are clear; yet, if not done properly, the detriments can be significant. This is particularly true today with the advent of inexpensive online advertising. Care must be taken to comply with the laws of every jurisdiction into which an advertisement may be launched. By working with an experienced business lawyer, you will reduce your business's potential exposure.

CHAPTER 2

Interviewing, Hiring, and Other Preemployment Considerations

In this chapter we consider several items that employers should keep in mind when interviewing and hiring new employees. Additionally, we will discuss several matters that applicants for employment should be aware of to ensure their legal rights are not being violated. It should be noted that when discussing requirements employers must comply with under federal law during the hiring process, employees should be similarly informed of these requirements. This is because an employer's failure to comply with federal laws regulating the hiring process gives rise to an applicant's right to enforce those laws through appropriate administrative or other means.

EMPLOYMENT APPLICATIONS, INTERVIEWS, AND DRUG TESTING—QUESTIONS EMPLOYERS CAN AND CANNOT ASK

Job applications and applicant interviews are foundational to formation of successful, long-term employer-employee relationships from the mutual perspectives of both employers and employees alike. Care, however, must be exercised by employers in both the design and use of legally compliant employment application forms as well as the conduct of interviews of candidates. Failure to carefully craft the employment application and interview questions ensures entanglement in a web of laws and regulations at the federal, state, and local levels of government designed to protect the rights of persons seeking employment. Whenever engaging in the hiring of employees, employers would be well advised to err on the side of caution and seek advice from qualified professionals including legal counsel, always being mindful of the inherent imbalance of power between employers and employee applicants.

While by no means exhaustive, the following guidelines, drawn from federal laws prohibiting discrimination in employment, may hopefully assist employers to avoid the potentially costly consequences of asking prohibited questions on employment applications or during job interviews. These types of questions have been found directly or indirectly to violate federal laws and regulations by revealing an applicant's membership in a protected class of individuals (described later in this chapter).

As will become apparent from careful reading of the following examples, whether a question posed to a candidate during the interview process is lawful or unlawful depends largely on the way the question is asked by the employer. A knowledgeable employer may thus legally craft questions in both application forms and during interviews that produce relevant information necessary to the evaluation of candidates' qualifications for employment. If, however, unartfully asked, the question posed to applicants may be found to be unlawful. Such mistakes can result in financially harmful consequences to the employer.

It must also be noted that when seeking to hire an employee, uniform employment applications should be utilized. Likewise, when interviewing candidates, a uniform set of interview questions should be prepared in writing and in advance of the interview. Because both application forms and interview questions should be prepared in advance of all interviews, it would be wise for employers to consult legal counsel to review their content in advance of their use to ensure they are compliant with all laws at the federal, state, and local level.

Also, when conducting in-person, telephonic, or video interviews of applicants, the best practice is to have a panel of three or more qualified individuals, diverse in both fields of expertise and demographics, conduct the interviews. The individual members of the panel should then independently score/evaluate all candidates on a uniform form containing the various qualifications for the position to be filled. A qualified interview panel ensures there are several witnesses present throughout the interview process, avoiding a "he said, she said" issue should a candidate challenge his unsuccessful candidacy for employment. Additionally, the use of a panel results in a more objective assessment by means of the panel's consolidated scoring of each candidate's qualifications.

Like all other aspects of the employment relationship, an employer's hiring process must be free from discrimination under all applicable federal, state, and local employment laws. In order to be nondiscriminatory, employers may not ask applicants questions that would reveal characteristics protected under various federal laws, such as race, color, age, national origin, religion, sex, veteran status/military status, disability or genetic information. Furthermore, many states and local jurisdictions protect both employment applicants as well as current employees based on these characteristics. Employers are well advised to check state and local laws in their jurisdiction to ensure they are compliant with those requirements as well.

FEDERAL LAWS PROHIBITING JOB DISCRIMINATION

As mentioned above, there are numerous federal laws that prohibit discrimination in employment, discussed more fully in Chapter 9. These laws are foundational to the development of lawful employment applications and interviews of candidates. The federal laws applicable to the hiring process are as follows:

- Title VII of the Civil Rights Act of 1964 (Title VII), which prohibits employment discrimination based on race, color, religion, sex, or national origin;
- The Equal Pay Act of 1963 (EPA), which protects men and women who perform substantially equal work in the same establishment from sex-based wage discrimination;
- The Age Discrimination in Employment Act of 1967 (ADEA), which protects individuals who are forty years of age or older;
- Titles I and V of the Americans with Disabilities Act of 1990, as amended (ADA), which prohibit employment discrimination against qualified individuals with disabilities in the private sector, and in state and local governments as well;

- Sections 501 and 505 of the Rehabilitation Act of 1973, which prohibit discrimination against qualified individuals with disabilities who work in the federal government;
- Title II of the Genetic Information Nondiscrimination Act of 2008 (GINA), which prohibits employment discrimination based on genetic information about an applicant, employee, or former employee; and
- The Civil Rights Act of 1991, which, among other things, provides monetary damages in cases of intentional employment discrimination.

The US Equal Employment Opportunity Commission (EEOC) enforces the foregoing federal laws. EEOC also provides oversight and coordination of all federal equal employment opportunity regulations, practices, and policies. Following the COVID-19 crisis in early 2020, EEOC has provided significant guidance on its impact upon both the ADA, the Rehabilitation Act and other EEO laws as employees return to work. EEOC's guidance in these emerging areas of the law will be discussed in Chapter 9 of this book.

We will now discuss how these federal laws and regulations impact applications and interviews for employment.

EMPLOYMENT APPLICATIONS AND INTERVIEWS

Employment applications and interviews, when properly designed and administered, should provide the employer an opportunity to make specific inquiries into an applicant's work and educational history in a standardized, nondiscriminatory format. An objective and uniform collection of employment data from applicants is beneficial to an employer. With the data collected it should become relatively easier to identify those candidates who meet the minimum qualifications for the position, and which candidate, in particular, is the strongest in those areas most desirable to the employer.

Note that even if a candidate has provided a potential employer with a résumé, the candidate should still be required to submit a completed employment application form. This is because the latter, if properly designed by the employer, will draw out additional and relevant information an applicant may not have included on their résumé. Employment applications must, however, be carefully worded to comply with the before-mentioned federal, state, and local laws.

Examples of What to *Exclude* from Employment Application Forms—Pursuant to Federal Law

Employers must avoid certain questions on application forms, particularly those that may even unintentionally reveal whether the applicant is a member of a protected class of persons under federal laws. It is also important to avoid any questions on employment applications that may either directly or indirectly reveal, or could even be perceived as a dislike for, a protected characteristic. The following five areas—Citizenship, Gender, Age, Salary History and Disability—are examples of areas to avoid:

Citizenship. Because discrimination based on national origin is illegal, questions about a person's citizenship may reflect perceived discrimination based on national origin. Furthermore, because citizens of other countries are legally able to work in the United States after meeting certain immigration requirements, employers should not ask whether an applicant is a US citizen. To avoid potential problems in this area, an employer may simply ask whether an applicant is legally authorized to work in the United States (this is discussed more fully in Chapter 8).

Gender. Because gender discrimination is illegal, it is also unlawful to use a different standard when evaluating a female applicant versus a male applicant. Questions that reveal the applicant's sex, marital status, number or ages of children or dependents, or provisions for childcare, as well as questions concerning pregnancy, childbearing, or birth control are legally prohibited.

Age. Because discrimination against persons who are forty years of age or older is unlawful, employment application questions that request a person's age, date of birth, or date of high school graduation should be avoided. Alternatively, an employer may simply ask whether an applicant is at least eighteen years of age or possesses the necessary work permits to work for the employer. Many states also prohibit discrimination on the basis of age with some even providing similar protections to workers younger than forty. If, however, there are minimum age requirement for a job in order to comply with a law or for insurance purposes, an employer is permitted to ask whether an applicant meets those age requirements.

Salary History. Because salary history may reflect past discriminatory practices of an applicant's prior employers, questions concerning an applicant's salary history may perpetuate those discriminatory offenses. Employers subject to laws prohibiting discriminatory practices at either the federal or state levels should therefore remove salary history questions from their employment application forms and train managers responsible for conducting applicant interviews to similarly avoid these types of questions during the interview. Employers are, however, legally permitted to provide a candidate with the starting salary or salary range for the position being interviewed for and inquire whether it would be acceptable to a candidate if offered the position. Before advising a candidate of the starting salary for the position being interviewed for and inquiring whether it would be acceptable, it would be wise to first admonish the applicant not to reveal their salary history when answering the question.

Disability. Discrimination based upon disability or even perceived disability is prohibited by law. Therefore, employment application questions about disabilities, medical treatment, medications taken, addictions, or the amount of sick leave taken in his last position are generally not permitted.

Finally, in rare circumstances, such as when an employer is a federal contractor and may thus be subject to certain federal regulations, such employers may be required to inquire concerning an applicant's race, ethnicity, gender, veteran status, disability, or other protected characteristic in order to promote and monitor equal employment opportunities. A pre-offer invitation to self-identify the foregoing characteristics may therefore be included in the federal contractor's application materials for a position, but must be thereafter maintained separately from the all other application materials.

Additional Information to *Exclude* from Application Forms and Interviews

Criminal Conviction Inquiries. Several states and local jurisdictions expressly prohibit employers from asking about criminal convictions on employment applications, and may also require employers to wait until after a conditional offer of employment has been made before making such inquiries. Additionally, EEOC has at least taken the position that employers should avoid asking about criminal histories on employment applications. EEOC's rationale for this prohibition is that an employer is more likely to objectively assess the relevance of an applicant's conviction if it becomes known only after the employer has already vetted the applicant's qualifications and experience. Following disclosure of any criminal convictions after a conditional offer of employment has been made, however, an employer may decline to hire the convicted applicant.

Social Security Number. While federal law does not prohibit employers from asking for a Social Security number on employment applications, it is not considered a best practice because of the threat of identity theft and other privacy concerns. Note that some states have enacted laws with specific requirements for protecting individuals' Social Security numbers. Ensure your business practices are in compliance with such state laws whenever applicable.

Information to Be *Included* on Employment Applications

Employment applications should include the following job-related components:

Availability. In this section, applicants should be asked to list their availability, such as full-time, part-time, and coverage for certain shifts if necessary, to make sure the applicant's availability is in line with its staffing needs.

Job History. In this section, applicants should be asked to provide current and previous positions held, length of employment at each job, and the reasons for leaving each previous job.

Education and Professional Designations. In this section, applicants should be asked to provide any degrees earned, the names of the institutions attended, and whenever applicable, any professional licenses and certifications currently held.

References. This section of the employment application requests applicants to provide a list of references.

Attestation. This is a statement the applicant signs attesting to the truthfulness and completeness of the information provided on his employment application. Employers should consider including language that it may take disciplinary action, up to and including termination of employment, at any time, should any of the information provided prove to be false or misleading.

IN PLAIN ENGLISH

Attestation is a legal acknowledgment of the truth and accuracy of a document as well as to any answers to questions contained in that document. It also confirms that a proper process was followed with respect to the document.

"At-Will" Statement. It is a best practice to include an "at-will" statement above the signature line to provide the applicant with notice that either the employer or the employee can terminate the employment relationship at any time, with or without notice, and for any lawful or no reason at all. While most states recognize employment is at will, many states also recognize exceptions to that general rule based upon various public policy exceptions. Because this area of law is evolving, both employers and employees alike are well advised to seek legal counsel in their state jurisdictions before acting.

EEO Statement. It is advisable that every application for employment include a statement that the company is an equal opportunity employer ("EEO statement"). This statement advises applicants that the employer's recruiting and hiring practices are based solely on job-related criteria and that it does not discriminate on the basis of an applicant's membership in any federal, state, or locally protected class of protected individuals.

Conclusions on Applications and Interviews for Employment

Employment applications and interviews are essential components of the hiring process. But it is also important that the application for employment and questions asked during interviews are carefully drafted and comply with all relevant federal, state, and local requirements.

An employer would be well advised to first prepare drafts of both an application form and a uniform set of questions to be asked of each job applicant when interviewed. The drafts should then be reviewed by an employment attorney to determine whether they are designed to reveal only lawful, job-related information and that no questions are unlawful or improper. Should errors be found in the drafts reviewed, legal counsel should be asked to revise wherever necessary in order to be legally compliant. Then, during the hiring process, the employer should adhere to the legally approved application form and written list of prepared questions uniformly with each candidate considered for hire.

Should, however, a candidate unexpectedly volunteer information concerning protected status, the employer should immediately redirect the interview to elicit only job-related information that will be helpful in assessing whether the candidate is qualified for the position. It is important to not use the volunteered information concerning protected status when making employment decisions.

DRUG SCREENING TESTS

By now everyone recognizes that many employers, usually during the final stages of the hiring process, require applicants to submit to drug screen testing, administered by independent and certified drug test laboratories that the employer pays for. Many job applicants, however, may feel uncomfortable submitting their bodily fluids to such testing and feel the drug screen tests themselves are unduly intrusive into areas of personal privacy concerning their activities during off-duty hours. Applicants may also object to the methodologies used in administering such tests including requiring them to provide, under supervision, a urine sample. While such testing was frequently challenged in both courts and before arbitrators in the 1980s as employers began with greater frequency to administer drug screen tests to both applicants for employment as well as members of their workforce, at this late stage it has become clear employers have the right, when exercised properly, to do so. The applicant's options are thus limited to the following: (1) the applicant can either comply with the employer's legitimate requirement and undergo a drug screen test; or (2) withdraw his application for employment from further consideration by the employer. Existing employees likewise face a Hobson's choice in this regard: (1) submit to drug screen testing that may be periodic, random or for cause following certain events in the workplace such as an industrial accident; or (2) be terminated from their employment due to insubordination in refusing to do so. Still, applicants for employment and even existing employees may reasonably question why it is necessary that employers require them to submit to drug screen testing at all.

The answer to this question is twofold. In a few limited industries which are particularly safety sensitive employers are required by laws and regulations to require applicants for certain jobs, such as those requiring a commercial drivers' license in order to operate heavy vehicles, to undergo drug and alcohol screen testing. Also, other employers regulated by such federal agencies as Federal Highway Administration, Federal Aviation Administration, and the U.S. Coast Guard are required by law to perform such tests. Thus, employers in the trucking, aviation, and mass transit industries, as well as employers who contract to perform services for the Department of Defense and NASA, simply have no choice other than to require drug screen testing of applicants seeking employment with them.

Still other employers who are not required by either law or regulation to require applicants for employment to undergo drug screen testing voluntarily choose to do so. The reasons for their decision in this regard are primarily economic in nature. Employers are required by state laws to carry workers' compensation insurance thereby providing a forum for relief to those members of their workforce who are unfortunately injured while working on the job. Those insurance carriers who offer to provide workers' compensation insurance to employers, however, may offer employers substantial discounts in premium paid when the employer voluntarily implements policies to maintain drug-free workplaces, including requirements to drug screen test all applicants for employment. Also, employers will likely want to limit their exposure to liability for personal injury due to workplace accidents both to their workers and members of the public who may be physically harmed by an employee during performance of duties within the scope of their work. If, however, it is found an employee involved in such a work-related accident was under the influence of drugs or alcohol at the time of the injury, the employer's exposure to liability is increased and may result in substantial judgments against it. Finally, numerous studies have conclusively demonstrated the financial losses to employers resulting from drug and alcohol use by their employees in the forms of (1) lost productivity, (2) increased absenteeism and tardiness, and (3) increased workplace injuries and resulting workers' compensations claims all result in increased production costs and diminished profitability.

While employers thus have the right to administer drug screen tests to its applicants for employment and existing workforce, as with most situations in the workplace its right to do so is not unlimited. What then are the outer limits of employers' right to conduct drug screen testing?

Both courts and state legislatures have recognized that drug testing by its very nature does impact the privacy rights of both current employees and applicants for employment. It is recognized that when an employee or applicant submits to drug screen testing, the results may reveal things in addition to whether the person tested is currently under the influence of drugs. This is because the science of drug screen tests reveals the metabolites of certain drugs, which are compounds excreted by the liver due to processing the drugs that have been ingested, are present in the urine of the person being tested. The test results thus reveal whether a person has used the drug tested for at some undetermined time in the past. The test results furthermore determine the quantity of the metabolites which are present in the urine. But that quantity of metabolites found is also unable to determine with any degree of accuracy when the drug was ingested or whether at the time of submitting a urine sample for testing the applicant or current employee was impaired from fully performing the duties of his job. Such drug screen testing may furthermore reveal the use of legal, prescribed medications which in turn may be indicative of various medical conditions that the employee or applicant would rather the employer not know about.

Also, state and federal laws may place some limitations on when, how and under what circumstances drug screen testing may be performed. Because these tests require the collection of bodily fluids, usually urine, and often under controlled and supervised conditions, the manner in which these tests are performed may raise legitimate issues of personal privacy. Because the law recognizes that current employees enjoy greater rights in their continued employment than is recognized by an applicant for employment, the former's rights are generally greater than the latter's in this area of the law.

Drug screen testing can give rise to a claim of disability discrimination. As noted above, drug screen testing can reveal the presence of drugs that may be legal and lawfully prescribed as medication for a medical condition. Thus, if an applicant for employment is denied employment due to the presence of a lawfully prescribed medication used in treating a disability, denial of employment on that grounds may be a violation of the ADA and the employer found liable for back pay.

An employer must also be careful in the manner in which it administers drug screen testing. If it is found the employer's practice is to administer drug screen testing only to certain groups of applicants or employees based on their race or other protected classifications, the employer may well be found to have unlawfully discriminated in the hiring or termination of those persons based on prohibited grounds.

The manner and limitations on drug screen testing have been fertile ground for state legislatures to regulate through statute. Does your state permit drug screen testing of applicants for employment at any time in the hiring process or only once a conditional offer of employment is made? Does your state permit drug screen testing of employee only if management and supervisors also submit to such testing? Does your state require if an employer conducts drug screen testing that it must advise job applicants by written notice or on the written application form of such a requirement to do so? To obtain the answers to these questions and many more applicable to the particular state in which you are located, you would be well advised to consult competent legal counsel.

Rules and attitudes concerning the use of marijuana have evolved considerably over the years. While still illegal under federal law, use of both medical and recreational marijuana has increasingly become lawful under many state laws. While at one time drug screen tests that showed the presence of the metabolite for marijuana in a urine sample above a specified cutoff level was considered legitimate grounds for denying employment or even terminating the employment of a current employee, the legalization at the state level of marijuana has caused many to rethink that result and question whether those standards should be continued.

At least the courts, however, seem to confirm an employer can deny employment to applicants who test positive for use of marijuana due to the presence of its metabolites in urine samples. The California Supreme Court, for example, has ruled that despite a state law allowing medical use of marijuana, that law applies only to bar criminal prosecution and not for purposes of prohibiting employers from denying employment to applicants for employment. Similarly, the Colorado Supreme Court has permitted an employer to terminate the employment of an employee who tested positive for marijuana even though it was ingested for medical reasons during off-duty hours.

At this point only a few states have specifically prohibited an employer from discriminatorily terminating the employment of an employee or denying employment to an applicant for use of medically prescribed marijuana. Because this is a rapidly emerging area of employment law and is specific to each state, those concerned should consult with competent counsel whenever assessing their legal rights and responsibilities.

During the hiring process, many employers require applicants for employment to take a drug screen test, usually once an applicant reaches the final stages of the process. Applicants may ask why employers require drug screen testing of them in the first place. Applicants may also question whether they must agree to take such tests. Applicants may furthermore ask whether they possess any legal rights in the drug screening process. This section of Chapter 2 will answer the foregoing questions and briefly explain the rules applicable to drug screen testing.

The Legal Limits on Drug Screen Testing

Courts and legislatures, however, are not unmindful of the reality that drug screen testing impinges upon applicants' rights of privacy. Drug screen tests do not reveal an applicant's current drug use or level of job impairment at the time administered. Drug tests, typically administered pursuant to a urine samples provided by an applicant, test for the level of certain metabolites, which are intermediate substances produced by human metabolism, found in the sample examined as ingested drugs are metabolized in the liver and then excreted into the applicant's urine. Drug screen tests therefore are only indicative that certain drugs were used at some unspecified time in the past, and may also include even the ingestion of legally prescribed medications and drug use on the employee's own time and while away from the employer's workplace. Adding to their invasiveness, drug screen testing procedures require the applicant or employee to surrender bodily fluids, such as blood or more commonly urine, oftentimes under the close supervision of another person in order to avoid specimen tampering by the applicant or employee taking the drug screen test.

Because drug screen testing is unavoidably invasive to one's privacy, some state and federal laws have placed restrictions on when, how, and whether it can be done. Generally, current employees have greater legal rights in this gray area of the law than do applicants for employment. This distinction is based on the premise that employees hold greater vested interests in their employment, which could be lost should they test positive for drugs. Job applicants, on the other hand, merely stand to lose a lesser interest in potential employment should they test positive for drugs.

Prospective employers, however, cannot force a job applicant to take a drug test. Prospective employers can, however, require an applicant for employment to take a drug test and pass the test as a precondition of their employment so long as they follow minimal rules when doing so. If a job applicant does not wish to take a drug screen test, however, the applicant is legally permitted to decline from doing so but will thereby remove the applicant from further consideration by an employer.

The following are some of the legal limits that may apply to applicant drug screen testing:

Some prescribed medications turn up during drug screen testing and some drugs that would otherwise be illegal (such as opiates) are legitimately prescribed for certain medical conditions. If an applicant for employment is turned down from employment because of a positive drug screen test due to these drugs, and the applicant's medication was legally prescribed for a disability, the employer could become financially liable for the consequences. Before administering a drug screen test, employers (or more precisely the testing laboratory they have contracted with to administer testing) should require an applicant to disclose in writing any prescribed medications currently being taken.

If an employer singles out certain groups of applicants, for example, by race or disability for drug testing, it could face discrimination claims under federal law. Where testing is permitted, it may be legally permissible for an employer to single out certain job classifications for testing (such as applicants for safety-sensitive positions). The employer, however, must uniformly test all applicants for those safety-sensitive positions in the same manner.

Violation of state-required procedures. Although virtually all states allow applicant drug screen testing, many impose procedural and other requirements on employers when they do so. For example, some states allow a drug screen test only after the applicant has received a conditional offer of employment pending passage of a drug screen test. A number of states also require employers who administer drug screen tests to provide written notification of such to applicants or indicate on job postings that such testing is required by the employer.

Invasion of privacy. Even when drug testing is otherwise permitted, an applicant's privacy rights may be still be violated due to the manner in which the test is administered. Requiring an applicant to disrobe while in the presence of someone and providing a urine sample, for example, may be a violation of the applicant's privacy rights.

Medical and Recreational Marijuana

More than twenty states currently allow residents to use marijuana for medical purposes. Also, eleven states currently allow residents to use marijuana recreationally. "Medical marijuana" or "compassionate use" laws typically require the user to have a written doctor's authorization to use marijuana, often for particular diseases or disabilities. If a patient meets the criteria, that patient cannot be prosecuted under state law for crimes relating to the use, possession, or cultivation of a specified quantity of marijuana. Federal drug laws, however, still apply.

If an applicant lives in one of these states and has a valid prescription for marijuana used for medical purposes or resides in a state where recreational use has been legalized, the applicant may ask whether an employer can refuse employment based on a positive drug screen test for this legally prescribed drug. So far at least, in most states, the answer appears to be "yes." The California Supreme Court, for example, has ruled that the state's medical marijuana law applies only to criminal prosecution and not to any workplace prohibitions. Likewise, the Colorado Supreme Court has also held that an employer may terminate an employee for off-duty use of medical marijuana, even though the use was lawful under Colorado state law.

A handful of states, however, have passed specific laws prohibiting an employer from discriminating against an employee or applicant for their lawful use of medical marijuana or requiring an employer to reasonably accommodate such employees in the workplace. This area of law is relatively new, however, and in all cases dealing with use of marijuana and applications for employment, legal counsel should be consulted to determine the applicable state laws.

GENETIC INFORMATION NONDISCRIMINATION ACT (GINA)

In passing the Genetic Information Nondiscrimination Act (GINA) of 2008, Congress noted the advances in genetics that have opened new opportunities for medical progress. Those advances include the early detection of illnesses, the ability to take steps to reduce the likelihood individuals will contract a particular disorder, and the development of better therapies that are more effective against disease or have fewer side effects than current treatments. Congress observed, however, these advances have also given rise to the potential misuse of genetic information to discriminate in health insurance and employment opportunities. As noted by Congress, the current explosion in the science of genetics, and the history of sterilization laws by the states based on early genetic science, compelled Congressional action in this area.

Furthermore, it was noted that Congress had already been informed of examples of genetic discrimination in the workplace. These include the use of preemployment genetic screening at Lawrence Berkeley Laboratory, which led to a court decision in favor of the employees in *Norman-Bloodsaw v. Lawrence Berkeley Laboratory* (135 F.3d 1260, 1269 (9th Cir. 1998)). Congress thus concluded it clearly had a compelling public interest in relieving the fear of discrimination and in prohibiting its actual practice in employment and health insurance.

The EEOC enforces GINA's Title II provisions dealing with genetic discrimination in employment. Title II of GINA prohibits genetic information discrimination in employment.

Pursuant to GINA, employers are prohibited from (1) discriminating based on genetic information in hiring, firing, and other employment actions, and (2) requesting, requiring, or purchasing genetic information with respect to employees or family members of employees.

Limited exceptions to the foregoing prohibitions are provided by GINA for purposes of monitoring compliance with Occupational Safety and Health Act (OSHA), Federal Mine Safety and Health Act, or Family Medical Leave Act (FMLA) requirements.

Under GINA, it is illegal for employers to discriminate against employees or employment applicants because of their genetic information. GINA thus prohibits the use of genetic information in making employment decisions, restricts employers, and other covered entities, including employment agencies, labor unions, and joint labor-management training and apprenticeship programs, from requesting, requiring, or purchasing genetic information, and strictly limits disclosure of genetic information.

Genetic Information Defined

Genetic information includes information about an individual's genetic tests and the genetic tests of an individual's family members, as well as information about the manifestation of a disease or disorder in an individual's family members (i.e., family medical history). Family medical history is included in the definition of genetic information because that information can be used to determine whether someone has an increased risk of getting a disease, disorder, or condition in the future. Genetic information also includes an individual's request for, or receipt of, genetic services, or the participation in clinical research that includes genetic services by the individual or a family member of the individual, and the genetic information of a fetus carried by an individual or by a pregnant woman who is a family member of the individual and the genetic information of any embryo legally held by the individual or family member using assisted reproductive technology.

IN PLAIN ENGLISH

While the term "genetic information" is quite complex and the legal definition is very technical, in plain English this deals with the traits that are transmitted from one generation to another.

Discrimination under GINA

GINA forbids discrimination on the basis of genetic information when it comes to any aspect of employment, including hiring, firing, pay, job assignments, promotions, layoffs, training, fringe benefits, or any other term or condition of employment. An employer may never use genetic information to make an employment decision because genetic information is not relevant to an individual's current ability to work. Under GINA, it is also illegal to "retaliate" against an applicant or employee for filing a charge of discrimination, for participating in a discrimination proceeding (such as a discrimination investigation or lawsuit), or for otherwise opposing discrimination.

Harassment under GINA

It is also illegal under GINA to harass a person because of that individual's genetic information. Harassment can include making offensive or derogatory remarks about an applicant or employee's genetic information, or about the genetic information of a relative of the applicant or employee. Although GINA does not prohibit simple teasing, offhand comments, or isolated incidents that are not sufficiently serious, harassment is illegal when it is so severe or pervasive that it creates a hostile or offensive work environment or when it results in an adverse employment decision (such as the employee being fired or demoted). The harasser can be the victim's supervisor, a supervisor in another area of the workplace, a coworker, or someone who is not an employee, such as a client or customer of the employer.

Exceptions to Prohibition against Obtaining Genetic Information

It will usually be unlawful for an employer to obtain genetic information. There are, however, six narrow exceptions to this prohibition as follows:

- Inadvertent acquisitions of genetic information do not violate GINA, such as in situations where a manager or supervisor overhears someone talking about a family member's illness;

- Genetic information (such as family medical history) may be obtained as part of health or genetic services, including wellness programs, offered by the employer on a voluntary basis, if certain specific requirements are met;
- Family medical history may be acquired as part of the certification process for FMLA leave (or leave under similar state or local laws or pursuant to an employer policy), where an employee is asking for leave to care for a family member with a serious health condition;
- Genetic information may be acquired through commercially and publicly available documents like newspapers, as long as the employer is not searching those sources with the intent of finding genetic information or accessing sources from which they are likely to acquire genetic information (such as websites and online discussion groups that focus on issues such as genetic testing of individuals and genetic discrimination);
- Genetic information may be acquired through a genetic monitoring program that monitors the biological effects of toxic substances in the workplace where the monitoring is required by law or, under carefully defined conditions, where the program is voluntary; and
- Acquisition of genetic information of employees by employers who engage in DNA testing for law enforcement purposes such as a forensic lab or for purposes of human remains identification is permitted, but the genetic information may only be used for analysis of DNA markers for quality control to detect sample contamination.

Confidentiality

Finally, it is also unlawful for an employer to disclose genetic information about applicants for employment or employees. Employers must keep genetic information confidential and in a separate medical file. (Genetic information may be kept in the same file as other medical information in compliance with the Americans with Disabilities Act.) There are limited exceptions to this nondisclosure rule. Such exceptions that provide for the disclosure of relevant genetic information include disclosure to government officials investigating compliance with Title II of GINA and disclosures made pursuant to court order.

FAIR CREDIT REPORTING ACT (FCRA)

Before You Get Background Information

EEOC

In all cases, make sure that you're treating everyone equally. It is illegal to check the background of applicants and employees when that decision is based on a person's race, national origin, color, sex, religion, disability, genetic information (including family medical history), or age (40 or older). For example, asking only people of a certain race about their financial histories or criminal records is evidence of discrimination.

Except in rare circumstances, do not try to get an applicant's or employee's genetic information, which includes family medical history. Even if you have that information, do not use it to make an employment decision. (For more information about this law, see the EEOC's publications explaining the Genetic Information Nondiscrimination Act, or GINA.) Do not ask any medical questions before a conditional job offer has been made. If the person has already started the job, do not ask medical questions unless you have objective evidence that the individual is unable to do the job or poses a safety risk because of a medical condition.

FTC

If you get background information (for example, a credit or criminal background report) from a company in the business of compiling background information, there are additional procedures the FCRA requires beforehand:

- Tell the applicant or employee you might use the information for decisions about their employment. This notice must be in writing and in a stand-alone format. The notice cannot be in an employment application. You can include some minor additional information in the notice (like a brief description of the nature of consumer reports), but only if it does not confuse or detract from the notice;
- If you are asking a company to provide an "investigative report"—a report based on personal interviews concerning

a person's character, general reputation, personal characteristics, and lifestyle—you must also tell the applicant or employee of their right to a description of the nature and scope of the investigation;

- Get the applicant's or employee's written permission to do the background check. This can be part of the document you use to notify the person that you will get the report. If you want the authorization to allow you to get background reports throughout the person's employment, make sure you say so clearly and conspicuously; and
- Certify to the company from which you are getting the report that you:
    - notified the applicant and got their permission to get a background report;
    - complied with all of the FCRA requirements; and
    - will not discriminate against the applicant or employee, or otherwise misuse the information in violation of federal or state equal opportunity laws or regulations.

Using Background Information

EEOC

Any background information you receive from any source must not be used to discriminate in violation of federal law. This means that you should:

- Apply the same standards to everyone, regardless of their race, national origin, color, sex, religion, disability, genetic information (including family medical history), or age (40 or older). For example, if you do not reject applicants of one ethnicity with certain financial histories or criminal records, you cannot reject applicants of other ethnicities because they have the same or similar financial histories or criminal records;
- Take special care when basing employment decisions on background problems that may be more common among people of a certain race, color, national origin, sex, or religion; among people who have a disability; or among people age 40 or older. For example, employers should not use a policy or practice that excludes people with certain criminal

records if the policy or practice significantly disadvantages individuals of a particular race, national origin, or another protected characteristic, and does not accurately predict who will be a responsible, reliable, or safe employee. In legal terms, the policy or practice has a "disparate impact" and is not "job related and consistent with business necessity"; and
- Be prepared to make exceptions for problems revealed during a background check that were caused by a disability. For example, if you are inclined not to hire a person because of a problem caused by a disability, you should allow the person to demonstrate their ability to do the job—despite the negative background information—unless doing so would cause significant financial or operational difficulty.

FTC

When taking an adverse action (for example, not hiring an applicant or firing an employee) **based on background information obtained through a company in the business of compiling background information,** the FCRA has additional requirements:

- Before you take an adverse employment action, you must give the applicant or employee:
    - a notice that includes a copy of the consumer report you relied on to make your decision; and
    - a copy of "A Summary of Your Rights Under the Fair Credit Reporting Act," which you should have received from the company that sold you the report.

By giving the person the notice in advance, the person has an opportunity to review the report and explain any negative information.

- After you take an adverse employment action, you must tell the applicant or employee (orally, in writing, or electronically):
    - that the individual was rejected because of information in the report;
    - the name, address, and phone number of the company that sold the report;

- that the company selling the report did not make the hiring decision, and cannot give specific reasons for it; and
- that the individual has a right to dispute the accuracy or completeness of the report, and to get an additional free report from the reporting company within 60 days.

Disposing of Background Information

EEOC

Any personnel or employment records you make or keep (including all application forms, regardless of whether the applicant was hired, and other records related to hiring) must be preserved for one year after the records were made, or after a personnel action was taken, whichever comes later. (The EEOC extends this requirement to two years for educational institutions and for state and local governments. The Department of Labor also extends this requirement to two years for federal contractors that have at least 150 employees and a government contract of at least $150,000.) If the applicant or employee files a charge of discrimination, you must maintain the records until the case is concluded.

FTC

Once you have satisfied all applicable recordkeeping requirements, you may dispose of any background reports you received. However, the law requires that you dispose of the reports—and any information gathered from them—securely. That can include burning, pulverizing, or shredding paper documents and disposing of electronic information so that it cannot be read or reconstructed. For more information, see "Disposing of Consumer Report Information? Rule Tells How" at http://www.business.ftc.gov/documents/alt152-disposing-consumer-report-information-rule-tells-how.

EMPLOYEE POLYGRAPH PROTECTION ACT OF 1988 (EPPA)

The Employee Polygraph Protection Act of 1988 (EPPA) is administered and enforced by the US Department of Labor's Wage and Hour Division. The EPPA applies to most private employers but does not, however, cover federal, state, and local government agencies.

Basic EPPA Provisions/Requirements

The EPPA prohibits most private employers from using lie detector tests, either for preemployment screening or during the course of employment. Employers generally may not require or request an employee or applicant to take a lie detector test, or discharge, discipline, or discriminate against an employee or job applicant for refusing to do so or exercising other rights under the EPPA.

Employers may not use or inquire about the results of a lie detector test or discharge or discriminate against an employee or applicant on the basis of the results of a test, or for filing a complaint or for participating in a proceeding under the EPPA.

Subject to restrictions, the EPPA permits polygraph tests to be administered to certain job applicants of security service firms (armored car, burglar alarm, and security guard) and of pharmaceutical manufacturers, distributors, and dispensers.

Subject to restrictions, the EPPA also permits polygraph testing of certain employees of private firms who are reasonably suspected of involvement in a workplace incident such as theft or embezzlement that resulted in specific economic loss or injury to the employer.

Where polygraph examinations are allowed, they are subject to strict standards for the conduct of the test, including the pretest, testing, and post-testing phases. An examiner must be licensed, if required by a state in which the test is to be conducted, and must be bonded or have professional liability coverage. The EPPA strictly limits the disclosure of information obtained during a polygraph test.

Employee Rights under the EPPA

The EPPA provides that employees have a right to employment opportunities without being subjected to lie detector tests, unless a specific exemption as discussed above applies. Where polygraph examinations are allowed, they are subject to strict standards at the pretest, testing, and post-testing stages. Specific notices must be given to employees or prospective employees. The EPPA also provides employees the right to file a lawsuit for violations. In addition, Wage and Hour Division accepts complaints of alleged EPPA violations.

Recordkeeping, Reporting, Notices, and Posters

Poster. Every employer subject to EPPA must post and keep posted on its premises a notice explaining the EPPA. The notice must be posted in a prominent and conspicuous place in every establishment of the employer where it can be readily observed by employees and applicants for employment. There is no size requirement for the poster or requirement as to whether it must be written in Spanish or English.

Notices. There are specific notices that must be given to individual being tested ("examinees") and examiners in instances where polygraph tests are permitted. When a polygraph test is administered pursuant to the economic loss or injury exemption mentioned above, the employer is required to provide the examinee with a statement prior to the test, in a language understood by the examinee, which fully explains the specific incident or activity being investigated and the basis for testing particular employees. The statement must contain, at a minimum, the following:

1. An identification with particulars of the specific economic loss or injury to the business of the employer;
2. A description of the employee's access to the property that is the subject of the investigation;
3. A detailed description of the basis of the employer's reasonable suspicion that the employee was involved in the incident or activity under investigation; and
4. The signature of a person (other than the polygraph examiner) authorized to legally bind the employer.

Every employer who requests an employee or job applicant to submit to a polygraph examination pursuant to the investigation, drug manufacturer or security services EPPA exemptions must provide:

1. Reasonable written notice of the date, time, and place of the examination and the examinee's right to consult with legal counsel or an employee representative before each phase of the test;
2. Written notice of the nature and characteristics of the polygraph instrument and examination;
3. Extensive written notice explaining the examinee's rights, including a list of prohibited questions and topics, the examinee's right to terminate the examination, and the

examinee's right to file a complaint with the Department of Labor alleging violations of EPPA; and

4. Employers must also provide written notice to the examiner identifying the persons to be examined.

Recordkeeping. In the limited instances where the EPPA permits the administration of polygraph tests, recordkeeping requirements apply both to employers and polygraph examiners. Employers and polygraph examiners must retain records identified in the law for a minimum of three years from the date the polygraph examination is conducted (or from the date the examination is requested if no examination is conducted). Employers investigating an economic loss or injury must maintain a copy of the statement that sets forth the specific incident or activity under investigation, the basis for testing that particular employee, and proof of service of that statement to the examinee. Employers who manufacture, distribute, or dispense controlled substances must maintain records specifically identifying the loss or injury in question and the nature of the employee's access to the person or property that is the subject of the investigation. Every employer who requests an employee or prospective employee to submit to a polygraph examination pursuant to EPPA exemptions must maintain:

1. A copy of the written statement that sets forth the time and place of the examination and the examinee's right to consult with an attorney;
2. A copy of the written notice provided by the employer to the examiner identifying the persons to be examined;
3. Copies of all opinions, reports, or other records furnished to the employer by the examiner relating to the examinations;
4. All polygraph examiners must maintain all opinions, reports, charts, written questions, lists, and other records relating to polygraph tests of the person being tested, as well as records of the number of examinations conducted by that examiner each day, and the duration of each test period; and
5. All exempt private-sector employers and polygraph examiners hired to conduct examinations must keep the required records safe and accessible at the place or places of employment or business or at one or more established central

recordkeeping offices. If the records are maintained at a central recordkeeping office, the records must be made available within seventy-two hours following notice from the Secretary of Labor or an authorized representative.

IN PLAIN ENGLISH

The Employee Polygraph Protection Act of 1988 exemptions are: 1) polygraph tests conducted pursuant to an ongoing investigation, 2) tests conducted by drug manufacturers, and 3) tests conducted in the security service industry.

Penalties/Sanctions

The Secretary of Labor can bring court action to restrain violators and assess penalties. An employer who violates the law may be liable to the employee or prospective employee for appropriate legal and equitable relief, which may include employment, reinstatement, promotion, and payment of lost wages and benefits.

Any person against whom a penalty is assessed may, within thirty days of the notice of assessment, request a hearing before an administrative law judge. If dissatisfied with the administrative law judge's decision, that person may request a review of the decision by the Administrative Review Board, which the Secretary of Labor has designated to issue final agency decisions. Final determinations on violations are enforceable in court.

Relation to State, Local, and Other Federal Laws

The EPPA generally does not override any provision of any state or local law or any collective bargaining agreement that is more restrictive with respect to lie detector tests.

WRITTEN JOB DESCRIPTIONS

Before ever beginning the hiring process, it is critical for an employer to have a written and well-thought-out job description for all positions including that to be filled. Having written descriptions accomplishes many important tasks that protect and assist an employer's business and employees such as:

- Serving as a reference guide for determining comparable industry salaries;
- Helping to maximize dollars spent on employee compensation for the position by ensuring the experience and skills necessary for the job are detailed and matched to prospective applicants;
- Functioning as a foundation for developing interview questions;
- Detailing information about the position that can be incorporated into "help wanted" ads;
- Discouraging employees from refusing to do a task because "it is not my job";
- Providing a basis for employee reviews, salary increases, setting goals, and growth paths; and
- Serving as legal documentation that can be useful in the event an employee files a wrongful termination or discrimination lawsuit against the employer.

An effective job description details the primary functions of the job, how the tasks will be carried out, and the necessary skills needed to perform the job effectively. It should anticipate employee growth and potential problems due to misunderstanding. An effective job description should do more than just describe the position; it should also address potential questions about the job in the future.

An effective job description should therefore address the following areas:

- **Job Title.** Provides clarity regarding the type of position, its interface with other positions, and its relative hierarchy within the organization;
- **Salary Range.** Specifies the starting, midrange, and maximum salary for the position. Also includes information about how employees may be eligible for additional compensation such as sales commissions, performance bonuses, and annual raises.
- **Purpose and Objectives.** Provides a general statement, summarizing in a few sentences the purpose and objectives of the position;

- **Specific Duties.** Provides a detailed list of specific duties and tasks in their order of importance. The list of duties should detail every activity that will take a percentage of the employee's time and include any accountability the employee may have for meeting the stated purpose and objectives of the position;
- **Description of Reporting Structure.** Provides a detailed description of any and all roles the employee will play. It should include their own supervisory roles, if applicable, as well as whom the employee reports to directly and indirectly. If the employee is to work closely with other employees or departments, include that information as well. If the job requires considerable interaction with many different coworkers, it may be helpful to include a company-wide organizational flowchart.
- **Experience and Skills.** Be as specific as possible when detailing the experience and skills required to perform the job. For example, if the position involves the use of a computer, list the type(s) of software and hardware customarily used to perform the job.
- **Description of Ideal Candidate,** List other skills and experience that an ideal candidate would possess but are not absolutely necessary to be considered for the job.
- **Work Location and Schedule.** List the location of the job and the typical days and hours of the position. Also mention whether the job may require availability outside usual working hours, either often or on occasion, and whether it will require travel, and, if so, the percentage of time spent traveling.
- **Other Duties as Assigned.** Inclusion of "other duties as assigned" in a job description allows the employer to add new tasks to the position as they are needed and hopefully avoid having the employee resist being asked to do something not in the job description. In some cases, it may be beneficial to clarify beyond the generic "other duties" and be more descriptive—for example, "other clerical duties as assigned" or other duties as assigned by a particular department or person.

IN PLAIN ENGLISH

A flowchart is a diagram that shows the structure of an organization and how tasks are handled by that organization. It assists the viewer in understanding how an organization works and who is in charge of particular projects, departments, groups, or the like. It can also be used to show how a particular project or task is accomplished.

Restrictions on Employees' Actions by Their Prior Employers

It is quite common for employers to require new employees to sign an employment contract such as the one discussed in Chapter 3. Those employment contracts frequently include restrictions regarding competition by the employee during employment and after employment terminates, restrictions on solicitation for business during employment and after employment terminates, and provisions advising the employee of the fact the employee has been provided with trade secrets that may not be used or disclosed without receiving express written permission from the employer. In addition, in the course of employment many employees create intellectual property such as literature, advertising, or music, all of which are protected by copyright and unless otherwise agreed belong to the employer (see Chapter 10 for a more detailed discussion of this subject).

IN PLAIN ENGLISH

Intellectual property is property that includes products of the mind such as copyrights, trademarks, patents, trade secrets, and other rights that protect creative products.

Noncompetition restrictions are frequently addressed by state law. A list of those statues is found in Appendix A of this book. Non-solicitation restrictions may also be addressed in cases and it is important to determine whether those type of restrictions are enforceable in the state of employment. Every state in the United States restricts the use of trade secrets. This subject is discussed more fully in Chapter 10 of this book.

Other forms of intellectual property including, names, symbols, or logos used to identify the source of a product or service (trademarks) or inventions that may be protected as trade secrets, or where appropriate, patented, are discussed in Chapter 10 of this book and are also frequently covered by employment contracts.

It is therefore essential for applicants to provide prospective employers with copies of any employment contracts the applicant signed with prior employers. This is because the employment contract with prior employers may contain language that prohibits the individual from using intellectual property of the prior employer or which restricts the individual from performing certain tasks. Certainly, if the applicant has had numerous prior positions, the applicant should not be required to provide every employment contract signed. It would only be necessary for the prospective employer to review those employment contracts that may remain in effect at the time of the new hiring. It is likely that contracts that are older than five years will not have non-compete or non-solicitation provisions still in effect, though other intellectual property restrictions will likely be operative and a prospective employee should be advised of this fact.

Interviewers should advise applicants not to use copyrighted material created for former employers, not to use trademarks created for former employers or trade secrets while working for former employers. A provision in the employment contract should address these issues. It is also important for perspective employees not to infringe on existing patents.

A candid discussion of these issues during the interview process is very important, and interviewers should have a checklist of subjects to discuss so that any important information is not inadvertently omitted.

DISCRIMINATION IN HIRING IN THE FEDERAL SECTOR

Other federal laws, not enforced by EEOC, also prohibit discrimination and reprisals against federal employees and applicants for employment. The Civil Service Reform Act of 1978 (CSRA) contains a number of prohibitions, known as "prohibited personnel practices," which are designed to promote overall fairness in federal personnel actions. The CSRA prohibits any federal employee who has authority to take certain personnel actions from discriminating for or against federal employees or applicants for employment on the bases of race, color, national origin, religion, sex, age, or disability. It also provides that certain personnel actions cannot be based on attributes or conduct that do not adversely affect employee performance, such as marital status and political affiliation. The Office of Personnel Management (OPM) has furthermore interpreted the prohibition of discrimination based on conduct to include discrimination based on sexual orientation. The CSRA also prohibits reprisal against federal employees or applicants for whistleblowing, or for exercising an appeal, complaint, or grievance right. The CSRA is enforced by both the Office of Special Counsel (OSC) and the Merit Systems Protection Board (MSPB).

DISCRIMINATION IN OTHER ASPECTS OF THE EMPLOYMENT RELATIONSHIP

While the discussion of various federal laws prohibiting discrimination in employment has thus far focused on the hiring process, it cannot be overlooked that those same statutes also prohibit discrimination during the entire employment relationship after hiring. Discriminatory practices in employment are found under Title VII, the Americans with Disabilities Act, the Genetic Information Nondiscrimination Act, and the Age Discrimination in Employment Act, which prohibit discrimination in any aspect of employment, including:

- hiring (discussed earlier) and firing;
- compensation, assignment, or classification of employees;
- transfer, promotion, layoff, or recall;
- job advertisements;
- recruitment;
- testing;
- use of company facilities;
- training and apprenticeship programs;
- fringe benefits;
- pay, retirement plans, and disability leave; or
- other terms and conditions of employment.

Discriminatory practices under the before-listed laws, discussed in greater detail below, include the following conduct by employers:

- harassment on the basis of race, color, religion, sex, national origin, disability, genetic information, or age;
- retaliation against an individual for filing a charge of discrimination, participating in an investigation, or opposing discriminatory practices;

- employment decisions based on stereotypes or assumptions about the abilities, traits, or performance of individuals of a certain sex, race, age, religion, or ethnic group, or individuals with disabilities, or based on myths or assumptions about an individual's genetic information; and
- denying employment opportunities to a person because of marriage to, or association with, an individual of a particular race, religion, national origin, or an individual with a disability. Title VII also prohibits discrimination because of participation in schools or places of worship associated with a particular racial, ethnic, or religious group.

Employers are furthermore required to post notices to all employees advising them of their rights under the laws which EEOC enforces and their right to be free from retaliation. Such notices must be accessible, as needed, to persons with visual or other disabilities that affect reading.

Many states and municipalities have also enacted protections against discrimination and harassment based on sexual orientation, status as a parent, marital status, and political affiliation.

FEDERAL LAWS PROHIBITING DISCRIMINATION IN THE EMPLOYMENT RELATIONSHIP

Title VII

Title VII prohibits not only intentional discrimination, but also practices that have the effect of discriminating against individuals because of their race, color, national origin, religion, or sex. National origin discrimination is illegal discrimination against an individual because of birthplace, ancestry, culture, or linguistic characteristics common to a specific ethnic group. A rule requiring that employees speak only English on the job may violate Title VII unless an employer shows that the requirement is necessary for conducting its business. If the employer believes such a rule is necessary, employees must be informed when English is required and the consequences for violating the rule.

IN PLAIN ENGLISH

Discrimination in and of itself is not illegal. For example, an individual can discriminate against a particular product or service for the individual's personal use so long as the reason for not using that product or service is not unlawful. Unlawful discrimination refers to discrimination on the basis of race, creed, disability, national origin, religion, and the like.

The Immigration Reform and Control Act (IRCA) of 1986 requires employers to assure that employees hired are legally authorized to work in the United States. It should be cautioned, however, an employer who requests employment verification only for individuals of a particular national origin, or individuals who appear to be or sound foreign, may be in violation of both Title VII and IRCA. Verification must therefore be obtained from all applicants and employees. Employers who impose citizenship requirements or give preferences to US citizens in hiring or employment opportunities may also violate IRCA.

Employers are required to provide religious accommodation under Title VII. An employer is required to reasonably accommodate the religious belief of an employee or prospective employee, unless doing so would impose an undue hardship.

Title VII's broad prohibitions against sex discrimination specifically cover:

- **Sexual Harassment.** This includes practices ranging from direct requests for sexual favors to workplace conditions that create a "hostile environment" for persons of either gender, including same-sex harassment. Note, the hostile environment standard also applies to harassment on the bases of race, color, national origin, religion, age, and disability.
- **Pregnancy Based Discrimination.** Pregnancy, childbirth, and related medical conditions must be treated in the same way as other temporary illnesses or conditions.

Additionally, rights are also available to parents and others under the Family and Medical Leave Act (FMLA) enforced by the US Department of Labor.

Age Discrimination in Employment Act (ADEA)

The Age Discrimination in Employment Act's broad ban against age discrimination also specifically prohibits:

- statements or specifications in job notices or advertisements of age preference and limitations. An age limit may only be specified in the rare circumstance where age has been proven to be a bona fide occupational qualification (BFOQ);
- discrimination on the basis of age by apprenticeship programs, including joint labor-management apprenticeship programs; and
- denial of benefits to older employees. An employer may reduce benefits based on age only if the cost of providing the reduced benefits to older workers is the same as the cost of providing benefits to younger workers.

Equal Pay Act (EPA)

The Equal Pay Act prohibits discrimination on the basis of sex in the payment of wages or benefits, where men and women perform work of similar skill, effort, and responsibility for the same employer under similar working conditions.

Note, however, that:

- Employers may not reduce wages of either sex to equalize pay between men and women;
- A violation of the EPA may occur where a different wage was/is paid to a person who worked in the same job before or after an employee of the opposite sex; and.
- A violation may also occur where a labor union causes the employer to violate the law.

Titles I and V of the Americans with Disabilities Act (ADA)

The ADA prohibits discrimination on the basis of disability in all employment practices. It is necessary to understand several important ADA definitions in order to know who is protected by the law and what constitutes illegal discrimination:

"Individual with a Disability"

An individual with a disability under the ADA is a person who has a physical or mental impairment that substantially limits one or more major life activities, has a record of such impairment, or is regarded as having a disability. An entity subject to the ADA regards someone as having a disability when it takes an action prohibited by the ADA based on an actual or perceived impairment, except if the impairment is both transitory (lasting or expected to last six months or less) and minor. Major life activities are basic activities that most people in the general population can perform with little or no difficulty such as walking, breathing, seeing, hearing, speaking, learning, thinking, and eating. Major life activities also include the operation of a major bodily function, such as functions of the immune system and normal cell growth, as well as brain, neurological, and hormonal functions.

"Qualified"

An individual with a disability is "qualified" if the individual satisfies skill, experience, education, and other job-related requirements of the position held or desired, and who, with or without reasonable accommodation, can perform the essential functions of that position.

"Reasonable Accommodation"

Reasonable accommodation may include, but is not limited to, making existing facilities used by employees readily accessible to and usable by persons with disabilities, job restructuring, modification of work schedules, providing additional unpaid leave, reassignment to a vacant position, acquiring or modifying equipment or devices, adjusting or modifying examinations, training materials, or policies, and providing qualified readers or interpreters. Reasonable accommodation may be necessary to apply for a job, to perform job functions, or to enjoy the benefits and privileges of employment that are enjoyed by people without disabilities. An employer is not required to lower production standards to make an accommodation. An employer generally is not obligated to provide personal-use items such as eyeglasses or hearing aids. A person who only meets the "regarded as" definition of disability is not entitled to receive a reasonable accommodation.

"Undue Hardship"

An employer is required to make a reasonable accommodation to a qualified individual with a disability unless doing so would impose an undue hardship on the operation of the employer's business. Undue hardship means an action that requires significant difficulty or expense when considered in relation to factors such as a business's size, financial resources, and the nature and structure of its operation.

"Prohibited Inquiries and Examinations"

Before making an offer of employment, an employer may not ask job applicants about the existence, nature, or severity of a disability. Applicants may be asked about their ability to perform job functions. A job offer may be conditioned on the results of a medical examination, but only if the examination is required for all entering employees in the same job category. Medical examinations of employees must be job-related and consistent with business necessity.

"Drug and Alcohol Use"

Employees and applicants currently engaging in the illegal use of drugs are not protected by the ADA when an employer acts on the basis of such use. Tests for illegal use of drugs are not considered medical examinations and, therefore, are not subject to the ADA's restrictions on medical examinations. Employers may hold individuals who are illegally using drugs and individuals with alcoholism to the same standards of performance as other employees.

The Civil Rights Act of 1991 (CRA)

The Civil Rights Act of 1991 made major changes in the federal laws against employment discrimination enforced by EEOC. Enacted in part to reverse several Supreme Court decisions that limited the rights of persons protected by these laws, CRA also provides additional protections. The CRA authorizes compensatory and punitive damages in cases of intentional discrimination, and provides for obtaining attorneys' fees and the possibility of jury trials. It also directs the EEOC to expand its technical assistance and outreach activities.

IN PLAIN ENGLISH

Compensatory damages are actual damages such as lost wages. Punitive damages are imposed as a penalty and for the purpose of discouraging future similar violations. Punitive damages are only awarded in cases where the improper act is not merely accidental.

Title II of the Genetic Information Nondiscrimination Act of 2008 (GINA)

GINA prohibits discrimination against applicants, employees, and former employees on the basis of genetic information. This includes a prohibition on the use of genetic information in all employment decisions; restrictions on the ability of employers and other covered entities to request or to acquire genetic information, with limited exceptions; and a requirement to maintain the confidentiality of any genetic information acquired, with limited exceptions.

EMPLOYERS AND OTHER ENTITIES COVERED BY EEO LAWS

Title VII, the ADA, and GINA cover all private employers, state and local governments, and educational institutions that employ fifteen or more individuals. These laws also cover private and public employment agencies, labor organizations, and joint labor-management committees controlling apprenticeship and training.

The ADEA covers all private employers with twenty or more employees, state and local governments (including school districts), employment agencies, and labor organizations.

The EPA covers all employers who are covered by the Fair Labor Standards Act. Virtually all employers are subject to FLSA's provisions.

Title VII, the ADEA, GINA, and the EPA also cover the federal government. In addition, the federal government is covered by Sections 501 and 505 of the Rehabilitation Act of 1973, as amended, which incorporate the requirements of the ADA. However, different procedures are used for processing complaints of federal discrimination. For more information on how to file a complaint of federal discrimination, contact the EEO office of the federal agency where the alleged discrimination occurred.

The CSRA (not enforced by EEOC) covers most federal agency employees except employees of a government corporation, the FBI, the CIA, the Defense Intelligence Agency, the National Security Agency, and as determined by the president, any executive agency or unit thereof, the principal function of which is the conduct of foreign intelligence or counterintelligence activities, or the General Accounting Office.

FILING CHARGES WITH EEOC

Applicants for employment or employees who believe an employer has violated one of the rights enforced by EEOC as outlined above in either the hiring process or during their employment may seek remedy before EEOC. The following outline provides applicants and employees with the necessary steps for initiating and processing a charge of unlawful employment discrimination practices before EEOC.

Eligibility to File a Charge of Discrimination

- Any individual who believes that their employment rights have been violated may file a charge of discrimination with EEOC.
- In addition, an individual, organization, or agency may file a charge on behalf of another person in order to protect the aggrieved person's identity.

How to File a Charge of Discrimination with EEOC

- A charge may be filed by mail or in person at the nearest EEOC office. Individuals may consult their local telephone directory (US Government listing) or call (800) 669–4000 (voice) or (800) 669–6820 (TTY) to contact the nearest EEOC office for more information on specific procedures for filing a charge.
- Individuals who need an accommodation in order to file a charge (e.g., sign language interpreter, print materials in an accessible format) should inform the EEOC field office so appropriate arrangements can be made.

- Federal employees or applicants for employment should consult EEOC's fact sheet concerning Federal Sector Equal Employment Opportunity Complaint Processing.

Information Necessary to File a Charge of Discrimination with EEOC

- The complaining party's name, address, and telephone number.
- The name, address, and telephone number of the respondent employer, employment agency, or union that is alleged to have discriminated, and number of employees (or union members), if known.
- A short description of the alleged violation (the event that caused the complaining party to believe that their rights were violated).
- The date(s) of the alleged violation(s).

Important Time Limits for Filing a Charge of Discrimination with EEOC

All laws enforced by EEOC, except the Equal Pay Act, require filing a charge with EEOC before a private lawsuit may be filed in court. There are strict and detailed time limits within which charges must be filed:

- A charge must be filed with EEOC within 180 days from the date of the alleged violation, in order to protect the charging party's rights.
- This 180-day filing deadline is extended to 300 days if the charge also is covered by a state or local antidiscrimination law. For ADEA charges, only state laws extend the filing limit to 300 days.
- These time limits do not apply to claims under the Equal Pay Act, because under the Equal Pay Act persons do not have to first file a charge with EEOC in order to have the right to go to court. However, because many EPA claims also raise Title VII sex discrimination issues, it may be advisable to file charges under both laws within the time limits indicated.

- To protect legal rights, it is always best to contact EEOC promptly when discrimination is suspected.
- Federal employees or applicants for employment should see the fact sheet about Federal Sector Equal Employment Opportunity Complaint Processing (available online at http://www.eeoc.gov).

State and Local Agencies' Enforcement of State and Local Discrimination Laws

Many states and local government entities have antidiscrimination laws and agencies responsible for enforcing those laws. EEOC refers to these agencies as Fair Employment Practices Agencies (FEPAs). Through the use of "work sharing agreements," EEOC and the FEPAs avoid duplication of effort while at the same time ensuring that a charging party's rights are protected under both federal and state law.

- If a charge is filed with a FEPA and is also covered by federal law, the FEPA "dual files" the charge with EEOC to protect federal rights. The charge usually will be retained by the FEPA for handling.
- If a charge is filed with EEOC and also is covered by state or local law, EEOC "dual files" the charge with the state or local FEPA, but ordinarily retains the charge for handling.

After a Charge Is Filed with EEOC

The employer is notified that the charge has been filed. From this point there are a number of ways a charge may be handled.

- A charge may be assigned for priority investigation if the initial facts appear to support a violation of law. When the evidence is less strong, the charge may be assigned for follow-up investigation to determine whether it is likely that a violation has occurred.
- EEOC can seek to settle a charge at any stage of the investigation if the charging party and the employer express an interest in doing so. If settlement efforts are not successful, the investigation continues.

- In investigating a charge, EEOC may make written requests for information, interview people, review documents, and, as needed, visit the facility where the alleged discrimination occurred. When the investigation is complete, EEOC will discuss the evidence with the charging party or employer, as appropriate.
- The charge may be selected for EEOC's mediation program if both the charging party and the employer express an interest in this option. Mediation is offered as an alternative to a lengthy investigation. Participation in the mediation program is confidential, voluntary, and requires consent from both charging party and employer. If mediation is unsuccessful, the charge is returned for investigation.
- A charge may be dismissed at any point if, in the agency's best judgment, further investigation will not establish a violation of the law. A charge may be dismissed at the time it is filed, if an initial in-depth interview does not produce evidence to support the claim. When a charge is dismissed, a notice is issued in accordance with the law, which gives the charging party ninety days in which to file a lawsuit.

EEOC's Resolution of Discrimination Charges

- If the evidence obtained in an investigation does not establish that discrimination occurred, this will be explained to the charging party. A required notice is then issued, closing the case and giving the charging party ninety days in which to file a lawsuit.
- If the evidence establishes that discrimination has occurred, the employer and the charging party will be informed of this in a letter of determination that explains the finding. EEOC will then attempt to work with the employer to develop a remedy for the discrimination.
- If the case is successfully resolved, or if a case has earlier been successfully mediated or settled, neither EEOC nor the charging party may go to court unless the resolution, mediation, or settlement agreement is not honored.

- If EEOC is unable to successfully resolve the case, the agency will decide whether to bring suit in federal court. If EEOC decides not to sue, it will issue a notice closing the case and giving the charging party ninety days in which to file a lawsuit. In Title VII and ADA cases against state or local governments, the Department of Justice takes these actions.
- Federal employees or applicants for employment should see the fact sheet about Federal Sector Equal Employment Opportunity Complaint Processing (available online at www.eeoc.gov).

Filing a Discrimination Lawsuit in Court

A charging party may file a lawsuit within ninety days after receiving a notice of a "right to sue" from EEOC, as stated above. Under Title VII, the ADA, and GINA, a charging party also can request a notice of "right to sue" from EEOC 180 days after the charge was first filed with EEOC and may then bring suit within ninety days after receiving this notice. Under the ADEA, a suit may be filed at any time sixty days after filing a charge with EEOC, but not later than ninety days after EEOC gives notice that it has completed action on the charge.

Under the EPA, a lawsuit must be filed within two years (three years for willful violations) of the discriminatory act, which in most cases is payment of a discriminatory lower wage.

Potential Remedies for Unlawful Employment Discrimination

The "relief" or remedies available for employment discrimination, whether caused by intentional acts or by practices that have a discriminatory effect, may include:

- back pay;
- hiring;
- promotion;
- reinstatement;
- front pay;
- reasonable accommodation; or
- other actions that will make an individual "whole."

IN PLAIN ENGLISH

"To make a person whole" is to provide that individual with the benefit that person should have received if the improper act had not occurred.

Remedies also may include payment of:

- attorney fees,
- expert witness fees, and
- court costs.

Under most EEOC-enforced laws, compensatory and punitive damages also may be available where intentional discrimination is found. Damages may be available to compensate for actual monetary losses, for future monetary losses, and for mental anguish and inconvenience. Punitive damages also may be available if an employer acted with malice or reckless indifference. Punitive damages are not available against the federal, state, or local governments.

In cases concerning reasonable accommodation under the ADA, compensatory or punitive damages may not be awarded to the charging party if an employer can demonstrate that "good faith" efforts were made to provide reasonable accommodation.

An employer may be required to post notices to all employees addressing the violations of a specific charge and advising them of their rights under the laws EEOC enforces and their right to be free from retaliation. Such notices must be accessible for persons with visual or other disabilities that affect reading.

The employer also may be required to take corrective or preventive actions to cure the source of the identified discrimination and minimize the chance of its recurrence, as well as discontinue the specific discriminatory practices involved in the case.

EMPLOYER DEFENSES TO TITLE VII, ADA, AND ADEA CLAIMS

Business Necessity. Business necessity is an employer's defense related to a decision that is based on the requirements of the business and is consistent with other business decisions. To establish business necessity, the employer must prove that the practice is job related.

Bona Fide Occupational Qualification. Bona fide occupational qualification is when an employer is allowed to hire employees based on qualities or attributions that would be discrimination when considered in other contexts. An employer must prove that the bona fide occupational liability for potential discrimination is job related.

There are certain industries that are required to hire employees based on a quality that would in other terms be considered discriminatory. These industries include religious organizations and schools, the modeling industry, and the entertainment industry. If an employer is going to hire based on bona fide occupational qualifications, it is best to ensure that it really is necessary to the operation of the business by consulting an attorney who can provide a measure of objectivity.

Seniority Systems. The Age Discrimination Act was enacted in order to prohibit employers from discriminating against individuals because of their age. A seniority system is a way to determine employment advantages based on the length of service of employees. It should offer rewards and opportunities to employees who have been with the employer for longer periods of time.

It is unlawful for the seniority system to require older employees to retire because of their age. All employees are also entitled to the same amount of pay and to the same benefits.

A seniority system would only be considered discriminatory if it did not allow an employee to enjoy the benefits that come with seniority because of their gender, race, or religion. It is not meant to be discriminatory; it is a way to reward employees that have provided their services for a long period of time.

PROBATIONARY PERIODS

When an individual is hired, it is quite common for the individual to be subject to a probationary period. Care should be taken when drafting the employment contract not to state that the employee who successfully completes the probationary period will become "permanent," because this might be interpreted as that the employee's employment can never be terminated. Instead the agreement should provide that when the probationary period is successfully completed, the individual will become a "regular" employee. "Regular employee" should be defined as an individual who is entitled to certain additional benefits such as medical or dental insurance, life insurance, pension plans, vacation, and the like. (This subject is discussed more fully in Chapter 8 of this book.) It should be made clear that the employment remains "at-will" even if the employee becomes a "regular employee."

The probationary period should only be for a reasonable amount of time, commonly three to six months, so the new employee's work can be evaluated during that period. If the probationary period is too short, the evaluation is likely to be inadequate. On the other hand, if the probationary period is too long, the new employee may become unhappy with the relationship, which would not benefit that individual or the employer.

It is quite common that an explanation of the probationary arrangement be spelled out in an Employee Handbook, which is discussed in detail in Chapter 6 of this book.

INDEPENDENT CONTRACTORS IN A GIG ECONOMY

While an "independent contractor" is different from an employee, the exact definition of independent contractor is not set in concrete. To prevent any unwanted surprises, it is essential to define the exact business relationship between the employee and the employer prior to beginning work.

"Independent Contractor" Defined

There are three different sources in which the classification of independent contract can be found. What makes an individual an independent contractor has been outlined by common-law principles, the FLSA, and finally, decisions in courts.

The IRS and many states have adopted common-law principles of agency to define an independent contractor. These rules focus primarily on the level of control that an employer has over a service or product, meaning, whether or not the employer actually defines what is being performed and the way that task will be accomplished.

Common-law principles of agency furthermore define independent contractor status by the method of compensation. If a person is on an employer's payroll and receives a steady paycheck, clearly that person is intended by the parties to be an "employee" rather than an "independent contractor," who likely receives payment in a different manner. Other considerations relevant to identifying someone as an independent contractor may include:

- If the worker supplies their own equipment, materials, and tools;
- If all necessary materials are not supplied by the employer;
- If the worker can be discharged at any time and can choose whether or not to come to work without fear of losing employment;
- If the worker controls the hours of employment, thus indicating they are acting as an independent contractor; and
- Whether the work performed is temporary or permanent.

Again, the nature of the work performed will assist in defining the relationship. When work is considered integral to the employer's business, it is more likely that the person is an employee. On the other hand, work that is temporary and nonintegral may imply independent contractor status.

In an attempt to interpret provisions of the FLSA and discern between employee and independent contractor status, some courts and federal agencies have employed the "economic realities test." That test looks at the dependence of the worker on the business for which the individual performs work. If a person gains a large portion of their salary from that business, chances are that person qualifies as an employee. The test also includes such factors as the level of skill employed, the integral or nonintegral nature of the work, intent of the parties, and payment of Social Security taxes and benefits.

Outside of the FLSA, courts sometimes ask the following questions to determine the status of a work relationship:

- What is the degree of control over work and who exercises that control?
- What is each party's level of loss in the relationship?
- Who has paid for materials, supplies, and/or equipment?
- What type of skill is required for work?
- Is there a degree of permanence?
- Is the worker an integral part of the business?

These courts also use the "right to control" test. When the hiring party controls the way work is carried out and a product is delivered, the relationship between the parties is that of an employer/employee. If, on the other hand, an employer does not have authority over how a party accomplishes the work but simply give requests or provides an outline, the relationship between the parties is that of hiring party/independent contractor.

EMPLOYER TAX LIABILITY

An employer's tax liability is determined by the worker's employment status. When a worker is an "employee," employers must pay state and federal unemployment tax, Social Security tax, and workers' compensation/disability premiums to a state insurance fund. When a worker is an "independent contractor," the hiring party is not required to make any of these payments.

Should employers incorrectly define a worker as an independent contractor, they may find themselves liable for past taxes, including FICA and federal unemployment tax. Safe harbors, which allow employers to use the independent contractor status and avoid penalties, include prior practice of treating similar employees as independent contractors and the existence of a prior IRS audit where no taxes were required to be paid.

In conclusion, there are certain factors that define whether a worker is an independent contractor, such as not relying on the business as the sole source of income, working at their pace as defined by an agreement, being ineligible for employer-provided benefits, and retaining a degree of control and independence over the work that is being performed. While the independent contractor is their own boss, work remains within the parameters of whatever oral or written contract exists between the employer and the person performing the work. An employee, on the other hand, relies on the business of the employer for a steady income, gives up elements of control and independence over the work being performed, and in turn is eligible for certain benefits and works within the established rules of the workplace.

TEMP AGENCIES AND EMPLOYEES

Occasionally employers will need the assistance of temporary employees for the purpose of assisting for a short period of time or for assisting with a specific limited project. In situations such as this, it is appropriate to hire a temporary employee rather than a "regular employee" who may not be needed after the limited project is completed. While it is certainly possible to advertise for a temporary employee, as discussed in Chapter 1 of this book, there are temporary agencies available that focus on obtaining these types of employees as well.

A temporary employee should be interviewed in the same manner as a "regular employee," even though the temporary employee's position is limited. This is because the temporary employee will likely have the same types of restrictions and limitations discussed earlier in this chapter. These would include, for example, noncompetition restrictions, non-solicitation restrictions, and intellectual property restrictions. The same care and diligence should be devoted to hiring temporary employees as is used to hire "regular" employees. The only difference between the two types of employees is the fact that temporary employees will only be employed for a limited time.

If a company is presented with a contract by an employment agency, whether a temp agency or a regular employment agency, then that contract should be reviewed by an experienced attorney before it is signed. This is because contracts with agencies may have provisions that could be problematic for employers in the future, and it is better to be prudent when the relationship begins rather than unhappy when attempting to terminate it. Issues that can arise include an agreement that the employer not hire individuals without paying the agency a commission even if the agency is not responsible for obtaining the new employee. Other problems that could result relate to situations in which the agency receives a commission for individuals who have not been properly screened despite the understanding that screening is important.

CONCLUSION

From a careful reading of this chapter, it should become apparent to the reader that there are multiple considerations for employees and employers alike during both the preemployment and initial phases of the employment relationship including: (1) preparing a useful employment application, (2) interviewing candidates for positions, and (3) hiring new employees, all of which are key to the establishment of successful, long-term relationships. Many of those considerations are essentially practical in nature, such as designing a useful employment application for a particular enterprise and how to conduct meaningful interviews of prospective employees, both of which are necessary tools to assist an employer in its ultimate search and hiring of the best qualified candidates for particular positions.

Once employment begins, however, there are still further considerations that need to be dealt with in that phase of the relationship including: (1) construction of a useful employee handbook to provide new employees a "road map" with which to navigate the relationship over the years ahead; (2) providing them with the necessary "onboarding" prerequisites to successfully begin their employment journey; and (3) carefully crafting written job descriptions to avoid confusion and potential misunderstandings during the relationship.

Throughout both the preemployment and employment phases of the relationship, there are a myriad of unavoidably complex federal, state, and local rules which must be adhered to, including but not limited to, (1) Title VII, (2) the EPA, (3) the ADEA, (4) Titles I and V of the ADA, (5) Sections 501 and 505 of the Rehabilitation Act of 1973, (6) Title II of GINA, and (7) the CRA, all of which must be scrupulously complied with by the employer in order to avoid becoming ensnared in costly, time-consuming, and distracting litigation. In order to make both the preemployment and employment phases of the employment relationship run smoothly and efficiently so the enterprise may ultimately succeed, it is necessary for employers to closely coordinate its plans, routine activities, and consequential actions in the foregoing respects with competent employment counsel, as has been repeatedly recommended by the authors throughout Chapter 2 and others of this book.

CHAPTER 3

Basics of Contracts

Contracts are an essential part of virtually every business for both employees and employers. Clearly, the entire field of contract law cannot be covered here, but, by becoming aware of some of the ramifications of contract law, you will see where you need to be cautious. In this chapter we will cover contract fundamentals. In later chapters we present specific kinds of employment contracts.

CONTRACT BASICS

A contract is a legally binding promise or set of promises. The law requires that the parties to a contract perform the promises they have made to each other. In the event of nonperformance—usually called a breach—the law provides remedies to the injured party. For the purposes of this discussion, it will be assumed that the contract is between two people, though it frequently involves business organizations, as well. It should be noted that when business organizations are involved, there are additional considerations, such as whether the person acting on behalf of the business has appropriate authority, how that authority must be evidenced and, regardless of authority, whether that individual's act will be deemed within the appropriate scope of the business. These issues complicate the analysis. You should discuss these issues with your attorney.

The three basic elements of every contract are the offer, the acceptance, and the consideration. To illustrate these elements, suppose a human resources manager meets with a prospective employee and explains what employment opportunities are available in the company (the offer). The prospective employee says that the job presented is perfect and acceptable (the acceptance). They agree on a salary (the consideration). That is the basic framework, but a great many variations can be played on that theme.

TYPES OF CONTRACTS

Contracts may be express or implied. They may be oral or written. There are generally at least two types of contracts that must be in writing if they are to be legally enforceable:

1. any contract that, by its terms, cannot be completed in less than one year, and
2. any contract that involves the sale of goods for over $500.

EXPRESS CONTRACTS

An express contract is one in which all the details are spelled out. It can be either oral or written. If you are going to the trouble of expressing contractual terms, you should put your understanding in writing. For example, a company might make a contract with a retail store for six dozen gallons of apple cider to be delivered by the company on October 1, at a price of $1.75 per gallon, to be paid within thirty days of receipt. This scenario is fairly straightforward. If either party fails to live up to any material part of the contract, a breach has occurred. The other party may withhold performance of the party's obligation until receiving assurance that the breaching party will perform. In the event no such assurance is forthcoming, the aggrieved party may have a cause of action and sue for breach of contract.

If the apple cider is delivered on October 15 and the store had advertised the availability of the special apple cider during the week of October 1, time was an important consideration and the store would not be required to accept the late shipment. If time is not a material consideration, then, even with the slight delay, this probably would be considered substantial performance and the store would have to accept the delivery.

IMPLIED CONTRACTS

Implied contracts are usually not reduced to writing and need not be very complicated. An example might be if you call a supplier to order five boxes of computer paper without making any express statement that you will pay for the paper. The promise to pay is implied in the order and is enforceable when the paper is delivered.

With implied contracts, however, things can often become a lot stickier. Suppose a manufacturer of notepads asks you to send over a supply of a new kind of glue you have just begun marketing to try it out. You deliver a generous amount. The notepad manufacturer likes the glue, uses it up, and is overheard commenting that it is the best glue yet for the manufacture of notepads. Is there an implied contract to purchase in this arrangement? That depends on whether you are normally in the business of giving away large, free samples of new products.

UNDERSTANDING CONTRACT PRINCIPLES

In order to understand the principles of offer, acceptance, and consideration, you should examine them in the context of several potential situations for hypothetical business owner, Pat Smith. Smith is an automobile dealer who has an impressive collection of vintage cars in mint condition. Let us look at the following situations and see whether an enforceable contract comes into existence.

- At a cocktail party, Jones expresses an interest in Smith's cars. It looks like the market value of your cars keeps going up, Jones tells Smith. I'm going to buy one while I can still afford it.

  Is this a contract? If so, what are the terms of the offer—the particular car, the specific price? No, this is not really an offer that Smith can accept. It is nothing more than an opinion or a vague expression of intent.
- Brown offers to pay $14,000 for one of Smith's cars that she saw in an auto show several weeks ago. At the show, it was listed at $14,500, but Smith agrees to accept the lower price.

  Is this an enforceable contract? Yes! Brown has offered, in unambiguous terms, to pay a specific amount for a specific car and Smith has accepted the offer. A binding contract exists.
- One day, Jones shows up at Smith's car lot and sees a particular car for which he offers $14,500. Smith accepts and

promises to transfer title the next week, at which time Jones will pay for it. An hour later Brown shows up. She likes the same car and offers Smith $16,000 for it.

Can Smith accept the later offer? No—a contract exists with Jones. An offer was made and accepted. The fact that the object has not yet been delivered or paid for does not make the contract any less binding.

- Green discusses certain renovations he would like Smith to perform on a particular car Smith has just acquired. He offers to pay $16,000 for the car if the final product is satisfactory to him. Green approves preliminary sketches and Smith completes the work. But when Green arrives to pick up his car, he refuses to accept it because it does not satisfy him.

  Is there a contract in this case? Green is making the offer in this case, but the offer is conditional upon his satisfaction with the completed work. Smith can only accept the offer by producing something that meets Green's subjective standards—a risky proposition. There is no enforceable contract for payment until such time as Green indicates that the completed work is satisfactory.

  If Green comes to Smith's car lot and says that the car is satisfactory but then, when Smith delivers it, says he has changed his mind, it is too late. The contract became binding at the moment he indicated the work to be satisfactory. If he then refuses to accept it, he would be breaching his contract.

PROVING AN AGREEMENT

Contracts are enforceable only if they can be proven. All the hypothetical examples mentioned could have been oral contracts, but a great amount of detail is often lost in the course of remembering a conversation. The best practice, of course, is to get it in writing. The function of a written contract is not only that of proof, but to make very clear the understanding of the parties regarding the agreement and the terms of the contract.

Some business owners prefer to do business strictly on the basis of a handshake, particularly with their immediate suppliers and retailers. The assumption seems to be that the best business relations are those based upon mutual trust alone. Although there may be some validity to this, business owners really should put all agreements in writing. Far too many trusting people have suffered adverse consequences because of their reliance upon the sanctity of oral contracts.

Under even the best of business relationships, it is still possible that one or both parties might forget the terms of an oral agreement. It is also possible that both parties might have quite different perceptions about the precise terms of the agreement reached. When the agreement is put into writing, however, there is much less doubt as to the terms of the arrangement. Thus, a written contract generally functions as a safeguard against subsequent misunderstandings or forgetful minds.

Perhaps the principal problem with oral contracts lies in the fact that they cannot always be proven or enforced. Proof of oral contracts typically centers around the conflicting testimony of the parties involved. If one of the parties is not able to establish by a preponderance of evidence (more likely than not) that their version of the contract is the correct one, then the oral contract may be considered nonexistent—as though it had never been made. The same result might occur if the parties cannot remember the precise terms of the agreement.

WHEN WRITTEN CONTRACTS ARE NECESSARY

Even if an oral contract is established, it may not always be enforceable. As already noted, there are some agreements that must be in writing in order to be legally enforceable.

An early law that was designed to prevent fraud and perjury, known as the Statute of Frauds, provides that any contract that, by its terms, cannot be fully performed within one year must be in writing. This rule is narrowly interpreted, so if there is any possibility, no matter how remote, that the contract could be fully performed within one year, the contract need not be reduced to writing.

For example, if a company agreed to provide another company with a fixed quantity of merchandise each year for a period of five years, the contract would have to be in writing. By the very terms of the agreement, there is no way the contract could be performed within one year. If, on the other hand, the contract called for the company to deliver a fixed quantity of merchandise to another company within a period of five years, the contract would not have to be in writing under the Statute of Frauds.

It is possible, though perhaps not probable, that the company could provide all of the merchandise within the first year. The fact that the company does not actually complete performance of the contract within one year is immaterial. So long as complete performance within one year is within the realm of possibility, the contract need not be in writing to be enforceable.

The Statute of Frauds further provides that any contract for the sale of goods valued at $500 or more is not enforceable unless it has been put into writing and signed by the party against whom enforcement is being sought. The fact that a contract for a price in excess of $500 is not in writing does not void the agreement or render it illegal. The parties are free to perform the oral arrangement, but if one party refuses to perform, the other will be unable to legally enforce the agreement.

The law defines goods as all things that are movable at the time the contract is made, except for the money used as payment. The real question becomes whether a particular contract involves the sale of goods for a price of $500 or more. Although the answer would generally seem to be fairly clear, ambiguities may arise.

Agreements involving land, buildings, and certain real estate leases must also be in writing to be legally enforceable. The law with respect to real estate varies from state to state and, if you are involved in a real estate transaction, you should work with an experienced attorney.

In addition, some states have identified specific contracts that are enforceable only if in writing regardless of the other rules which would otherwise apply. For example, Oregon state law prescribes that a contract for landscape work, regardless of its duration or price, must be in writing.

ESSENTIALS TO PUT IN WRITING

A contract should be written in simple language that both parties can understand and should spell out the terms of the agreement.

A contract should include the following:

- the date of the agreement;
- identification of the parties (i.e., the buyer and seller in the case of sale of goods or services);

- a description of the goods or services involved;
- the price or other consideration; and
- the signatures of the parties involved.

To supplement these basics, an agreement should spell out whatever other terms might be applicable, such as pricing arrangements, payment schedules, insurance coverage, and benefits. Many transactions are important enough that additional clauses covering certain contingencies should be added as well.

Finally, it should be noted that a written document that leaves out essential terms of the contract presents many of the same problems of proof and ambiguity as an oral contract.

IN PLAIN ENGLISH

The terms of the contract should be well conceived, clearly drafted, conspicuous (i.e., not in tiny print that no one can read), and in plain English, so everyone can understand them.

NO-COST WRITTEN AGREEMENTS

At this point, owners of small businesses might object, asserting that they do not have the time, energy, or patience to draft contracts. After all, they are in business to make a product or sell a service, not to formulate written contracts steeped in legal jargon.

Fortunately, the businessperson will not always be required to do this, because the supplier or retailer may be willing to draft a satisfactory contract. In the employment context, union shops will generally have established contracts. In nonunion shops, employers may have form contracts of their own. However, be wary of signing any form contracts—they will almost invariably be one-sided, with all terms in favor of whoever paid to have them drafted. You should carefully read, and be sure that you understand, every contract before you sign it. If you do not completely understand any part of a contract, then you should consult with an attorney in order to be sure that you are willing to be bound by that contract.

As a second alternative, the businessperson could employ an attorney to draft contracts. However, this might be cost-effective only for substantial transactions. With respect to smaller transactions, the legal fees may be much larger than the benefits derived from having a written contract.

The Uniform Commercial Code (UCC) provides businesses with a third and, perhaps the best, alternative. While the UCC applies only to the sale of goods, in situations where it applies, businesses need not draft contracts or rely on anyone else (a supplier, retailer, or attorney) to do so.

CONFIRMING MEMORANDUM

The UCC provides that, where both parties are merchants and one party sends to the other a written confirmation of an oral contract within a reasonable time after that contract was made and the recipient does not object to the confirming memorandum within ten days of its receipt, the contract will be deemed enforceable.

A merchant is defined as any person who normally deals in goods of the kind sold or who, because of occupation, represents themselves as having knowledge or skill peculiar to the practices or goods involved in the transaction. Most businesspeople will be considered merchants.

It should be emphasized that the sole effect of the confirming memorandum is that neither party can use the Statute of Frauds as a defense, assuming that the recipient fails to object within ten days after receipt. The party sending the confirming memorandum must still prove that an oral contract was made prior to or at the same time as the written confirmation. (However, once such proof is offered, neither party can raise the Statute of Frauds to avoid enforcement of the agreement.)

The advantage of the confirming memorandum over a written contract lies in the fact that the confirming memorandum can be used without the active participation of the other contracting party. It would suffice, for example, to simply state "this memorandum is to confirm our oral agreement."

Because you would then still have to prove the terms of that agreement, it would be useful to provide a bit more detail in the confirming memorandum, such as the subject of the contract, the date it was made, and the price or other consideration to be paid. Thus, you might draft something like the following:

> This memorandum is to confirm our oral agreement made on July 3, 2020, pursuant to which supplier agreed to deliver to purchaser

on or before September 19, 2020, 5,000 sheets of letterhead for the purchase price of $600.

The advantages of providing some detail in the confirming memorandum are twofold. First, in the event of a dispute, you could introduce the memorandum as proof of the terms of the oral agreement. Second, the recipient of the memorandum will be precluded from offering any proof regarding the terms of the oral contract that contradicts the terms contained in the memorandum. The recipient or, for that matter, the party sending the memorandum, can introduce proof only regarding the terms of the oral contract that are consistent with the terms, if any, found in the memorandum.

Thus, the purchaser in the example would be precluded from claiming that the contract called for delivery of 10,000 sheets of letterhead because the quantity was stated in the written memo and not objected to. On the other hand, the purchaser would be permitted to testify that the oral contract required the supplier to engrave the letterhead in a specific way, because this testimony would not be inconsistent with the terms stated in the memorandum.

IN PLAIN ENGLISH

If drafting a complete written contract proves too burdensome or too costly, the businessperson should submit a memorandum in confirmation of the oral contract. This at least surpasses the initial barrier raised by the Statute of Frauds. Moreover, by recounting the terms in the memorandum, the businessperson is in a much better position to prove the oral contract at a later date.

Even though the UCC does not provide a method whereby an employee can use a confirming memorandum for the purpose of confirming an oral employment contract, an employee can nevertheless use the confirming memorandum to prevent the other party who does not object in a timely manner from disputing the items stated in the memorandum. In fact, a confirming memorandum could very well state that if the recipient does not object or clarify the items set forth in this memorandum within a prescribed period of time then the individual providing the memorandum will treat the silence as acceptance.

ADDITIONAL TERMS

One party to a contract can prevent the other from adding or inventing terms that are not spelled out in the confirming memorandum by ending the memorandum with a clause requiring all other provisions to be contained in a written and signed document. Such a clause might read as follows.

> This is the entire agreement between the parties and no modification, alteration, or additional terms shall be enforceable unless in writing and signed by both parties.

If you use such a clause, be sure there are no additional agreed-to terms that have not been included in the written document. A court will generally be confined to the four corners of the document when trying to determine what was agreed to between the parties. This means that nothing more than what is on the paper containing the agreement will be allowed as evidence.

An exception to this rule is that a court may allow oral evidence for the purpose of interpreting ambiguities or explaining the meaning of certain technical terms. The court may also permit the other parties to introduce evidence of past practices in connection with the contract in question, in connection with other agreements between the parties, or even in connection with contracts between other parties.

Businesspeople should not rely on oral contracts alone, because they offer little protection in the event of a dispute. The best protection is afforded by a written contract. It is a truism that oral contracts are not worth the paper they are written on.

CONTRACTING ONLINE

In 2000, the Electronic Signatures in Global and National Commerce Act (E-SIGN) became effective. This act was intended, among other things, to encourage online commerce and provide the parties who take advantage of it with the ability to contract in cyberspace.

Where a contract is required to be in writing, parties can decide to contract electronically by affirmatively agreeing to do so. When a company dealing with a consumer is required to provide a contract or notice in writing, that company must both seek the customer's consent to receipt of an electronic document and verify that the document can be accessed and retained by the consumer. For example, the company must notify the customer of the hardware and software requirements for accessing the document.

Once a consumer consents to electronic receipt of documents, the consumer must notify the company of any change in email address. If the customer desires to withdraw their consent to electronic receipt, the location where documents can be sent must be disclosed to the company, as well.

Online contracting is available only when there is a method for preserving the electronic contracts and other relevant data electronically. This will eliminate the need for warehousing hard copies of the documents for online contracting. No special technology must be used for online contracting and the parties are free to establish their own vehicle for accomplishing the act's requirements. Electronically signed documents can be encrypted if the parties agree. In fact, this is likely to be the standard procedure, at least at the initial stages of the development of the online process of contracting.

CONCLUSION

We have now provided you with some of the fundamentals of contract law, which are important for you to understand. In the next chapter we will discuss specific employment contracts and the issues that may arise in the employment context. Later chapters will add additional useful information for both employers and employees.

CHAPTER 4

Union Shops

Employers frequently ask what can be done to avoid union efforts to organize their workforce? The answer is easily stated although its fulfillment will undoubtedly require sustained effort and ongoing vigilance by the employer. The answer is as follows: At all times treat the members of your workforce with dignity and respect and reward their labor with fair wages and fringe benefits. There is an old adage in labor relations that states, "An employer gets the union it deserves."

A BRIEF SUMMARY OF THE HISTORICAL BACKGROUND OF COLLECTIVE BARGAINING AND LABOR UNIONS

One highly regulated area of employment law concerns specialized contracts of employment referred to as "collective bargaining agreements" existing between employers and labor unions.

The history of federal labor laws was extremely turbulent and evidences many hard-fought battles between employers and trade unions in both the federal courts and Congress along the difficult journey to a framework of federal laws and court cases. Numerous laws were enacted for the purpose of regulating the relationship between employers and unions. These laws include the Wagner Act of 1935, Taft-Hartley Act of 1947, and Landrum-Griffin Act of 1959.

During the nineteenth century, the forces of labor and management met on a decidedly imbalanced playing field as labor fought to improve wages and working conditions for workers on the one hand while employers sought to maximize retention of profits and control on the other. Union efforts to improve the economic welfare of the workforce, however, were met with formidable resistance from federal courts. This included, among other things, use of (a) criminal prosecution claiming that unionization interferes with and restrains trade and (b) orders by judges who were not friendly toward labor unions that prohibited strikes, picketing, and product boycotts. Employers were able to use court orders known as injunctions to prevent union activity. These orders were very effective, because they were speedy, and violating them could subject the individual to criminal prosecution.

IN PLAIN ENGLISH

Product boycotts involve situations where employees would advise everyone they communicated with that the identified product should not be purchased because it was created by employees who were not paid fair wages for the work they did. It was hoped that the employer would realize reduced sales and agree to increase wages in order to be able to increase sale of those products.

IN PLAIN ENGLISH

An injunction is a court order that prohibits an individual or group of individuals from doing something, and if the individual or group does not comply with the order, the individual or group could be criminally prosecuted.

Employers were also successful in preventing union activities by filing lawsuits claiming that the union activity was unlawful. Federal antitrust statutes, including the Sherman Act of 1890 and Clayton Act of 1914, provided still further obstacles to union activities. These laws were used by employers to control wages, continue the working conditions the unions were attempting to change, and to subject the unions to significant economic penalties. The irony is that those laws were created with the purpose of controlling employers and not for their benefit.

Eventually, judges changed their attitude toward unions, and many judges became less willing to issue and enforce injunctions against labor unions. The US Congress also began to be sympathetic to the needs of labor unions, and laws were passed to protect the rights of employees. Timing was also favorable to changes in national labor relations policies as the twilight years of the nineteenth century witnessed economic recession and the dawn of the twentieth century revealed the horrors of the First World War. The resulting National War Labor Board introduced the principle of employee freedom to organize in and bargain collectively with employers through trade unions free from employer interference. In 1898, the Erdman Act introduced to the railroad industry principles for the peaceful resolution of disputes through third-party mediation and conciliation efforts, a prohibition against termination from employment for union membership, and the outlawing of so-called "yellow dog contracts," forbidding employees from joining unions. In 1908, the US Supreme Court declared the Erdman Act to be unconstitutional. The Railway Labor Act of 1926 containing similar protections was born, and was eventually upheld in 1930 by a more progressive majority of the Supreme Court.

IN PLAIN ENGLISH

Mediation is a process whereby an independent person who acts neutral, like a referee, assists the employer and the union in working out an acceptable resolution of any dispute they have between them. The mediator does not make any decisions; instead, the mediator merely assists the parties in working out their differences. Conciliation is sometimes used instead of mediation and, in some situations, conciliation is used to define the process of mediation.

The early decades of the twentieth century also witnessed dramatic changes in federal legislation by a more worker-friendly Congress with the goal of protecting the rights of labor to organize and engage in concerted activities to improve the wages and working conditions of workers. The Norris-LaGuardia Act of 1932 declared as public policy that employees were permitted to organize and bargain collectively, free from employer coercion and sought to achieve that goal by regulating, and in most cases, prohibiting issuance of injunctions in a "labor dispute." Peaceful strikes, picketing, and boycotts were thus sheltered from the injunction in most cases and in those limited instances where injunction was appropriate the length was limited, a trial by jury was guaranteed for issuance of an early injunction and the judge who issued the injunction was prohibited from presiding over any later proceedings for violation.

Until the mid-1930s, however, Congress applied a more hands-off policy toward the often-combative conflicts between unions and employers, with each side left to their own economic weapons to bring pressure to bear upon their opposition. For unions, that economic pressure came in the form of the strike and picketing of the employers' premises. For employers, that economic pressure was discharging striking workers and locking them out of the employer's premises. This hands-off approach, however, inevitably led to highly emotional and combative conflicts between labor and management that often escalated quickly into outright physical violence and bloodshed.

With the Wagner Act of 1935, often referred to as the National Labor Relations Act ("NLRA"), however, Congress began to take a more proactive and rational approach to a national labor relations policy. NLRA declared as federally protected "the right to self-organization, to form, join, or assist labor organizations, to bargain collectively through representatives of their own choosing, and to engage in concerted activities for the purpose of collective bargaining or other mutual aid or protection." NLRA also declared illegal certain employer acts, known as "unfair labor practices" such as restraint, interference, or coercion of employees in the exercise of their rights to organize. The NLRA also restricted employers by prohibiting discrimination in terms of employment so as to discourage union membership and the employers' refusal to bargain in good faith with the majority employee representative.

NLRA unfair labor practices were furthermore to be monitored through judicial-type proceedings before a newly created three-member (later expanded to five members) National Labor Relations Board ("NLRB"). The NLRB was further charged with authority to conduct secret-ballot elections for purposes of a group of common interest employees ("a bargaining unit") and selecting a labor organization to represent them for purposes of dealing with their employer. The NLRA ultimately withstood constitutional challenge and was approved by the Supreme Court in *NLRB v. Jones & Laughlin Steel Corp.*

With the enactment of the NLRA came a dramatic rise in union membership, increased union awareness and power, collective bargaining, and increased strikes. Unfortunately, the increase in union activity was also accompanied by a degree of corruption and undemocratic practices in internal union affairs. As union activity increased, the NLRB became more active by aggressively pursuing employers with claims for unfair labor practices.

IN PLAIN ENGLISH

"Collective bargaining" is defined as negotiations by groups of employees for salaries, other benefits, and working conditions.

The rise in unionization resulted in pushback from Congress and in the passing of the Taft-Hartley Act of 1947. This Act separated the criminal and civil processes in labor relations. The Office of General Counsel is responsible for handling the criminal proceedings and the NLRB itself is responsible for handling the civil or administrative proceedings. The Taft-Hartley Act impacted employers and supervisors in several ways, such as excluding supervisors and independent contractors from NLRA coverage, adding additional free speech protections for employers, and prohibiting employers from requiring union membership prior to hiring (this is referred to as the "closed shop"). The Taft-Hartley Act also impacted employees and unions as well by providing employees with the right to decline joining the union process. This act also granted the US Court of Appeals greater authority to review NLRB findings and remedies.

In 1959, the NLRA was again amended by the Landrum-Griffin Act to address corruption within union leadership by requiring elaborate reporting requirements to the US Department of Labor and a "bill of rights" for union members covering such matters as internal union elections, eligibility for internal union offices, and union disciplinary procedures.

With this historical overview in mind, we will now turn to the subject of union access to the employer's premises for the purposes of unionizing employees.

CAN AN EMPLOYER'S PROPERTY BE LAWFULLY ACCESSED FOR PURPOSES OF TRYING TO UNIONIZE?

It may come as a surprise to some employers that the answer to the above question is generally "yes." Questions concerning union access to employer's property for purposes of exercising rights under the NLRA, however, are complex and often very fact specific. Any employer considering preparing and spreading a "no union solicitation rule" on its premises would therefore be well advised to first discuss the matter with a competent attorney familiar with this area of labor law. Similarly, union organizers should become familiar with this area of the law when faced with an employer's "no union solicitation rule" in order to properly comply with legal requirements. The following brief overview of this area may prove helpful when discussing these issues with your attorney or within the union.

Access to an employer's premises for purposes of employee solicitation on behalf of a union may potentially occur by either: (1) an employee of an employer who is a union supporter during working or nonworking hours; or (2) a nonemployee of the employer such as a professional organizer employed by a union. Whether it is legal for an employer to refuse to grant this type of access under each circumstance depends on the below factors. We will first discuss access by an employer's own employees for union solicitation purposes.

SOLICITATION BY EMPLOYEES OF THE EMPLOYER

Whether an employer is required to allow employees on their property for the purpose of promoting a union depends on a balancing of the competing interests of (a) NRLA rights that outlaw employer interference with employee organized activities on the one hand and (b) the employer's interests in imposing limitations on the time and manner in which employees may solicit on behalf of a union.

An employer will usually announce a "no solicitation rule" prohibiting employee promotion of a union or from handing out pro-union literature on its premises by threatening discipline either in advance of or in the midst of a union election campaign. In 1945, the US Supreme Court declared such a rule to be invalid, though there were some exceptions. Under the Supreme Court's analysis, it does not need to be proven that the employer's rule against promoting a union actually interfered with a union's ability to communicate with the employee. The Court also found that it did not need to be proven that the employer's reason for having such a rule was to intentionally discourage union efforts in its workforce. Such a rule is presumed to be an unreasonable obstacle to unionization and, therefore, discriminatory in the absence of evidence that special circumstances make the rule necessary in order to maintain production or discipline.

To comply with the Supreme Court's ruling, however, care must be taken in the no-solicitation rule to distinguish between "working hours" and "working time." While the term "working hours" is normally understood to apply to all time between when an employee "clocks in" at the beginning of their work shift and "clocks out" at the end of their workday, "working time" applies only to those hours when the employee is actually engaged in the performance of work. An employer's general ban against solicitation during all "working hours" (which would include both breaks and lunchtime) will be found to be automatically in violation of the prohibition against "restraint, interference, or coercion," while a more specific restriction only against solicitation during times when work is actually being performed would not run afoul of the NLRA unless it is communicated or applied in such a way that it affects employees on the times mentioned above. An employer can overcome the above restrictions if the rule is necessary for efficiency, safety, or discipline. One example is when the employer produces aircraft and spacecraft. Another exception is in retail businesses where the rule prohibits employees from engaging in union solicitation in places where there may be customers, such as the sales floor, elevators, or stairways.

Also regarding the area of solicitation on the employer's property, an employer's no-solicitation rules prohibiting all distribution of union literature (i.e., pamphlets) in working areas including those times when no work is being performed is more allowable than oral solicitation provisions due to the potential creation of litter and the relative ease with which employees can carry leaflets to nonworking areas for distribution and perusal during nonworking times. A blanket no-distribution ban on such literature will, however, be presumed illegal if it applies to nonworking time and to areas on the employer's premises, such as a company parking lot, which are other than areas where work is actually performed.

The presumed validity of no-solicitation rules concerning working time, however, may be overcome by the NLRB's General Counsel when there is specific proof the rule was adopted for discriminatory purposes with a specific desire to inhibit union communication with employees. If an employer permits working-time solicitation to other organizations, such as for athletic events or charities, or permits solicitation of an *anti-union* nature, it will be deemed to evidence a discriminatory motive and any presumed business rationale for the employer's no-solicitation policy will thus be seriously undermined.

The timing of the announcement of no solicitation rules by itself, however, is irrelevant. While the presumed validity of a "no-solicitation during work time" rule will *not* be overcome simply by the timing of its announcement or reactivation, a case for unlawful discrimination due to the timing of the rule may be reinforced by other employer unfair labor practices or permission granted to other entities to engage in solicitation. The burden will then shift to the employer to establish that the no solicitation rule is necessary for production or discipline.

Union Pins and Buttons

The wearing of union pins or buttons also falls within the domain of no-solicitation rules. The wearing and display of such items by employees are treated as protected activity. Unlike no-solicitation rules, however, even when the employer's ban against wearing such pins and buttons is limited to hours when work is actually being performed and not to all working time, there is no presumption of the rule's validity and the burden is on the employer to demonstrate that special circumstances warrant interference with those protected activities such as when specific words on a union button provoke other employees to serious anger, will affront the employer's customers, or distract employees from tasks requiring substantial concentration.

Evidence concerning the employer's permission to allow employees to wear other pins and only disallow the wearing of union pins may serve as further evidence of discrimination against the union and thus unlawful interference.

Collective Bargaining Agreements' Relaxation of NLRA Protections Concerning No-Solicitation Rules

Contractually agreed upon no-solicitation rules may be denied enforcement by the NLRB when doing so would effectively permit the current union to waive the right of employees campaigning for a competing union or against unionization altogether. This rule concerning contractually agreed no-solicitation rules has also been extended to the distribution of campaign literature during nonworking time and nonworking areas by candidates for the union election of officers.

Some unions have attempted to invoke the Supreme Court rule regarding the presumption of illegality of no-solicitation rules under circumstances where employees who are not working return to the employer's property and attempt to solicit on behalf of the union employees who are working but on their breaks or lunchtimes. Such attempts have been rejected by both the NLRB and one federal court of appeals. These attempts by off-duty employees were regarded as similar to that of a nonemployee and therefore can be excluded without reason from the employer's property during their nonworking time.

NONEMPLOYEE SOLICITATION ON BEHALF OF UNIONS

While the above outlines the rules concerning employee solicitations on behalf of unions, it should be noted the rules concerning nonemployee solicitation have been far more restrictive. Thus, the Supreme Court concluded:

> It is our judgment . . . that an employer may validly post his property against nonemployee distribution of union literature if reasonable efforts by the union through other available channels of communication will enable it to reach the employees with its message and if the employer's notice or order does not discriminate against the union by allowing other distribution.

Later decisions, however, have held that in those instances where it is not practical to promote the union to employees off company premises because of the employees' location, the employer is required to open its premises to nonemployee union organizers under reasonable conditions. Such has been applied to (1) a remote logging camp or a mining camp on a distant island, (2) sailors aboard shipping tankers, and (3) mountain-resort employees who spend both working and nonworking time on the employer's premises. Once again, however, if the employer prohibits access to its premises only to nonemployee union organizers but permits other nonemployees (such as groups promoting recreational activities, political groups, or charitable organizations, etc.) upon its property to solicit or communicate for other nonunion purposes, the presumed validity of the exclusionary rule is defeated.

While unions have attempted to find constitutionally protected free speech rights in instances where nonemployee union organizers solicit employees on employer property, those efforts have proven unsuccessful. It may thus be concluded that with the limited exception of "company towns," any asserted right of both employees and nonemployees to solicit on employer property cannot be based on federal Constitution guarantees to free speech but must instead be based on the above analysis of the NLRA and any accommodation between employee rights under the NLRA and the property rights of employers.

IN PLAIN ENGLISH

While there are only a few towns that are exclusively for a company, they do exist. These are towns which are owned by the company. All of the stores and amenities are owned and maintained by the company. Only company employees live in those towns.

CAPTIVE AUDIENCE SPEECHES

It should be added that employers may lawfully assemble its employees on its premises during working hours for purposes of delivering an anti-union address to them, referred to as "captive audience" speeches. Unless the employer's no-solicitation rule is unlawfully overbroad to include forbidding union solicitation during nonworking time during working hours such as during employee breaks and lunches, an employer does not commit an unfair labor practice by denying a union's request for an "equal time" opportunity to reply. Moreover, an employer's denial of equal time is ordinarily presumed to be lawful even though the employer's solicitation is forced and unlawful (and thus subject to remedy though the filing of an unfair labor practice). If the NLRB's General Counsel can demonstrate the union is seriously incapacitated from reply communications to employees through alternative means, then the employer's denial of equal time is unlawful.

ACCESS TO THE NAMES AND ADDRESSES OF AN EMPLOYER'S EMPLOYEES

Finally, on a topic related to union access of the employer's premises, the NLRB held that within one week of the agreement upon or the ordering of a representation election, the employer is obliged to furnish to the NLRB for transmittal to the union the names and addresses of all employees eligible to vote in the election.

HYPOTHETICAL EXAMPLE

The following hypothetical is provided for purposes of illustrating some of the major principles discussed in this chapter.

Floe's Fabulous Flip-Flops ("FFFF"), based in Fabulous Fairbanks, manufactures casual footwear for women and men at its adjacent plant, which it then sells to customers at its many retail stores throughout the United States, When rumors began to circulate that certain FFFF employees were discussing among themselves taking steps through the NLRB to seek collective bargaining representation from United Sole Workers of America (USW), FFFF's senior managers announced and distributed to all employees a written company-wide no-solicitation and dress code policy ("policy") declaring, "No shoes, No socks, and No solicitation!" Among its many prohibitions, FFFF's new policy strictly forbade employees while at work in either its manufacturing or retail operations from soliciting other employees to join or otherwise support any union efforts to organize FFFF's workforce during "working hours," including employee rest breaks and lunch breaks. According to FFFF's no-solicitation policy, any employee discovered violating the policy would be immediately fired from employment.

TJ, a longtime associate working in FFFF's Rodeo Drive store, receives a copy of FFFF's policy. Following conclusion of TJ's shift that afternoon, TJ visits the offices of NLRB Region 21 in Los Angeles to discuss FFFF's no-solicitation policy with a member of its General Counsel staff. TJ thereafter initiates a Charge Against Employer, alleging that FFFF's no-solicitation policy violates NLRA. What would be the probable outcome of the unfair labor practice charge prosecuted by NLRB's General Counsel against FFFF?

- Consistent with the union access principles discussed above, with regard to employees in its manufacturing facility, FFFF may lawfully announce and distribute the foregoing no-solicitation rule if changed to limited solicitations by employees when work is actually being performed.
- FFFF's plan, when applied to its manufacturing operations, would also not violate NLRA if it excluded times when employees are not engaged in the actual performance of work duties such as during their rest breaks and meal breaks.
- FFFF's no-solicitation rule when applied to the distribution of union literature in its factory would not violate NLRA if it prohibited distribution of literature in areas of the plant where work is performed due to hazards created by littering and the relative ease of distribution and perusal by

employees of union literature in nonwork areas during nonworking time.

- FFFF's rule would furthermore not run afoul of NLRA prohibitions regarding solicitation even during nonworking time if applied to its retail operations forbidding employee solicitations while present on the retail floor and in other store areas such as stairways and elevators accessible by customers.

FFFF's rule prohibiting solicitation on employer premises by nonemployees or employees who are off duty would not violate constitutionally protected free speech rights.

CONCLUSION

By treating members of the workforce with dignity and respect and paying them a fair wage and fringe benefits for their work, there is little incentive for their seeking assistance from a union to negotiate and thereafter "police" collective bargaining agreements containing contractually guaranteed wages, hours, and other terms and conditions of employment.

After all, what rational worker would voluntarily pay costly dues out of their paycheck to pay a union to represent them when dealing with their employer unless the employer's practices gives them cause to do so? It is certainly not easy for unions to organize a group of workers. It therefore follows that an employer must first set the stage for a union to organize its workforce by treating them in a manner perceived to be disrespectful and/or paying them less than their counterparts employed in similar industries who are represented by a union.

On the other side of the equation, an employer may wish to consider the consequences should his workforce become organized by a union representing them when dealing with management. Under those circumstances, the employer loses control over a portion of its enterprise concerning the management of its workforce, which become governed by the terms and conditions specified in a resulting collective bargaining agreement with the union. Moreover, the employer, in all likelihood, will feel the need when faced with vigorous union advocates to retain expert assistance on its own side of the bargaining table during often difficult negotiations leading to an initial collective bargaining agreement and each time the agreement is up for renewal.

Also, during the term of the collective bargaining agreement, grievances may be filed by the union, which is charged with policing the agreement challenging the employer's claim violations of the agreement. The employer may once again feel compelled to retain expert representation, often by skilled attorneys, to defend itself against the union's grievance should it go to arbitration and thus incur the necessary time and expenses in doing so, including, at minimum, significant legal costs. And that is a best-case scenario when the employer wins in arbitration. Employers should also consider, however, the additional financial costs and loss of credibility in the eyes of the union should the employer lose the case in arbitration and be required to pay damages potentially in the thousands of dollars to its aggrieved employees. It all becomes quite costly, distracting, and time consuming.

CHAPTER 5

Collective Bargaining Agreements

INTRODUCTION

Perhaps one of the most significant legislative achievements of the twentieth century for the protection of the private sector's workforce was Congress's passage of the National Labor Relations Act ("NLRA"). The history of the law's development and evolution is discussed more fully in Chapter 4. While limited in scope to workers in the private sector (and thus inapplicable to public-sector employees at the federal, state, and municipal government levels, as well as to agricultural workers), the NLRA nevertheless provides an orderly system whereby employees may (1) choose to organize into bargaining units composed of workers with a similar community of interests thereby creating a new labor organization ("union"), or (2) select a preexisting union to represent them by means of free and transparent elections for collective bargaining purposes. Once a union has been selected it will thereafter represent the employees' interests at the bargaining table by engaging their employer in negotiations over the terms of wages, hours, and other conditions of employment that ultimately are converted into a written collective bargaining agreement. This agreement will govern the employment relationship with the union member's employer for a mutually agreed upon period of time.

The NLRA thirdly provides legal protections to workers and their union representatives so that they can engage in good-faith bargaining over the terms of collective bargaining agreements. The NLRA also protects these individuals' participation in various forms of activities in furtherance of their exercise of rights protected by the NLRA. These activities include the right to quasi-judicial hearings before administrative law judges of the National Labor Relations Board ("NLRB") to adjudicate various charges of alleged unfair labor practice violations of the NLRA.

IN PLAIN ENGLISH

Quasi-judicial means that it is not actually a traditional court. It resembles a court and follows similar procedures. An example of this would be a proceeding handled by an administrative law judge rather than a traditional state or federal judge.

This chapter, concerning collective bargaining in the private sector, is divided into three distinct but connected areas. First discussed is the law governing organizing workers into appropriate bargaining units and the conduct of free elections to determine whether bargaining unit members wish or do not wish to be represented by a union for collective bargaining purposes. Secondly, we shall discuss the law governing the rights of the union, if selected to represent the bargaining unit, when engaging in collective bargaining with an employer. These negotiations concern the terms and conditions of employment that later become the union contract and collective bargaining agreement. Lastly, we shall discuss the law governing the rights of employees to engage in protected activities on behalf of themselves and their coworkers without being discriminated against or otherwise penalized for their exercise of protected activities under the NLRA.

You should be aware of the fact that this chapter simply provides a general overview of this complex area of law governing collective bargaining relationships in the private sector. A far more detailed and comprehensive resource for research in this area may be found in *The Developing Labor Law: The Board, the Courts, and the National Labor Relations Act* by John Higgins and published by the American Bar Association. This is a very technical book and would likely be a good resource for your employment attorney. The best way for you to handle an employment-related problem is for you engage the services of a competent attorney, many of whom specialize in the area of traditional labor law and exclusively represent either individual employees and unions or employers.

THE NATIONAL LABOR RELATIONS ACT (NLRA)

The NLRA, it should be initially noted, is decidedly pro–collective bargaining in its vision concerning the national interest of providing an orderly mechanism for the resolution of disputes that inevitably arise within of the employer-employee relationship. Indeed, the NLRA's stated purpose is to define and protect the rights of employees as well as employers, to encourage collective bargaining, and to eliminate certain practices on the part of labor and management that are harmful to the general public welfare.

The NLRA states and defines the rights of employees in the private sector to organize and bargain collectively with their employers through representatives of their own choosing or alternatively to decline to do so. To ensure that employees can freely choose their own representatives for purposes of collective bargaining (or choose not to be represented), the NLRA establishes procedures by which employees can exercise their choice by means of secret-ballot elections conducted by NLRB staff. Furthermore, to protect the rights of employees and employers alike, and to prevent labor disputes that would adversely affect the rights of the general public, Congress has defined certain practices of employers and unions as "unfair labor practices," which are prohibited by the law.

The NLRA is principally administered and enforced by the National Labor Relations Board (NLRB) and its Office of the General Counsel acting through fifty-two regional and field offices located in major cities across the United States. The General Counsel and staff of the NLRB's Regional Offices investigate and prosecute unfair labor practice cases on behalf of individuals and businesses that file complaints. The office also conducts representation elections to determine employee union representatives. The presidentally appointed five-member NLRB decides cases involving charges of unfair labor practices and determines representation election questions as referred from its regional offices.

IN PLAIN ENGLISH

This is an attorney appointed by the president of the United States for a four-year term to head the legal department for the National Labor Relations Board. The current general counsel is Peter B. Robb.

COLLECTIVE BARGAINING AND REPRESENTATION OF EMPLOYEES

Collective bargaining as defined by NLRA Section 8(d) requires an employer and the representative of its employees to meet at reasonable times, confer in good faith about certain matters, and to put into writing any agreement reached if requested by either party (all Section references in this chapter at to the National Labor Relations Act unless otherwise specified). The parties must confer in "good faith" (a term of art defined through NLRB and federal court cases) with respect to wages, hours, other terms or conditions of employment, the negotiation of an agreement, and any questions arising under an agreement.

IN PLAIN ENGLISH

"Good faith" is defined as an honest intent to do some action without taking advantage over another person or to fulfill a promise, even when some legal technicality is not satisfied. This term is used in many areas of the law and it has different meanings depending on the context in which it is used. For purposes of the National Labor Relations Act it is defined by numerous employment cases.

It is an unfair labor practice for either party to refuse to bargain collectively with the other. That obligation to bargain in good faith, however, does not compel either party to agree to a proposal of the other, nor does it require either party to make a concession to the other.

Section 9(a) provides that employee representatives "designated or selected for the purposes of collective bargaining by the majority of the employees in a unit appropriate for such purposes, shall be the exclusive representatives of all the employees in such unit for the purposes of collective bargaining."

Appropriate Bargaining Units

What is an appropriate bargaining unit? A bargaining unit is a group of two or more employees who share a community of interest regarding their wages, hours, and other terms and conditions of employment and may reasonably be grouped together for purposes of collective bargaining. The determination of what is an appropriate unit for such purposes is, under the NLRA, left to the NLRB's discretion. Section 9(b) states that the NLRB shall decide in each representation case whether, "in order to assure to employees the fullest freedom in exercising the rights guaranteed by this Act [NLRA], the unit appropriate for the purposes of collective bargaining shall be the employer unit, craft unit, plant unit, or subdivision thereof."

Generally speaking, the appropriateness of a bargaining unit is determined on the basis of a community of interest of the employees involved. Those who have the same or substantially similar interests concerning wages, hours, and working conditions are grouped together in a bargaining unit. In determining whether a proposed unit is appropriate, the following factors are also considered:

- Any history of collective bargaining.
- The desires of the employees concerned.
- The extent to which the employees are organized. Section 9(c)(5), however, forbids the NLRB from giving this factor controlling weight.

Exclusions from Bargaining Units

Who can or cannot be included in a bargaining unit? A unit may cover the employees in one plant of an employer, or it may cover employees in two or more plants of the same employer. It should be noted that a bargaining unit can include only persons who are "employees" within the meaning of the NLRA. As referenced earlier, the NLRA excludes from its coverage certain individuals such as agricultural laborers, independent contractors, supervisors, and persons in managerial positions, from the meaning of "employees." None of these individuals can thus be included in a bargaining unit established by the NLRB.

In addition, the NLRB, as a matter of policy, excludes from a bargaining unit an employee who acts in a confidential capacity (a confidential employee) to an employer's labor relations officials.

Once an employee representative has been designated by a majority of the employees in an appropriate bargaining unit, the NLRA makes that representative the *exclusive* bargaining agent for all employees in the unit. As the exclusive bargaining agent for the unit, the union has a duty to represent all employees in the unit fairly and equally without regard to their union membership or activities (the duty of fair representation). Once a collective-bargaining representative has been designated or selected by its employees, it is illegal for an employer to bargain with anyone other than the designated representative for members of that unit or for the unit itself.

Section 9(a) provides that any individual employee or group of employees shall have the right at any time to present grievances to their employer and to have such grievances heard without the intervention of the bargaining representative, provided:

- The hearing is not inconsistent with the terms of any collective-bargaining agreement then in effect; and
- The bargaining representative has been given the opportunity to be present at such a hearing.

How Are Bargaining Representatives Selected

The NLRA requires that an employer bargain with the representative selected by its employees. The most common method by which employees can select a bargaining representative is a secret-ballot representation election conducted by the NLRB staff. There are a number of cases both in front of the administrative law judges and in traditional courts that involve these types of elections. This is a complex area of employment law, and if you are involved with union elections you should enlist the aid of an experienced attorney.

The Rights of Employees

The rights of employees are principally set forth in Section 7. Examples of the rights protected by Section 7 are as follows:

- Forming or attempting to form a union among the employees of a company.
- Joining a union whether the union is recognized by the employer as the representative of a bargaining unit or not.
- Assisting a union in organizing the employees of an employer.
- Going out on strike (a refusal to work) to secure better working conditions of employment.
- Refraining from activity on behalf of a union.

Union-Security Agreements

Pursuant to the NLRA, unions may be elected to provide representation services to members of a bargaining unit. In exchange for providing those services, however, a union will seek a form of payment ("union dues") from bargaining unit members to defray the costs and expenses of providing those representational services.

The NLRA permits, under certain conditions, a union and an employer to enter into an agreement (a "union-security agreement") that *requires* bargaining unit members to make certain payments to the union from their paychecks (dues checkoffs) for purposes of providing representation services in order to *retain* their jobs. A union-security agreement cannot, however, require an *applicant* for employment to become a union member in order to be hired, and such a union-security agreement can also not require employees to actually *join* or *maintain membership in* a union in order to retain their jobs.

Under a valid union-security agreement, employees choosing to not become dues-paying members of a union may, however, be required, as with employees who actually do join the union, to pay full initiation fees and dues following a "grace period" after a collective-bargaining agreement becomes effective or after a new employee is hired. However, the most that can be required of nonmembers of the union who advise the union representing them that they object to the use of their payments of dues for nonrepresentational activities (such as for political campaign contributions) is that they pay their fair share of the union's costs resulting from providing actual representational services to all bargaining unit members. These services include collective bargaining with the employer, contract administration ("policing the agreement"), and grievance hearings (including arbitration through the grievance procedures in collective bargaining agreements).

Under a union-security agreement, employees who have religious objections to becoming union members or to financially supporting a union ("religious objectors") may be excused from paying any union dues or initiation fees. Religious objectors, however, may be required to make a comparable financial contribution to a nonreligious, nonlabor, tax-exempt organization instead of making payments to a union. Unions representing such employees may also charge them the reasonable costs associated with any grievances under the collective bargaining agreement processed upon their behalves.

STRIKES

Section 7 furthermore states, in part, "[e]mployees shall have the right to engage in other concerted activities for the purpose of collective bargaining or other mutual aid or protection." Strikes (the withholding of labor from an employer) are included among those concerted employee activities protected by this section. Section 13 also addresses the right to strike. It is clear from both Sections 7 and 13 that while the law guarantees the right of employees to strike, it does so cautiously. Sections 7 and 13 place limitations and qualifications on the exercise of an employee's right to strike.

The lawfulness of a strike may depend on the object or purpose of the strike, on its timing, or upon the conduct of the strikers involved while on the picket line.

Employees and employers who anticipate being involved in a strike action should proceed with extreme caution. Furthermore, it is important to seek the advice of competent legal counsel as such activities are likely to result in serious ramifications to the parties' ongoing labor-management relationship and could result in substantial economic damages.

Employees who strike for a lawful purpose fall into one of the following two classes: "economic strikers" and "unfair labor practice strikers." Both classes of strikers continue as employees under the NLRA during the course of the strike, but unfair labor practice strikers possess greater rights to reinstatement to their jobs following conclusion of the strike than economic strikers.

If the *object* of a strike is to obtain from the employer some form of *economic concession* such as higher wages, shorter hours, or better working conditions, the striking employees are called "economic strikers." Economic strikers retain their status as employees and cannot be discharged. They can, however, be replaced by their employer. If the employer has hired bona fide *permanent* replacements to fill the jobs of the economic strikers, then when the strikers apply to return to work unconditionally, the strikers are not legally entitled to immediate reinstatement at that time. If the economic strikers do not obtain regular and substantially equivalent employment with their employer, they are only entitled to recall to jobs for which they are qualified when such positions become available. As noted above, this is only if they, or their bargaining representative, make an unconditional request for reinstatement.

On the other hand, employees who strike in protest of an *unfair labor practice* committed by their employer are called "unfair labor practice strikers." Unfair labor practice strikers can neither be discharged *nor* permanently replaced. When the strike ends, unfair labor practice strikers, absent serious misconduct on their part during the strike, are entitled to have their jobs back. This is true even if replacement employees hired during the strike must be discharged in order to do so. It should be noted that misconduct while participating as pickets on the picket line qualifies as serious misconduct that could override the right of reemployment.

Given the distinctions between the rights of economic versus unfair labor practice strikers, it is important to recognize the perilous positions both employers and unions may be placed in with respect to strikes. A strike following a period of negotiations at the bargaining table that has failed to achieve an agreement is likely to be accompanied by unfair labor practice charge(s) claiming the employer has failed to bargain in good faith with the union. If employees then strike against the employer, the union will likely argue they are unfair labor practice strikers and thus entitled to immediate reinstatement following conclusion of the strike. The employer, on the other hand, may respond that the employees are in fact striking in order to extract economic concessions from the employer that the union was otherwise unable to achieve at the bargaining table. Thus, the strikers are economic strikers who are not entitled to immediate reinstatement following conclusion of the strike.

Untangling a strike's true intent is likely to be a complex, protracted, and legally expensive task, which must be adjudicated by the NLRB. Should the NLRB ultimately conclude that economic strikers or unfair labor practice strikers have unconditionally requested reinstatement and been unlawfully denied reinstatement by the employer, the NLRB may award such strikers back pay starting from the date they should have been reinstated. This can result in a substantial financial burden for employers.

The most logical, and potentially economically advantageous, solution to resolve such a legal dilemma, especially when the intent of a strike is ambiguous, is to draft the terms of striking employees' reinstatement into an agreed-upon settlement that includes a successor collective bargaining agreement. The Federal Mediation and Conciliation Service, which has offices in major cities throughout the United States, maintains a staff of highly skilled and experienced mediators who may be dispatched at no cost to the parties to mediate and potentially resolve these and other types of labor disputes.

IN PLAIN ENGLISH

A mediator is an individual who is retained by the parties to a dispute to assist them in resolving the dispute. The mediator is impartial and acts like a referee. The mediator does not have to be an attorney, though most of them are. The mediator's sole mission is to resolve the dispute. While services such as the Federal Mediation and Conciliation Service exist and offer their services free of charge, it is typical for mediation expenses to be equally divided between the parties in other situations.

A strike may be found unlawful, however, because an object or purpose of the strike is unlawful. For example, it is an unfair labor practice for an employer to discharge an employee for a failure to make certain lawful payments to the union when there is no union-security agreement in effect. A strike to compel an employer to do this in the absence of a lawful union-security agreement would be an example of a strike for an unlawful objective or purpose and, therefore, constitute an unlawful strike.

Furthermore, Section 8(b)(4) prohibits strikes for certain objectives even though the objectives are not necessarily unlawful when achieved by other means. For example, consider a strike to compel Employer A to cease doing business with Employer B. It would not be unlawful for Employer A to voluntarily stop doing business with Employer B. Nor is it unlawful for a union to merely request that it cease doing business with Employer B. It is, however, unlawful for the union to strike Employer A with an object of forcing that employer to cease doing business with Employer B.

A strike that violates a no-strike provision of a collective bargaining agreement is also not protected by the NLRA, and the striking employees can be discharged or otherwise disciplined for engaging in such a contractually prohibited strike. This is true unless the strike is called by the union to protest certain kinds of unfair labor practices being committed by the employer. It should also be noted that not all refusals to work are considered a "strike" and thus a violation of no-strike provisions of collective bargaining agreements. For example, a walkout by employees due to conditions abnormally dangerous to their health and safety, such as a defective ventilation system in a spray-painting shop, has been held not to violate a no-strike provision in the collective bargaining agreement.

Section 8(d) provides that when either party desires to terminate or change an existing collective bargaining agreement, it must comply with certain preconditions for doing so. If these preconditions are not met, however, a strike to terminate or change a contract is unlawful and participating strikers then lose their status as employees of the employer engaged in the labor dispute.

Strikers who engage in serious misconduct in the course of a strike may also be refused reinstatement to their former jobs with their employer. This applies to economic strikers and unfair labor practice strikers alike. Serious misconduct on the picket line has been held to include, for example, violence and threats of violence. The US Supreme Court has furthermore ruled that a so-called sit-down strike, that is, when employees stay inside an employer's plant but refuse to work, thereby preventing the employer from continuing its operations by use of replacement workers and thus depriving the owner of the use of his property, is not protected by the NLRA. Furthermore, examples of serious misconduct that may cause employees involved in strike activities to lose their right to reinstatement are:

- Strikers physically blocking persons from either entering or leaving a struck plant.
- Strikers threatening violence against non-striking employees.
- Strikers attacking management representatives.

Likewise, the right to picket an employer's premises is subject to certain limitations and qualifications. As with the right to strike, picketing can be prohibited due to its objective or timing, or due to misconduct while on the picket line.

UNFAIR LABOR PRACTICES OF EMPLOYERS

Potential unfair labor practices of employers are listed in Section 8(a) while those of unions are in Section 8(b). Section 8(e) furthermore lists an unfair labor practice that can be only be committed when both an employer and a union are acting in concert.

Section 8(a)(1)—Interference with Section 7 Rights

Any prohibited interference by an employer with the rights of employees to organize, form, join, or assist a labor organization, to bargain collectively, to engage in other concerted activities for mutual aid or protection, or to refrain from any or all of these activities, constitutes a violation of this section.

Examples of violations of Section 8(a)(1) includes employer conduct that may independently violate Section 8(a)(1). Examples of such independent violations are:

- Threatening employees with loss of jobs or benefits if they should join or vote for a union.
- Threatening to close down the plant if a union should be organized in it.
- Questioning employees about their union activities or membership in such circumstances as will tend to restrain or coerce the employees.
- Spying on union gatherings, or pretending to spy.
- Granting wage increases deliberately timed to discourage employees from forming or joining a union (the so-called "fist inside a velvet glove").

Section 8(a)(2)—Domination or Illegal Assistance and Support of a Labor Organization

Section 8(a)(2) makes it unlawful for an employer "to dominate or interfere with the formation or administration of any labor organization or contribute financial or other support to it." This section not only outlaws "company unions," which are dominated by the employer, but also forbids an employer from contributing money to a union it favors or giving a union improper advantages that are denied to rival labor organizations.

An employer violates NLRA Section 8(a)(2) by:

- Taking an active part in organizing a union or forming a committee to represent employees.
- Bringing pressure on employees to support a union financially, except in the enforcement of a lawful union-security agreement.
- Allowing one of several unions, competing to represent employees, to solicit authorization cards for representation on company premises during working hours and denying other unions the same privilege.

- Soliciting and obtaining from employees and applicants for employment, during the hiring procedure, applications for union membership and signed authorizations for the check-off of union dues.

Section 8(a)(3)—Discrimination Against Employees

Section 8(a)(3) makes it an unfair labor practice for an employer to discriminate against employees "in regard to hire or tenure of employment or any term or condition of employment" for the purpose of encouraging or discouraging membership in a labor organization. In general, the NLRA makes it illegal for an employer to discriminate in employment because of an employee's union or other group activity within the protection of the NLRA. A banding together of employees, even in the absence of a formal organization, may constitute a labor organization for purposes of Section 8(a)(3).

Discrimination within the meaning of the NLRA would include such action as refusing to hire, discharging, demoting, assigning to a less-desirable shift or job, or withholding benefits.

The NLRA does not limit an employer's right to discharge for economic reasons. This section does not limit an employer's right to discharge, transfer, or lay off an employee for genuine economic reasons or for such good cause as disobedience or deficient work performance. This right applies equally to employees who are active in support of a union and to those who are not.

Situations in which an employer disciplines an employee both because the employee has violated a work rule and because the employee has engaged in protected union activity are called "mixed motive cases." In these cases the burden of proof is initially on the union to establish the essential elements of a prohibited discrimination unfair labor practice, then shifts to the employer, and the discipline will be found unlawful unless the employer can establish that the employee would have received the same discipline even if the employee had not engaged in protected union activity.

An employer who has engaged in good-faith bargaining with a union may lock out the represented employees, sometimes even before an "impasse" is reached in the parties' negotiations if the employer does so to further its position in bargaining. A bargaining lockout may be found unlawful, however, if the employer is unlawfully refusing to bargain or is bargaining in bad faith.

IN PLAIN ENGLISH

"Impasse" refers to a situation in which no further progress is possible, especially because of disagreement; a deadlock.

Examples of illegal discrimination under Section 8(a)(3) include:

- Discharging employees because they urged other employees to join a union.
- Refusing to reinstate employees when jobs they are qualified to perform are open because they took part in a union's lawful strike.
- Granting of "superseniority" to those hired to replace employees engaged in a lawful strike.
- Demoting employees because they circulated a union petition among other employees asking the employer for an increase in pay.
- Discontinuing an operation at one plant and discharging the employees involved followed by opening the same operation at another plant with new employees because the employees at the first plant joined a union (a so-called "runaway shop").
- Refusing to hire qualified applicants for jobs because they belong to a union. It would likewise be a violation if the qualified applicants were refused employment because they did not belong to a union, or because they belonged to one union rather than another.

Section 8(a)(4)—Discrimination Due to NLRB Activity

Section 8(a)(4) makes it an unfair labor practice for an employer "to discharge or otherwise discriminate against an employee because the employee has filed charges or given testimony under [the National Labor Relations Act]."

Examples of violations of Section 8(a)(4) are:

- Refusing to reinstate employees when jobs they are otherwise qualified for are open because they filed charges with the NLRB claiming their layoffs were based on union activity.

- Demoting employees because they testified in an NLRB hearing.

Section 8(a)(5)—Refusal to Bargain in Good Faith

Section 8(a)(5) makes it illegal for an employer to refuse to bargain in good faith concerning wages, hours, and other conditions of employment with the representative selected by a majority of the employees in a bargaining unit appropriate for collective bargaining purposes.

Required subjects of bargaining are broadly interpreted by the NLRB. The duty to bargain in good faith covers all matters concerning rates of pay, wages, hours of employment, or other conditions of employment. These are called "mandatory" subjects of bargaining, about which the employer, as well as the employees' representative, must bargain in good faith. Remember, however, the law does not require "either party to agree to a proposal or require the making of a concession." In addition to wages and hours of work, mandatory subjects of bargaining include but are not limited to such matters as pensions for present employees, bonuses, group insurance, grievance procedures, safety practices, seniority, procedures for discharge, layoff, recall, or discipline, and union-security. Certain managerial decisions such as subcontracting, relocation, and other operational changes may not be mandatory subjects of bargaining, even though they affect employees' job security and working conditions. With "nonmandatory" subjects, the parties are free to bargain and to agree, but neither party may insist on bargaining such subjects over the objection of the other party.

What constitutes a violation of NLRA Section 8(a)(5)? An employer will be found to have violated Section 8(a)(5) if its conduct in bargaining, viewed in its entirety, indicates the employer did not negotiate with a good-faith intention to reach agreement (so called "surface bargaining"). However, the employer's good faith is not at issue when its conduct constitutes an out-and-out refusal to bargain on a mandatory subject of bargaining (a "per se bad faith" bargaining violation). For example, it is a violation for an employer, regardless of its good faith, to refuse to bargain about a subject that it believes is not a mandatory subject of bargaining, when in fact it is.

Finally, the duty of an employer to bargain in good faith includes the duty to refrain from unilateral action, that is, taking action on its own with respect to matters concerning which it is required to bargain, and from making changes in terms and conditions of employment without consulting the employees' representative.

Examples of Section 8(a)(5) violations are as follows:

- Refusing to meet with the employees' representative because the employees are out on strike.
- Insisting, until bargaining negotiations break down, on a contract provision that all employees will be polled by secret ballot before the union calls a strike.
- Refusing to supply the employees' representative with cost and other data concerning a group insurance plan covering the employees.
- Announcing a wage increase without consulting the employees' representative.
- Failing to bargain about the effects of a decision to close one of the employer's plants.

UNFAIR LABOR PRACTICES OF UNIONS

Section 8(b)(1)(A)—Restraint and Coercion of Employees

Section 8(b)(1)(A) forbids a labor organization or its agents from "restrain[ing] or coerce[ing] employees in the exercise of the rights guaranteed [by the law]." The section notes it is not intended to "impair the rights of a labor organization to prescribe its own rules" concerning membership in the labor organization. Like Sections 8(a)(1) for employers, Section 8(b)(1)(A) is violated by union conduct that independently restrains or coerces employees in the exercise of their rights.

Union conduct that is reasonably calculated to restrain or coerce employees in their rights violates Section 8(b)(1)(A) whether or not it succeeds in actually restraining or coercing employees.

Examples of restraint or coercion that violate Section 8(b)(1)(A) when done by a union or its agents include the following:

- Mass picketing in such numbers that non-striking employees are physically barred from entering the plant.
- Acts of force or violence on the picket line, or in connection with a strike.
- Threats to do bodily injury to non-striking employees.

- Threats to employees that they will lose their jobs unless they support the union's activities.
- Statements to employees who oppose the union that the employees will lose their jobs unless the union wins a majority in the plant.
- Entering into an agreement with an employer that recognizes the union as exclusive bargaining representative when it has not been chosen by a majority of the employees.
- Fining or expelling members for crossing a picket line that is unlawful under the NLRA or which violates a no-strike agreement.
- Fining employees for crossing a picket line after they have resigned from the union.
- Fining or expelling members for filing unfair labor practice charges with the NLRB or for participating in an investigation conducted by the NLRB.

The following are examples of restraint or coercion that violate Section 8(b)(1)(A) when done by a union that is the exclusive bargaining representative:

- Refusing to process a grievance in retaliation against an employee's criticism of union officers.
- Maintaining a seniority arrangement with an employer under which seniority is based on the employee's prior representation by the union elsewhere.
- Rejecting an application for referral to a job in a unit represented by the union based on the applicant's race or union activities.

Section 8(b)(1)(B)—Restraint and Coercion of Employers

Section 8(b)(1)(B) prohibits a labor organization from restraining or coercing an employer in the selection of a bargaining representative.

Examples of violations of Section 8(b)(1)(B):

- Insisting on meeting only with a company's owners and refusing to meet with the attorney the company has engaged to represent the company in contract negotiations, and threatening to strike to force the company to accept its demands.

- Striking members of an association of employers (such as the United Employers Association or the National Association of Colleges and Employers) that bargains with the union as the representative of the group of employers in order to compel the struck employers to sign individual contracts with the union.
- Insisting during contract negotiations that the employer agree to accept working conditions that will be established by a bargaining group to which it does not belong.
- Fining or expelling supervisors for the way they apply the bargaining contract while carrying out their supervisory functions or for crossing a picket line during a strike to perform their supervisory duties.

Section 8(b)(2)—Causing or Attempting to Cause Discrimination

Section 8(b)(2) makes it an unfair labor practice for a labor organization to cause an employer to discriminate against an employee in violation of Section 8(a)(3).

What violates Section 8(b)(2)? A union violates Section 8(b)(2), for example, by demanding an employer discriminate against employees because of their failure to make certain otherwise lawful payments to the union when there is no valid union-security agreement in effect. This section can also be violated by agreements or arrangements with employers that unlawfully condition employment or job benefits on union membership, on the performance of union membership obligations, or on arbitrary grounds. Union conduct affecting an employee's employment in a way that is contrary to provisions of the bargaining contract may likewise be violations of this section.

Examples of violations of Section 8(b)(2) are:

- Causing an employer to discharge employees because they circulated a petition urging a change in the union's method of selecting shop stewards.
- Causing an employer to discharge employees because they made speeches against a contract proposed by the union.
- Making a contract that requires an employer to hire only members of the union or employees "satisfactory" to the union.

- Causing an employer to reduce employees' seniority because they engaged in antiunion acts.
- Refusing referral or giving preference on the basis of race or union activities in making job referrals to units represented by the union.
- Seeking the discharge of an employee under a union-security agreement for failure to pay a fine levied by the union.

Section 8(b)(3)—Refusal to Bargain in Good Faith

Section 8(b)(3) makes it illegal for a labor organization to refuse to bargain in good faith with an employer about wages, hours, and other conditions of employment if it is the representative of that employer's employees. This section imposes on labor organizations the same duty to bargain in good faith that is imposed on employers by Section 8(a)(5).

Examples of violations of Section 8(b)(3). Section 8(b)(3) is violated by any of the following:

- Insisting on the inclusion of illegal provisions in a contract, such as a "closed shop" (must be a member of the union to be hired) or a discriminatory hiring hall.
- Refusing to negotiate on a proposal for a written contract.
- Striking against an employer who has bargained, and continues to bargain, on a multiemployer basis to compel it to bargain separately.
- Refusing to meet with the attorney designated by the employer as its representative in negotiations.
- Terminating an existing contract and striking for a new one without notifying the employer, the Federal Mediation and Conciliation Service, and the state mediation service, if any.
- Conditioning the execution of an agreement on inclusion of a provision that is not required such as a performance bond.
- Refusing to process a grievance because of the race, sex, or union activities of an employee for whom the union is the statutory bargaining representative.

IN PLAIN ENGLISH

A closed shop is a situation in which only members of the union involved are allowed to be employed. Most US states have laws prohibiting this conduct. These laws are often referred to as "right to work laws."

Section 8(b)(4)—Prohibited Strikes and Boycotts

Section 8(b)(4) prohibits a labor organization from engaging in strikes or boycotts or taking other specified actions to accomplish certain unlawful objectives or "objects" as they are called in the NLRA. Because this is a very technical and complex area of the law, and, because the violation can be very serious, it is essential to enlist the aid of an experienced attorney with respect to these types of issues. A union commits an unfair labor practice if it takes any of the kinds of action listed in clauses (i) and (ii) as a means of accomplishing any of the objects listed in the four subparagraphs thereof.

Examples of violations of Section 8(b)(4)(B):

- Picketing an employer to force it to stop doing business with another employer who has refused to recognize the union.
- Asking the employees of a plumbing contractor not to work on connecting up air-conditioning equipment manufactured by a nonunion employer whom the union is attempting to organize.
- Urging employees of a building contractor not to install doors that were made by a manufacturer that is nonunion or that employs members of a rival union.
- Telling an employer that its plant will be picketed if that employer continues to do business with an employer the union has designated as "unfair."

Section 8(b)(5)—Excessive or Discriminatory Membership Fees

Section 8(b)(5) makes it illegal for a union to charge employees who are covered by an authorized union-security agreement a membership fee "in an amount which the [NLRB] Board finds excessive or discriminatory under all the circumstances."

Examples of violations of this section include:

- Charging old employees who do not join the union until after a union-security agreement goes into effect an initiation fee of $15 while charging new employees only $5.
- Increasing the initiation fee from $75 to $250 and thus charging new members an amount equal to about four weeks' wages when other unions in the area charge a fee equal to about one half the employee's first week's pay.

Section 8(b)(6) (so-called "Featherbedding")

Section 8(b)(6) forbids a labor organization "to cause or attempt to cause an employer to pay or deliver or agree to pay or deliver any money or other thing of value, in the nature of an exaction, for services which are not performed or not to be performed."

IN PLAIN ENGLISH

Exaction is defined as demanding a payment or service from someone when such payment or service is not justified or otherwise required.

Section 8(b)(7)—Organizational and Recognitional Picketing by Noncertified Unions

Section 8(b)(7) prohibits a labor organization that is not currently certified as the employees' representative from picketing or threatening to picket with an objective of obtaining recognition by the employer ("recognitional picketing") or acceptance by its employees as their representative ("organizational picketing").

Section 8(e)—Entering a "Hot Cargo Agreement"

Section 8(e) makes it an unfair labor practice for an employer or a labor organization to enter a "hot cargo agreement" pursuant to which an employer agrees not to work on or handle any freight or product coming from any other employer with which the union has a dispute. This section applies equally to both unions and to employers. This discussion of Section 8(e) as an unfair labor practice of employers applies equally as a discussion of an unfair labor practice committed by unions as well.

Section 8(g)—Striking or Picketing a Health-Care Institution Without Notice

Section 8(g) prohibits a labor organization from engaging in a strike, picketing, or other concerted refusal to work at any health-care institution without first giving at least ten days' prior notice in writing to the institution and the Federal Mediation and Conciliation Service.

CONCLUSION

As discussed above, the objective of the NLRA is to avoid or reduce industrial strife and protect the public health, safety, and interest. The NLRA goal, can best be achieved by the parties or those who may become parties to an individual dispute. Voluntary adjustment of differences at the community and local levels is almost invariably the speediest, most satisfactory, and longest-lasting way of carrying out the objective of the NLRA. As noted throughout this book, it is essential for you to enlist the aid of an experienced attorney when dealing with the complex issues discussed in this chapter, because the penalties for violations may be significant, and the law is very complex.

CHAPTER 6

Creating Effective Employee Handbooks

Few of us would consider venturing on a road trip to some distant place we have never visited before without first consulting a reliable road map. The same is true when beginning a new employment relationship. The employee must first consult the employer's employee handbook, a special kind of "road map," to guide the employee through the navigation of the employment "journey."

As mentioned on the subject of new employee orientation in Chapter 7 of this book, every employer should have a well-thought-out and clearly written employee handbook setting forth in clear and understandable language (in plain English) its policies and procedures on such matters as sexual harassment prevention, nondiscrimination in employment, hours of work, security requirements, overtime pay, and the like. The handbook should make it clear to employees that it is not an employment contract and continued employment is strictly "at will." This provision will also benefit the employer. It should also cover trade secret protection as discussed in Chapter 10 of this book. This document should be drafted, or at least reviewed, by an attorney with experience in employment law, because there are numerous requirements for legal notices and other areas that a layperson or even employee handbook software may fail to properly address.

"EMPLOYEE HANDBOOK" DEFINED

An employee handbook is a relatively compact "booklet" for ease of reference that provides information and guidance to employees regarding their employer's history, business goals, shared values, practices, policies, and procedures. A properly prepared employee handbook provides a reliable resource for both employees and their employer to refer to when questions arise in the workplace and clearly defines the expectations of each party to the employment relationship. Employee handbooks also typically include a variety of other subject matters such as an employer's dress code and grooming standards, employee compensation, fringe benefits, sick time, and other paid leaves of absence.

Importantly, employee handbooks may serve as a preventative device for avoidance of potential litigation between disgruntled former employees and their employer. To ensure that all employees have received and reviewed the employee handbook, every employee should be required to sign and date an acknowledgment form created for that purpose when the employment relationship begins.

Moreover, an employee handbook establishes important legal protections for employers and defines the unique employment relationship between the business and its employees. For example, if an employer terminates the employment relationship, the "at will" provisions stated in the employee handbook should provide protection to the employer from legal liability due to a "wrongful termination" lawsuit, which are increasingly common today.

PRELIMINARY CONSIDERATIONS BEFORE CREATING AN EMPLOYEE HANDBOOK

Because the employee handbook is an employer's rulebook, it is the prevailing resource, for example, used when creating periodic employee performance reviews. It should also provide an orderly system for alternative dispute resolution ("ADA") should employment issues arise in the workplace, including both mediation and arbitration as discussed in Chapter 16 of this book. The employer's human resources specialist will frequently consult the handbook, employees will occasionally revisit it as issues arise, and the employer will scrutinize the handbook when periodically revising policies. By reviewing the employee handbook, employees should be able to determine from its contents how ideal employees are expected by their employer to perform their duties in the workplace and the standards they must work to attain and thereafter maintain throughout the employment relationship.

IN PLAIN ENGLISH

Mediation is a procedure whereby an individual known as a mediator acts like a referee in assisting the parties to a dispute in resolving that dispute. The mediator serves as a catalyst to the parties' voluntary resolution of their disputes and is not a decision maker. The mediator's role is to be impartial and aid the disputing parties in compromising their differences.

An arbitrator, on the other hand, is a decision maker—an arbitrator acts like a judge. Arbitration is similar to an actual court proceeding, though it is customarily conducted in an office rather than in court and with limited exception is final and binding on the parties.

An Employee Handbook Provides Protection against Lawsuits

Items to include in order to provide protection against costly litigation include (a) a written and signed acknowledgment of receipt of the employee handbook; (b) a disclaimer setting forth an at-will employment clause that provides in clear and unambiguous language that receipt of the employee handbook does not constitute an employment contract and is not a guarantee of future employment; and (c) an explanation that the employer retains its management right to change employment policies contained in the handbook at any time. Other matters included in the employee handbook are policies concerning sexual harassment prevention, nondiscrimination, termination from employment, a section on ADA dispute resolution, and numerous other provisions that relate to the employment relationship (discussed more fully later in this chapter). By clearly communicating these policies in an employee handbook, the employer advises employees what they can and cannot do in the workplace and what may be considered grounds for their discipline, up to and including termination from employment.

An Employee Handbook Provides a Window into an Employer's Culture and Shared Values

While many employee handbooks may appear similar in content, preparation of a customized employee handbook for a particular employer begins from inside the business organization and works outwardly in formation of its ultimate content. Therefore, in preparing an employee handbook for a particular employer, time and attention must be initially invested in a soul-searching assessment of the employer's unique culture, values, and goals for the future of its enterprise. After conducting such an assessment, the employer should adopt language in the employee handbook which reflects its identified culture, values, and goals. While the content of the employee handbook is extremely important, the overall tone conveyed to the reader must also be considered. Employees reading the employee handbook will thus receive a message from its content and tone concerning how the employer views employees, the employment relationship, and the manner in which employees should respond.

An Employee Handbook Is Not an Employment Contract

Chapter 3 of this book discusses the formation and contents of employment contracts. It should be emphasized, however, that there are a few but critical distinctions between employment contracts and employee handbooks. First and foremost, an employment contract is a legally binding document while an employee handbook is not binding on the employer, although it will outline various policies and procedures that employees are required to follow. Some of these policies and procedures are required by laws, such as those discussed in Chapters 9 and 10 of this book dealing with employee dignity, privacy, and reputation as well as ownership of work. Secondly, employee contracts are specific to each individual employee and therefore apply solely to that employee. An employment contract details the legal rights and obligations of the employer and the employees generally. Importantly, an employee must be consulted if an employer wishes to amend the terms of an employment contract, and the employee may decline to agree to any of the employer's proposed amendments. An employee handbook, on the other hand, details guidelines, policies, and procedures applicable to all the employer's employees, which may be changed at any time without consulting with the employees who are bound by its terms. This is because the employer should state in the handbook that it reserves the right to amend the handbook by providing a certain time period for notice of the amendment. The expected behaviors and practices contained in the employee handbook may or may not be required by laws outside of the employment relationship such as, with a few exceptions, the employer's attendance policy. It should be noted, however, that because employees cannot be expected to follow the requirements of any amendments to the employee handbook that the employee is unaware of, employees must first be clearly advised of any revisions to the employee handbook's terms, and a written acknowledgment of their receipt and understanding of those amendments must be signed by all employees.

REASONS TO CREATE EMPLOYEE HANDBOOKS

Employee handbooks provide employers an opportunity to detail their expectations of all staff members in a standardized, consistent format. They also assist in the establishment of the employer's standards of employee accountability. Additionally, employee handbooks provide a common platform with which to share the business organization's culture, values, and mission with its employees, and provide a resource for employees to consult regarding their compensation, benefits, and other policies applicable to them.

As a pragmatic matter, without a written handbook to consult, employees may be left with an incomplete understanding of their benefits and thus fail to fully appreciate and use all of the benefits they are entitled to receive from their employer. Most importantly, however, an employee handbook clearly communicates the employer's expected workplace behavior and performance standards for employees. Whenever issues arise concerning employee workplace behavior or performance, the clearly expressed terms of the employee handbook preclude an employee's claimed ignorance of employer expectations.

SMALL START-UP COMPANIES

When an employer is initially becoming established and employs only a handful of people, it may be tempting to believe there is no need to take time from a busy schedule to go to the trouble of creating an employee handbook. To the contrary, however, this is the ideal time when a small start-up is in the best position to focus on its long-term culture, vision, and goals, and then memorialize those ideals in an employee handbook so future growth and development may be guided by those goals. When just starting up, the employer is in a better position to organizationally define itself than when it is more mature and disagreements may arise among managers concerning the direction and process of moving forward. An employee handbook that is well thought out and visionary in its scope may serve as a useful reminder of the employer's goals and culture. Finally, once a business is well established, the way in which things are done by habit and custom may become "set in concrete," and more resistant to change. When an employee handbook is created in the beginning, it is easier, whenever necessary, to make specific modifications to it rather than create an employee handbook after a significant time period of operation without one.

FAMILY BUSINESSES

Each family unit has its own well-established and unique set of values, priorities, and goals. When family members form a business together, however, that business entity may be subject to a natural attempt to "graft" the family unit's rootstock with a "branch" of its business culture and values. This tendency may be useful when both cultures of the family unit and the family business are compatible and align well. But that may not always be an ideal business model. It is therefore a better practice when establishing a family business to perform an assessment of what the family business' culture will ultimately reflect. By giving careful consideration to the ultimate goal of what a family business should be and memorializing this business culture into an employee handbook, the family unit is required to examine its own existing culture and values, assess whether they are suitable for the business model being established, and place those goals and ideals into a written employee handbook. By doing so early, future conflict among family members, which may prove fatal to the business, may be reduced and both the family unit and the family business will likely benefit.

HOW TO PREPARE AN EFFECTIVE EMPLOYEE HANDBOOK

Just as with any important document that will be used during the ongoing employment relationship, preparation of an effective employee handbook begins with a detailed outline of those items to be included within it. When preparing the outline, however, an employer should begin by performing a realistic assessment of the business and its relationship to the employees who must perform all necessary tasks to make it successful, including its core values, business ethics, long-term goals, and vision for the future. Following creation of an outline, the employer then begins to add details to the outline under each item contained in the outline and discuss the information the employer wishes to communicate to its employees on those particular subjects. The employer then continues to then add further details under each item discussed and repeatedly revises the document as necessary until the employer is satisfied that the subjects covered have been thoroughly discussed, resulting in a workable rough draft of its employee handbook.

Importantly, however, once a rough draft has been completed to the best of an employer's abilities, have the document carefully reviewed by an experienced employment attorney. The employment counsel may then add language to the draft concerning any important matters that have been overlooked by the employer, or possibly delete other provisions that in the lawyer's experience may prove problematic in the future. Many employment attorneys have drafts of employee handbooks that they have prepared for other clients that may prove useful in tailoring a employee handbook for your business. Your lawyer may be willing to assist you in creating a unique employee handbook specifically for your business once you provide the lawyer with some fundamental information about your business, the benefits provided, and other information which you believe would be helpful. You should consult with your attorney in order to determine whether the lawyer will assist by creating the initial draft handbook or whether the lawyer recommends that you create the first draft. The greater the time, input, discussion, and careful consideration that is invested in preparation of an employee handbook, the more likely it will provide a solid foundation for the employment relationship with the employer's workforce for many years ahead.

ITEMS THAT SHOULD BE *INCLUDED* IN EMPLOYEE HANDBOOKS

1. **The Purpose of the Employee Handbook.** This section of the employee handbook provides a brief explanation of the employer's purpose.

2. **The Employer's Vision and Mission Statements.** This section succinctly summarizes what the employer does, its goals, core values, and mission.
3. **The Employer's Employment Policies.** This section provides a brief statement of the employer's commitment to adhere to all laws governing equal employment opportunity, nondiscrimination due to disabilities, and to provide for religious accommodations.
4. **Employee Conduct and Discipline.** This section provides employees with a detailed statement of the employer's expectations concerning work performance and conduct standards while in the workplace as well as disciplinary procedures and consequences that may result due to an employee's failure to abide by those expectations. Many employers utilize a system of progressive discipline for certain areas of misconduct with each succeeding offense receiving more severe disciplinary penalties. If a progressive disciplinary policy is adopted by an employer, it should be stressed that some transgression, such as violence in the workplace and theft, are considered so serious by the employer that they will result in the employee's immediate termination from employment even in the absence of prior progressive discipline. There are some offenses the employer may also wish to add and identify as falling under a so-called zero-tolerance policy (sometimes referred to as "one and done" violations) for which no prior discipline is necessary before termination from employment. Examples of such offenses include: use of cell phones while driving ("distracted driving"); sexual harassment of employees, customers, and suppliers (which may result in costly litigation and liability to the employer); or drug or alcohol use while on the employer's premises. Each employer must carefully consider its disciplinary policy, including any potential liability that may occur to itself due to commission of certain offenses by its employees. Areas for discipline should at minimum include:

i. Anti-Harassment and Discrimination Policies. This section of the employee handbook is a prohibition defining the employer's rules regarding harassment and discrimination. An employer must decide which behaviors qualify for discipline under these categories, where allegations of misconduct should be reported to the employer and how the employer will respond. There are, however, many state and federal laws pertaining to certain offenses in these areas as well. An employer's policies concerning these types of misconduct must accordingly comply with these legal requirements. Moreover, if inconsistencies exist between the employer's policies concerning these matters and laws and regulations on this subject, the employer must ensure its policies are interpreted and enforced in a manner consistent with all laws and regulations. To ensure an employer's anti-harassment and antidiscrimination policies are legally compliant with all federal, state, and local laws, they should be reviewed and uniformly administered in frequent consultation with an experienced employment attorney.

ii. The policies should also specify that they are applicable to all employees including the employer's officers, managers, and supervisors regardless of the level within the employer's hierarchy. Experience has provided valuable lessons that all employers must heed concerning potential and costly legal consequences that may arise due to commission of such offenses by members of the employer's management.

5. **Drug Testing and Substance Abuse.** This is a statement explaining whether mandatory drug testing of employees is required by the employer. It should furthermore detail how such drug testing, if administered by the employer, will be performed, whether it will uniformly occur on an annual basis, after a workplace accident or injury, or randomly. The handbook should specify what the disciplinary consequences are due to a failed drug screen test whether it be progressive discipline or zero tolerance. The distinction

between progressive discipline and zero-tolerance disciplinary policies is discussed in Chapter 15 of this book. This statement should also include all other policies regarding drug and alcohol use while on the employer's premises, including its parking lots, and the disciplinary consequences for violations.

6. **Timekeeping and Payroll Practices.** This section provides a statement outlining requirements under both state and federal law for payment of employee compensation. This statement should also include any employer policy concerning attendance, reporting of gratuities, and legal consequences that may result due to breaking any laws. It should furthermore provide all details of employee benefits provided by the employer including: (a) 401(k)s or similar retirement benefits; (b) paid time off; (c) any "perks" of employment, including eligibility requirements for receipt of this benefit and contact information for the outlined programs; (d) travel and expense reimbursements; and (e) health insurance.
7. **Time Off and Vacation Policies.** This section outlines federal and state mandatory leaves of absence (such as FMLA leave), holidays, paid vacation, sick leave, medical leave, military leave, and how employees should communicate or schedule these leaves of absence subject to their supervisor's approval. Employers should consult with an experienced attorney to ensure the stated medical leave policies are in full compliance with the complexities and intersections of the Family and Medical Leave Act of 1993, state-required maternity and paternity leaves of absence, as well as workers' compensation leave.
8. **Health, Safety, and Emergency Policies.** This section of the employee handbook includes the employer's policies and procedures regarding work-related injuries or accidents, possession of weapons, Occupational Safety and Health Act compliance, and how various workplace emergencies must be handled and reported.
9. **Separation Policy.** This statement explains the employer's policies and procedures for both voluntary and involuntary

terminations of the employment relationship. This section also sets forth the employer's expectations of its employees when separating from employment and in return the employer's expected obligations to the separating employee.

10. **Other Policies.** Other possible policies to be placed in employee handbooks include the following: (a) social media usage while in the workplace; (b) confidentiality policies explaining the employer's standards for protecting both its internal information as well information related to its clients; (c) use of the employer's equipment and software for personal reasons rather than the employer business; (d) conflicts of interest; (e) dress and grooming standards; (f) romantic and sexual relationships with coworkers; (g) smoking/vaping policies; and (h) nepotism.
11. **A Disclaimer/Acknowledgement Form.** As discussed above, a disclaimer form should be prepared stating that the employee handbook is not intended by the employer to create an employment contract. It should also require the employee to sign the document under language stating they have received, read, and understand the employee handbook and, furthermore, understand that they are responsible for complying with its terms. Have this form carefully reviewed by an experienced employment attorney and retain it in the employee's official personnel file.

IN PLAIN ENGLISH

Perk is defined as a benefit over and above the salary that is unique to the employer. This would include, for example, educational benefits, gym memberships, working meals, and workplace snacks and drinks.

Employees should read the employee handbook carefully. Be sure that it is understood, and if there are any questions regarding a provision, a supervisor should be consulted regarding those questions. If you, as an employee, think the item is important and unclear in the employee handbook, then you should request that the supervisor provide you with a written explanation of the item so that it will be available to you if a problem should arise.

That written explanation should be retained by you with the employee handbook.

ITEMS THAT SHOULD BE *EXCLUDED* FROM EMPLOYEE HANDBOOKS

As discussed above, there are many items that should be covered by employee handbooks. It is equally important to emphasize, however, that there are several items that should be excluded. While the list of items to be excluded from employee handbooks is shorter than the list of items to be included, items to be excluded are equally important and can have serious legal ramification to an employer should they be inadvertently included in the handbook.

It is therefore important to avoid use of several common phrases and topics in an employee handbook. Doing so may create potential "gray areas" that could lead to miscommunications of the employer's expectations of employees and may potentially have serious legal consequences. The following language should therefore be excluded from employee handbooks:

1. Any language that refers to or even implies job security guarantees. Avoid implying anything about employee job security by avoiding phrases such as when an employee becomes "permanent" or implies an employee's job may not be terminated "without good cause." Use of such phrases may be interpreted by employees (and potentially the courts) as implying the employment relationship cannot be terminated "at will" by the employer.
2. Any language that refers to the employment handbook as a comprehensive document. While it is important the employee handbook provides as much relevant information as possible to employees, do not omit warning employees that it is not to be construed as a comprehensive statement and may be changed at the employer's unilateral discretion. For example, although certain grounds for discipline may not be explicitly stated in the employee handbook's section on discipline, if an employer should conclude commission of a certain offense is too serious to ignore, the employer may still discipline the employee for that misbehavior so long as

it is clear in the employee handbook that the grounds for discipline have not been comprehensively stated.

3. By providing a disciplinary policy in its employee handbook, an employer should carefully avoid becoming "trapped" by detailing what specific levels of discipline will be administered for each particular offense comitted. Some employers have erred in this regard by attempting to be too precise in an effort to provide its supervisors with clear and uniform instructions on how to administer discipline to employees in each case. To provide flexibility to the employer in disciplining employees at various levels from warnings to terminations, employers should instead use general terms in the employee handbook to describe the types of offenses subject to discipline, such as "attendance," "theft," "violence," and "insubordination," which are inclusive of a broad range of misconduct, and then explain again in general language that each individual transgression must be independently assessed for purposes of determining the appropriate level of discipline based on its own unique facts and circumstances.

TASKS FOLLOWING DRAFTING AN EMPLOYEE HANDBOOK

1. The employer's management team should be thoroughly trained on all policies outlined in the employee handbook so they may, in turn, answer any questions from employees and thereafter uniformly enforce its provisions without discrimination.
2. The employer's employees should also be trained on all policies outlined in the employee handbook to provide them a clear understanding of all employer policies and give them an opportunity to ask clarifying questions before signing the handbook acknowledgment form discussed earlier in this chapter.
3. The employer should furthermore provide uniform procedures to periodically conduct refresher training either in person or online for employees and their supervisors

concerning the policies in the employee handbook and document receipt of that training by a signed acknowledgment form.

4. Revisit the employee handbook on a regular basis, at all times regarding it as a "living" document, and revise it accordingly as employment laws and regulations will inevitably change. Employers should ask an experienced employment attorney to alert them of any new developments on matters contained in the employee handbook including such areas as nondiscrimination in employment, retirement and employee benefits, changes in technology, overtime and minimum-wage law requirements, and then have an employment attorney revise the employee handbook and discuss it with the employer to ensure it remains fully compliant with all new laws, regulations, and court developments.

CONCLUSION

A well-conceived and drafted employee handbook is an essential tool for all businesses, no matter the nature of the enterprise or how large or small its workforce may be. The handbook is created by an employer working with its attorney to assist the employer's employees in successfully navigating the employment relationship by providing advanced written notification of the employer's standards and expectations for satisfactory job performance. An employee handbook is drafted without consultation with employees, may be unilaterally modified or adjusted at any time by the employer, and does not form an employment contract. Because of the practical and legal consequences of its language and use, however, employers would be well advised to consult an employment lawyer frequently in its creation, application, and periodic modifications to ensure both its terms and use remain fully compliant with all laws and regulations pertaining to the dynamic field of employment law. Employees who have questions or concerns about any of the items in the employee handbook should request clarification from the employee's supervisor or appropriate management representative.

CHAPTER 7

An Employee's First Day—Onboarding

Once a candidate has been interviewed, drug screened, background checked, offered employment, and signs an employment contract (discussed in Chapters 2 and 3 of this book), there are a number of very important "onboarding" items which must be addressed.

To begin with, the new employee is required to present proof of citizenship or at least proof that the individual is eligible to work in the United States. This means the employee must provide a "green card" to the employer. It is a good idea for employers to make copies of whatever document the new employee presents in this regard, which should then be filed in the employee's personnel file. Because it is unlawful for an employer to permit an individual to be employed if employee is not a US citizen or does not possess a green card, violation of this requirement has serious legal consequences to the employer and must therefore be strictly adhered to.

IN PLAIN ENGLISH

A green card is a document which a permanent resident alien is provided so that the individual can legally work in the United States. While this is the most common document for noncitizen employees, there are other documents that permit employment for noncitizens as well. For example, the noncitizen may have a work visa for temporary employment. For purposes

(Continue on next page)

of this book, we will use the term "green card" as the document noncitizen employees must provide regardless of the status of the noncitizen. If you have any doubt about whether the document provided by a noncitizen employee is valid for allowing that individual to work for you, you should check with an employment attorney or Homeland Security. For noncitizen employees who have any questions about the validity of the document to be provided to the new employer, then conferring with an immigration lawyer or Homeland Security is also recommended.

The new employee should also be provided a copy of the employer's employee handbook (discussed in detail in Chapter 6 of this book). It is important the new employee be required to sign a written acknowledgment indicating the handbook has been received, read, and is understood. The employer should therefore prepare in advance a written acknowledgment form to this effect that the new employee is then required to sign and date within just a few days after beginning employment. The signed acknowledgement form should likewise be placed in the new employee's personnel file. Employees should carefully read and be sure to completely understand the employee handbook or, if there are any questions, they should be asked and a written response requested so that the individual knows exactly what the rules of employment are. The employer's written response to the employee's questions should be retained by the employee with his copy of the employee handbook. The employee's personnel file should also contain all other important documents relevant to the individual's employment.

THE IMPORTANCE OF ONBOARDING

A well-prepared orientation program for new employees, known in human resources as "onboarding," is an important element in providing new employees with a warm and practical welcome. This in turn prepares the employee to succeed in the new employment relationship. By carefully preparing a well-thought-out onboarding program, an employer will be benefited in the following respects:

1. It minimizes legal risks to the employer, by reminding new employees to submit all employment documents by their deadlines;

2. It permits the parties to the employment relationship to focus on those items that are the most important once the new employee arrives for the first day on the job;
3. It makes the new employee more comfortable on the job due to the employer's advance preparation of the work space and related equipment and supplies; and
4. It creates a friendlier, more collaborative work environment for the entire workforce, as current employees will know when and how to welcome their new coworker.

SEXUAL HARASSMENT PAMPHLETS AND VIDEOS

Sexual harassment in the workplace presents a very serious and potentially costly danger for all of today's employers and employees. As such, new employees should be required to watch an instructional video on the subject of preventing sexual harassment. Such videos are relatively inexpensive and readily available from a number of online sources. It is a good idea for employers to have one of these videos available to its workforce at all times and to require annual review by all employees. Because the law evolves rapidly in this dynamic area, however, it is appropriate to obtain updated materials and videos at least once every three years.

Additionally, the employer should be sure that there are standing instructions to its employment attorney for updates regarding sexual harassment. At that time, it would be appropriate for the employer to obtain a more up-to-date video on sexual harassment prevention that includes the change(s) noted by legal counsel.

Some employers use pamphlets rather than videos for the above-mentioned purposes. The employer must determine which medium it feels would be the most effective for new and continuing members of its workforce. The choice of medium is, of course, entirely subjective, because some individuals learn better through oral instruction while others by visual instruction. As noted above, it is also wise to conduct annual refresher training on the topic of preventing sexual harassment regardless of medium. These refresher trainings may be accomplished using a computer and appropriate software designed for this purpose. Regardless of the medium of the training, it is important to document each employee's receipt of mandatory refresher training and file a record of such in the employee's personnel file.

IN PLAIN ENGLISH

While this section recommends the use of instructional videos or pamphlets, some employers actually have live presentations and others require employees to attend seminars conducted by industry or professional associations. The method by which the sexual harassment material is presented will likely vary depending upon the size, location, and preference of the employer. Regardless of the medium, the material presented must be up-to-date, comprehensive, and accurate.

ITEMS TO BE ACCOMPLISHED *BEFORE* A NEW EMPLOYEE'S FIRST DAY

A truly successful onboarding program, however, begins even before the employee's first day on the job. The following checklist serves as a guide to ensure the necessary onboarding items are completed prior to a new employee's first day. While the remaining material in this chapter is primarily addressed to the employer, new employees should read it and understand it in order to anticipate what to expect in the initial phase of the employment process.

☐ **Paperwork to Be Completed by New Employee. If appropriate for the employment relationship,** prepare a written employment contract (see Chapter 3 of this book) for the new employee to sign. All employment contracts when used should include the following content:

1. Job title and department assigned to;
2. Hours and days of employee's work schedule;
3. Length of employment;
4. Compensation and fringe benefits to be earned;
5. Employee job responsibilities consistent with position's job description (see discussion in this chapter under "job description");
6. Nondisclosure agreement (see discussion in Chapter 3 of this book);
7. Non-compete agreement (see discussion in Chapter 3 of this book);
8. Employee invention agreement;

9. Paid and unpaid leaves of absence policy; and
10. Grounds for discipline consistent with the employee handbook and any other rules of conduct (see discussion in Chapter 15 of this book).

☐ **Offer of Employment.** Send the new employee a written offer of employment. In this document the employer should detail the basics of the employer–employee relationship, which include:

1. New employee's job title;
2. Department assigned to;
3. Name and position of new employee's direct supervisor;
4. Work schedule (consistent with the written employment contract referenced above);
5. Starting date;
6. Compensation;
7. Fringe benefits;
8. Length of employment;
9. Date by which candidate needs to respond in writing to the offer of employment letter; and
10. The employer may wish to also attach the actual employment contract (discussed in Chapter 3 of this book) in which the terms of employment are detailed in order to answer any questions by the new employee and avoid any awkward or disruptive surprises and resulting misunderstandings following arrival for the first day of work.

☐ **Required Employment Forms.** Complete any employment forms required by federal, state, or local laws. These forms commonly include the following:

1. W-4 form;
2. I-9 form;
3. State tax withholding form;
4. Employee invention agreement form;
5. Direct deposit form; and
6. Health insurance form.

ADDITIONAL TASKS TO BE PERFORMED *BEFORE* A NEW EMPLOYEE'S FIRST DAY

Both employers and employees should be familiar with their respective roles and responsibilities when beginning the employment relationship. In this section, we will explain what we recommend for employers to welcome the new employee into the job. While this section is addressed to employers, a new employee should be familiar with it so that the new employee can be prepared to accomplish the required tasks.

☐ **Employers should ask their new employee to send them:**

1. Personal data to enter into the employer's human resources information system including ID or passport number, contact details, Social Security number, and tax identification number;
2. Bank account information if the employer uses direct deposit to pay its employees; and
3. Copies of any certificates, diplomas, or licenses required to perform the job.

☐ **Getting off on the right foot with a new employee is essential to the establishment of a lasting, long-term relationship. Employers should therefore send new employees a welcome letter/email, which includes:**

1. The date and arrival time of the employee's first day;
2. Map of the employer's work site, if applicable;
3. Review of the employer's dress code for employees; and
4. A first day and first week agenda of tasks to be completed, if foreseeable and possible.

☐ **Invite new employee to join employer's software applications, including:**

1. Email messaging software;
2. Any productivity tools used by the employer; and
3. Password security codes.

☐ **Announcement:**

Nothing can leave a bad first impression more than a new employee beginning employment in a sea of strangers without introduction and having someone find their way around unassisted. Employers can make the new employee's transition to the workplace easier by:

1. Sending an announcement to all employees introducing the new employee by name to ensure they are aware when the new employee will begin working and encouraging them to give their new team member a warm welcome;
2. Reminding the new employee's supervisor to also send a message to all their subordinates on the new employee's starting date reminding them of the new employee's arrival date and name;
3. Sending a reminder to all managers of the new employee's arrival date and ask them to coordinate the new employee's first-day duties; and
4. Send the new employee's personnel data to your accounting department (so that they can add the new employee to the payroll), IT team (so that they can help the new employee set up accounts on corporate software) and office manager (so they can set up the new employee's workstation).

IN PLAIN ENGLISH

While we have provided recommendations for employers with larger organizations, smaller employers should be aware of these items and determine which ones apply to their organization.

☐ **Prepare and provide the new employee with technological equipment which is either required or useful for the new employee's position.** This might include some of the following, though varying positions may require additional equipment. Employers should determine what equipment is necessary to the industry, profession, or tasks involved with the new employee's position.

1. Desk and/or laptop computers;

2. Desktop computer monitor;
3. Landline telephone and/or cell phone;
4. Computer mouse;
5. Computer keyboard;
6. A headset; and
7. Tools or equipment that may be required or necessary for the job to be performed. As noted above, the tools, equipment, or technology to be provided will vary depending upon the industry, profession, or task.

☐ **Arrange for new employee's ID card, building access key card, and personal locker, if applicable.**

☐ **Order new employee's business cards and/or name plates, if applicable.**

☐ **Place an order for a work uniform, if applicable.**

☐ **Prepare and send an onboarding "kit" to the new employee that includes:**

1. A copy of the employee handbook;
2. A welcome letter from the new employee's manager or CEO;
3. Computer setup instructions, if applicable;
4. Stationery supplies (notepads, pens, Post-it stickers), if needed;
5. A copy of the employer's organizational chart, if available;
6. Any available written information concerning the employer and/or its culture; and
7. A guide to any local cafés and restaurants to access for lunch breaks, if available.

☐ **Prepare tentative first day and first week agendas, which cover:**

1. A scheduled meeting to provide an employer overview, including its mission, teams, and policies;
2. Scheduled one-on-one meetings with manager and team members;

3. A time to complete human resources paperwork;
4. Role-specific training;
5. Product-related demonstrations; and
6. Team-building activities such as a group lunch.

☐ **Assign a coworker to assist the new employee through the first few weeks or months in the new employee's new work assignment.**

As previously noted, many of the items listed above relate to larger employers and are provided by us so that the material is complete. You should determine whether any or all of them would apply to your unique organization.

ORIENTATION DURING NEW EMPLOYEE'S FIRST DAY ON THE JOB

A well-thought-out employee orientation or onboarding program for new employees should provide a sound foundation for the new employee's employment relationship. The employer should therefore take the time and pay attention to details in order to provide the new employee with a thorough orientation, which includes among other things:

1. A detailed explanation regarding the days and hours of work and when employees must take mandatory rest and lunch breaks; an employer's failure to enforce statutorily required meal and rest breaks leaves the employer exposed to monetary damages often including penalties.
2. What holidays the employer observes and any rules for working overtime and resulting rates of pay;
3. Paid sick leave time and, whenever applicable, any rules concerning maternity and paternity leave benefits;
4. If the new employee is relocating from somewhere outside of the employer's geographic area, information concerning possible weather conditions affecting commuting to work by private vehicle and public transportation options; and
5. If not in the employer's handbook, office rules regarding absenteeism, tardiness, or any other situations that would require the employer to arrange for someone to fill in for the

absent employee and any disciplinary consequences that may flow from excessive absenteeism.

As mentioned previously, much, if not all of the above information should be contained in the employee handbook (discussed in greater detail in Chapter 6 of this book), but it is nevertheless a best practice to at least call the employee's attention to these matters on the first day of work, which underscores their importance.

Depending upon the nature of the employer's business, the new employee should also be advised and properly trained on all safety procedures, practices, and equipment used on the job. Safety procedures and equipment should also be explained and their importance stressed in the employee handbook as well. Also, the employer's dress code is important to the work environment and should be explained to the new employee. This explanation should include a discussion concerning inappropriate dress and, if appropriate, the danger of wearing loose-fitting garments when working around machinery, which would be a safety hazard. Appropriate documentation of all safety training received should be prepared with a signed acknowledgment form completed by the employee

When uniforms, personal protective equipment and safety footwear are required within the employer's workplace, the new employee should be informed and told if the uniform includes any safety devices. When uniforms are company specific, the new employee should be advised of the appropriate arrangements for obtaining them, or if generic, where they may be purchased. Also discuss with the new employee whether there is a reimbursement policy for out-of-pocket expenses with the new employee. Because personal hygiene in the workplace is also a necessity, new employees should be advised regarding any applicable grooming standards as well.

IN PLAIN ENGLISH

Safety devices include, but are not limited to, helmets, hearing protection devices, eye protection devices, specialized footwear, safety vests, harnesses, gloves, aprons, and the numerous other devices which are job-specific and are intended to protect the individual's safety on a particular job or the safety of customers.

To ensure that no items are overlooked, employers should prepare a written checklist of all of the things that should be addressed with the new employee on the first day on the job so that each item will be sufficiently covered in detail. For specific items to include in the checklist, please refer to the items discussed above. Once initially created by the employer, the checklist should be reviewed, revised whenever necessary, periodically reviewed and augmented by the employer's employment counsel to add any omitted items that are important to the employer's specific business. By doing so, an employer will have created a detailed checklist specific to its industry and workplace that should then be uniformly followed. Each item on the checklist should then be checked off as the new employee progresses through the first day orientation.

When some items require follow-up, the new employees' signing an acknowledgment form documenting that the individual has read and understands the provided employee handbook should be repeated.

CONCLUSION

If the employer has done a careful and thorough job during the hiring process and selected the most qualified individual to fill the position, the onboarding process should prove to be enjoyable, relatively easy to implement, and provide a solid foundation for a long-term, successful, and productive employment relationship. It is therefore important to provide the new employee with as much helpful information when the relationship begins so the new employee will feel welcomed into the organization and be able to perform the job the new employee has been carefully hired to fill to the satisfaction of the employer. The employee will, in return, receive satisfaction knowing that the job is being performed well and to the satisfaction of the employer.

The more an employer prepares for the initial orientation/onboarding process by following the above suggestions, the more likely the employment relationship is to be successful.

While most of the material in this chapter is addressed to the employer, it is important for employees to be aware of it as well. In this way, a new employee will be able to understand the "onboarding process" and be prepared to start the new job with a positive attitude.

CHAPTER 8

Regulation of Employee Wages and Hours

FAIR LABOR STANDARDS ACT

The Fair Labor Standards Act (FLSA) establishes the minimum wage (lowest hourly pay), overtime pay, recordkeeping, and child labor standards affecting full-time and part-time workers in the private sector and in federal, state, and local governments. The Wage and Hour Division of the US Department of Labor administers and enforces the FLSA with respect to private employment, state and local government employment, and federal employees of the Library of Congress, US Postal Service, Postal Rate Commission, and the Tennessee Valley Authority. The FLSA is enforced by the US Office of Personnel Management for employees of other Executive Branch agencies, and by the US Congress for covered employees of the Legislative Branch. Special rules apply to state and local government employment involving fire protection and law enforcement activities, volunteer services, and compensatory time off instead of cash overtime pay.

Some states, cities, and counties, however, have higher minimum wage rates. When a state, city, or county minimum wage rate is higher than the federal rate, employers are legally required to pay their employees the higher wage rate. States may not, however, establish minimum wage rates that are lower than the FLSA's minimum wage requirements. Be sure to research reliable resources at the state and local levels of government, such as state departments of labor where you operate your business or are employed to determine whether higher minimum wage rates apply in your circumstances.

FLSA's Basic Wage Standards

"Covered" and "nonexempt" workers (defined and discussed below) are entitled to a minimum wage of $7.25 per hour effective July 24, 2009. Covered, nonexempt workers must be paid overtime pay at a rate of not less than one and one-half times their regular pay rates after forty hours of work in a workweek. Wages required by the FLSA are due on the regular payday for the pay period covered. Deductions made from wages for such items as cash or merchandise shortages, employer-required uniforms, and tools of the trade are illegal to the extent they reduce the wages of employees below the minimum rate required by the FLSA or reduce the amount of overtime pay due under the FLSA. The FLSA contains some exemptions from these basic standards. Some apply to specific types of businesses, while others apply to specific kinds of work. While the FLSA does set basic minimum wage and overtime pay standards and regulates the employment of minors, there are a number of employment practices the FLSA does not regulate. The FLSA, for example, does not require:

- vacation, holiday, severance, or sick pay;
- meal or rest periods, holidays off, or vacations;
- premium pay for weekend or holiday work;
- pay raises or fringe benefits; or
- a discharge notice, reason for discharge, or immediate payment of final wages to employees whose employment has been terminated.

The FLSA also does not provide wage payment or collection procedures for an employee's usual or promised wages or commissions in excess of those required by the FLSA. Some states, however, have laws under which such claims (sometimes including fringe benefits, discussed in more detail in Chapter 17) may be filed. The FLSA also does not limit the number of hours in a day or days in a week an employee may be required or scheduled to work, including overtime hours, if the employee is at least sixteen years old. The above matters are for agreement between the employer and the employees or their authorized representatives.

FLSA's "Covered" Employees

The FLSA's application to businesses is quite broad and sweeping. All employees of certain enterprises having workers engaged in interstate commerce, producing goods for interstate commerce, or handling, selling, or otherwise working on goods or materials that have been moved in or produced for such commerce by any person, are "covered" by the FLSA. A covered enterprise is the related activities performed through unified operation or common control by any person or persons for a common business purpose and: (1) whose annual gross volume of sales made or business done is not less than $500,000 (exclusive of excise taxes at the retail level that are separately stated); (2) is engaged in the operation of a hospital, an institution primarily engaged in the care of the sick, the aged, or the mentally ill who reside on the premises; a school for mentally or physically disabled or gifted children; a preschool, an elementary or secondary school, or an institution of higher education (whether operated for profit or nonprofit); or (3) is an activity of a public agency. Any enterprise that was covered by the FLSA on March 31, 1990, and thereafter ceased to be covered because of the revised $500,000 test, continues to be subject to the overtime pay, child labor, and recordkeeping provisions of the FLSA.

IN PLAIN ENGLISH

Interstate commerce is defined as commerce between any two states or any state and US territory.

Employees of firms that are not covered enterprises under the FLSA still may be subject to its minimum wage, overtime pay, recordkeeping, and child labor provisions if they themselves are individually engaged in interstate commerce or in the production of goods for interstate commerce, or in any closely related process or occupation directly essential to such production. Such employees include those who: work in communications or transportation; regularly use the mails or telephones for interstate communication, or keep records of interstate transactions; handle, ship, or receive goods moving in interstate commerce; regularly cross state lines in the course of employment; or work for independent employers who contract to do clerical, custodial, maintenance, or other work for firms engaged in interstate commerce or in the production of goods for interstate commerce. Domestic service workers such as day workers, housekeepers, chauffeurs, cooks, or full-time babysitters are also covered if: (1) their cash wages from one employer in a calendar year meet a certain threshold amount, which is adjusted annually by the Social Security Administration; or (2) they work a total of more than eight hours a week for one or more employers.

FLSA's "Tipped" Employees

Tipped employees are individuals engaged in occupations in which they customarily and regularly receive more than $30 a month in tips. Employers may consider tips as part of wages, but employers must still pay at least $2.13 an hour in direct wages. An employer who elects to use the tip credit provision must inform the employee in advance, and must be able to show that the employee receives at least the applicable minimum wage when direct wages and the tip credit claimed are combined. If an employee's tips combined with their direct wages of at least $2.13 an hour do not equal the minimum hourly wage, the employer must make up the difference. Also, employees are entitled to keep all of their tips, except to the extent that they participate in a valid tip pooling or sharing arrangement.

IN PLAIN ENGLISH

Tip pooling arrangements are arrangements whereby employees who are tipped for the work they perform pool those tips and share in the pool based on criteria established by law. Employers are forbidden to receive any of the pooled tips.

Employer-Furnished Facilities

The reasonable cost or fair value of board, lodging, or other facilities customarily furnished by the employer for the employee's benefit may be considered part of wages. This would include situations where, for example, a religious leader is provided with a residence, camp counselors or property managers are provided with lodging, and factory workers are provided with breakfast and/or lunch. It could also include situations where lodging is provided in remote locations when employees are required to work in those locations—for example, oil platforms.

IN PLAIN ENGLISH

While providing lodging may be considered as part of an employee's compensation in some situations, working in an employee's home may be a problem. The performance of certain types of work in an employee's home, sometimes known as industrial homework, is prohibited under the

(Continue on next page)

law unless the employer has obtained prior certification from the Department of Labor. Restrictions apply in the manufacture of knitted outerwear, gloves and mittens, buttons and buckles, handkerchiefs, embroideries, and jewelry (where safety and health hazards are not involved). The manufacture of women's apparel (and jewelry under hazardous conditions) is generally prohibited.

FLSA's Subminimum Wage Provisions

The FLSA does provide for the employment of certain individuals at wage rates below the statutory minimum. Such individuals include student learners (vocational education students), as well as full-time students in retail or service establishments, agriculture, or institutions of higher education. Also included are individuals whose earning or productive capacity is impaired by a physical or mental disability, including those related to age or injury, for the work to be performed. Employment at less than the minimum wage is authorized to prevent curtailment of opportunities for employment of these individuals. Such employment is permitted only under certificates issued by the Wage and Hour Division of Department of Labor.

Youth Minimum Wage

A minimum wage of not less than $4.25 an hour is permitted for employees under twenty years of age during their first ninety consecutive calendar days of employment with an employer. Employers are prohibited from taking any action to displace employees in order to hire employees at the youth minimum wage. Also prohibited are partial displacements such as reducing employees' hours, wages, or employment benefits.

FLSA's Employee Exemptions

Some employees, as noted above, are exempt from the FLSA's overtime pay provisions or both its minimum wage and overtime pay provisions. Because such exemptions are generally narrowly defined under the FLSA, an employer should carefully check the exact terms and conditions for each exemption. The following are some examples of exemptions that are illustrative, but not all-inclusive. These examples are generally described and do not define the conditions for each exemption.

1. Exemptions from *Both* Minimum Wage and Overtime Pay:
   a. Executive, administrative, and professional employees (including teachers and academic administrative personnel in elementary and secondary schools), outside sales employees, and employees in certain computer-related occupations (as defined by Department of Labor regulations);
   b. Employees of certain seasonal amusement or recreational establishments, employees of certain small newspapers, seamen employed on foreign vessels, employees engaged in fishing operations, and employees engaged in newspaper delivery;
   c. Farmworkers employed by anyone who used no more than 500 "man-days" of farm labor in any calendar quarter of the preceding calendar year; and
   d. Casual babysitters and persons employed as companions to the elderly or infirm.
2. Exemptions from Overtime Pay *Only*:
   a. Certain commissioned employees of retail or service establishments; auto, truck, trailer, farm implement, boat, or aircraft sales-workers; or parts-clerks and mechanics servicing autos, trucks, or farm implements, who are employed by nonmanufacturing establishments primarily engaged in selling these items to ultimate purchasers;
   b. Employees of railroads and air carriers, taxi drivers, certain employees of motor carriers, seamen on American vessels, and local delivery employees paid on approved trip rate plans, announcers, news editors, and chief engineers of certain non-metropolitan broadcasting stations, and domestic service workers living in the employer's residence; and
   c. Employees of motion picture theaters.

Farmworkers' Partial Exemptions from Overtime Pay

Partial overtime pay exemptions apply to employees engaged in certain operations on agricultural commodities and to employees of certain bulk petroleum distributors. This might include, for example, individuals who pump gas and individuals who harvest produce on farms.

IN PLAIN ENGLISH

A partial overtime pay exemption is a situation in which overtime would normally be required but, because of the exemption, overtime payment is not required. This kind of situation is very limited and, before an employer attempts to rely on it, an experienced employment lawyer should be consulted.

Special Rules for Hospital and Residential Care Facilities

Hospitals and residential care facilities may adopt, by agreement with their employees, a fourteen-day work period instead of the usual seven-day workweek. This is permissible if the employees are paid at least time and one-half their regular rates for hours worked over eight in a day or eighty in a fourteen-day work period, whichever is the greater number of overtime hours. This type of arrangement is very common for adult foster care facilities and other residential facilities where disabled or elderly individuals reside. It is also common for hospital workers other than physicians, such as cleaning staff, security staff, medical technicians, and laboratory staff.

Other Special Rules for Remedial Education, Police, and Firefighters

Employees who lack a high school diploma, or who have not attained the educational level of the eighth grade, can be required by their employers to spend up to ten hours in a workweek engaged in remedial reading or training in other basic skills without receiving time and one-half overtime pay for these hours. However, the employees must receive their normal wages for hours spent in such training and the training must not be job-specific. Also, public agency fire departments and police departments may establish a work period ranging from seven to twenty-eight days in which overtime need only be paid after a specified number of hours in each work period.

FLSA's Child Labor Provisions

The FLSA's child labor provisions are designed to protect the educational opportunities of minors and prohibit their employment in jobs and under conditions detrimental to their health or well-being. The provisions include restrictions on hours of work for minors under sixteen and lists hazardous occupations orders for both farm and nonfarm jobs declared by the Secretary of Labor to be too dangerous for minors to perform.

Regulations governing child labor in nonfarm jobs differ somewhat from those pertaining to agricultural employment. In nonfarm work, the permissible jobs and hours of work, by age, are as follows: (1) Youths eighteen years or older may perform any job, whether hazardous or not, for unlimited hours; (2) Minors sixteen and seventeen years old may perform any nonhazardous job, for unlimited hours; (3) Minors fourteen and fifteen years old may work outside school hours in various nonmanufacturing, non-mining, nonhazardous jobs under the following conditions: no more than three hours on a school day, eighteen hours in a school week, eight hours on a nonschool day, or forty hours in a nonschool week. Also, work may not begin before 7:00 a.m. nor end after 7:00 p.m., except from June 1 through Labor Day, when evening hours are extended to 9:00 p.m. Under a special provision, youths fourteen and fifteen years old enrolled in an approved Work Experience and Career Exploration Program may be employed for up to twenty-three hours in school weeks and three hours on school days (including during school hours). In addition, academically oriented youths enrolled in an approved Work-Study Program may be employed during school hours. Fourteen is the minimum age for most nonfarm work. However, at any age, minors may: deliver newspapers, perform in radio, television, movie, or theatrical productions; work for parents in their solely owned nonfarm business (except in mining, manufacturing, or on hazardous jobs); or gather evergreens and make evergreen wreaths.

Farm Jobs (Child Labor)

In farm work, permissible jobs and hours of work, by age, are as follows: (1) Minors sixteen years and older may perform any job, whether hazardous or not, for unlimited hours; (2) Minors fourteen and fifteen years old may perform any nonhazardous farm job outside of school hours; (3) Minors twelve and thirteen years old may work outside of school hours in nonhazardous jobs, either with a parent's written consent or on the same farm as the parent(s); (4) Minors under twelve years old may perform jobs on farms owned or operated by parent(s), or with a parent's written consent, outside of school hours in nonhazardous jobs on farms not covered by minimum wage requirements. Minors of any age may be employed by their parents in any occupation on a farm owned or operated by their parents.

FLSA's Recordkeeping Requirements

The FLSA requires employers to keep records on wages, hours, and other items, as specified in Department of Labor recordkeeping regulations. Most of the information is of the kind generally maintained by employers in the ordinary course of business in compliance with other laws and regulations. The records do not have to be kept in any particular form, and time clocks need not be used.

With respect to a nonexempt employee subject to FLSA's minimum wage provisions or both the minimum wage and overtime pay provisions, the following records must be kept: (1) personal information, including employee's name, home address, occupation, gender, and birth date, if under nineteen years of age; (2) hour and day when workweek begins; (3) total hours worked each workday and each workweek; (4) total daily or weekly straight-time earnings; (5) regular hourly pay rate for any week when overtime is worked; (6) total overtime pay for the workweek; (7) deductions from or additions to wages; (8) total wages paid each pay period; and (9) date of payment and pay period covered.

Records required for exempt employees differ from those for nonexempt workers. Special information is required for homeworkers, for employees working under uncommon pay arrangements, for employees to whom lodging or other facilities are furnished, and for employees receiving remedial education.

FLSA AMENDMENTS UNDER THE AFFORDABLE CARE ACT

The Affordable Care Act (ACA), signed into law on March 23, 2010, amended FLSA's Section 7, to provide a break time requirement for nursing mothers.

Employers are required to provide reasonable break time for an employee to express breast milk for her nursing child for one year after the child's birth each time such employee has need to express the milk. Employers are also required to provide a place, other than a bathroom, that is shielded from view and free from intrusion from coworkers and the public, which may be used by an employee to express breast milk. The FLSA requirement of break time for nursing mothers to express breast milk does not preempt state laws that provide greater protections to employees (for example, providing compensated break time, providing break time for exempt employees, or providing break time beyond one year after the child's birth). Employers are required to provide a reasonable amount of break time to express milk as frequently as needed by the nursing mother. The frequency of breaks needed to express milk as well as the duration of each break will likely vary. A bathroom, even if private, is not a permissible location under the ACA. The location provided must be functional as a space for expressing breast milk. If the space is not dedicated to the nursing mother's use, it must be available when needed in order to meet the statutory requirement. A space temporarily created or converted into a space for expressing milk or made available when needed by the nursing mother is sufficient provided that the space is shielded from view, and free from any intrusion from coworkers and the public.

Only employees who are not exempt from FLSA's Section 7, which includes the FLSA's overtime pay requirements, are entitled to breaks to express milk. While employers are not required under the FLSA to provide breaks to nursing mothers who are exempt from FLSA's Section 7 (such as bona fide professional, executive and administrative employees), they may be obligated to provide such breaks under state laws.

Employers with fewer than fifty employees are not subject to the FLSA break time requirement if compliance with the provision would impose an undue hardship. Whether compliance would be an undue hardship is determined by looking at the difficulty or expense of compliance for a specific employer in comparison to the size, financial resources, nature, and structure of the employer's business. All employees who work for the covered employer, regardless of work site, are counted when determining whether this exemption may apply.

Employers are not required under the FLSA to compensate nursing mothers for breaks taken for the purpose of expressing milk. However, where employers already provide compensated breaks, an employee who uses that break time to express milk must be compensated in the same way that other employees are compensated for break time. In addition, the FLSA's general requirement that the employee must be completely relieved from duty or else the time must be compensated as work time applies.

FEDERAL CONTRACTOR LABOR STANDARDS

Minimum Wages of Federal Contract Workers

The Department of Labor published notice in the Federal Register announcing that effective January 1, 2020, Executive Order 13658's minimum wage rate, which generally must be paid to workers performing work on or in connection with covered federal contracts, increased to $10.80 per hour.

Effective January 1, 2020, as well, employees who perform work on or in connection with covered federal contracts and receive tips as part of their wages generally must be paid a minimum hourly wage of $7.55.

THE PORTAL-TO-PORTAL ACT

The FLSA of 1937, as discussed earlier in this chapter, regulates how covered employers must pay employees whom they employ to perform work on their behalves. The FLSA, however, defines "employ" very generally as, "to suffer or permit to work" but fails to explicitly define what constitutes actual "work."

Following FLSA's enactment, the US Supreme Court held that compensable time under the FLSA includes employees' activities "controlled or required by the employer and pursued necessarily and primarily for the benefit of the employer and his business," as well as "all time during which an employee is necessarily required to be on the employer's premises, on duty or at a prescribed workplace." The foregoing ambiguous definitions, however, provoked still further litigation and ultimately resulted in a pushback from a Republican-led Congress in its passage of the Portal-to-Portal Act of 1947.

The Portal-to-Portal Act provides that employers are not required to compensate employees for the following activities: (1) walking, riding, or traveling to and from the actual place of performance of the principal activity or activities that [an] employee is employed to perform; and (2) actions that are preliminary to or postliminary to the employee's principal activity or activities, which occur either prior to the time on any particular workday at which such employee commences, or subsequent to the time on any particular workday at which the employee ceases, such principal activity or activities. These standards make clear that compensable work time generally does not include time spent commuting to or from work. FLSA regulations further clarify that "[n]ormal travel from home to work is not work time" regardless of "whether [the employee] works at a fixed location or at different job sites."

Unlike ordinary commute time, however, the Portal-to-Portal Act provides that "travel from job site to job site during the workday must be counted as hours worked." At times, employers require their employees to travel away from their home communities overnight for purposes of performing work.

In these circumstances as well, the regulations provide that "[t]ravel away from home is clearly work time when it cuts across the employee's workday. The employee is simply substituting travel for other duties." It has furthermore been concluded that compensable time includes "all time spent in such travel during the hours which correspond to [the employee's] normal hours of work, including those hours on Saturday and Sunday which correspond to [the employee's] normal working hours on other days of the week." By way of an example, Wage and Hour regulations provide that "if an employee regularly works from 9:00 a.m. to 5:00 p.m., Monday through Friday, the travel time during these hours is work time on Saturday and Sunday as well as on the other days." As an enforcement policy, however, it should be noted that Wage and Hour Division "will not consider as work time that time spent in travel away from home outside of regular working hours as a passenger on an airplane, train, boat, bus, or automobile."

WAGE GARNISHMENT (CONSUMER CREDIT PROTECTION ACT)

A wage garnishment occurs when an employer is required to withhold earnings of an employee for the payment of a debt in accordance with a court order or other legal procedure, such as a debt owed by the employee to a credit card company. Title III of the Consumer Credit Protection Act (CCPA) prohibits an employer from discharging an employee because their earnings have been subject to garnishment for any single debt, regardless of the number of levies made or proceedings brought to collect it. CCPA does not, however, protect an employee from discharge if the employee's earnings have been subject to garnishment for a second or more debts.

The CCPA is administered by Department of Labor's Wage and Hour Division. CCPA limits garnishment for any employee or individual who receives earnings for personal services (including wages, salaries, commissions, bonuses, and periodic payments from a pension or retirement program). CCPA furthermore protects employees by limiting the amount of earnings that may be garnished in any workweek or pay period to the lesser of 25 percent of "disposable earnings" (defined below) or the amount by which disposable earnings are greater than thirty times the federal minimum hourly wage prescribed by FLSA's Section 6 (a) (1). The foregoing limit applies regardless of how many garnishment orders an employer receives. As discussed earlier in this chapter, the FLSA minimum wage is $7.25 per hour.

CCPA permits a greater amount of an employee's earnings to be garnished to enforce any order for the support of a person, such as spousal support or child support, and allows up to 50 percent of an employee's disposable earnings to be garnished for such support if the employee is supporting a current spouse or child who is not the subject of the support order, and up to 60 percent if the individual is not doing so. An additional 5 percent may be garnished for support payments over twelve weeks in arrears.

An employee's "disposable earnings" is the amount of earnings left after legally required deductions (e.g., federal, state and local taxes; the individual's share of Social Security, Medicare, and unemployment insurance taxes; and contributions to state employee retirement systems required by law) have been made. Other deductions not required by law (e.g., union dues, health and life insurance premiums, and charitable contributions) are not subtracted from earnings when the amount of disposable earnings for garnishment purposes is calculated.

CCPA restrictions on the amount of wages that can be garnished do not apply to certain bankruptcy court orders or debts due for federal or state taxes. Nor do they affect voluntary wage assignments, i.e., situations where employees voluntarily agree that their employers may turn over a specified amount of their earnings to a creditor.

CCPA will, in most cases, give employees the right to receive at least partial compensation for the personal services that they provide despite garnishment. This law also prohibits an employer from discharging an employee because of the garnishment of wages for any single indebtedness. Department of Labor's Wage and Hour Division accepts complaints of alleged CCPA violations.

CONCLUSION

It is clear that the material in this chapter is quite technical and complicated. For this reason, it is essential for an employer to work with an experienced employment attorney in order to be sure it is complying with the law. It is also important for employees who believe they are not being properly dealt with, in respect to any of the items discussed in this chapter, to contact an employment lawyer. The material addressed in this chapter is based upon the federal law. You must also be mindful of the fact that state, as well as local, law may apply. For this reason, whether you are an employer or an employee, you should definitely determine whether there are any applicable state or local laws that apply to your situation.

CHAPTER 9

On-the-Job Rights and Responsibilities—Employees' Dignity, Privacy, and Reputation

The rights and responsibilities between employers and employees concerning matters of dignity, privacy, and reputation in the workplace originate from four principal sources: (1) federal and state laws designed for employees' protections against certain practices committed by employers; (2) in the public sector, the US Constitution; (3) common-law tort principles developed by the courts over time in response to various wrongs committed against employees by employers; and (4) individual employment contracts between employees and employers (see Chapter 3), as well as collective bargaining agreements between unions and employers (see Chapter 4). In this chapter we will explore the various rights of dignity, privacy, and reputation enjoyed by employees while in the workplace and their employers' legal obligations to comply with them.

FEDERAL AND STATE LAWS

Discrimination in Employment

As earlier discussed in Chapter 2 of this book, interviewing, hiring, and other preemployment considerations that are prerequisites to the establishment of an employment relationship must comply with federal and state laws prohibiting discrimination in employment. Those same federal and state statutory obligations, however, apply with equal force throughout the resulting employment relationship once entered into. In addition to the Civil Rights Act (Title VII), employers must comply with numerous other antidiscrimination laws applicable to employment such as the Equal Pay Act (EPA), the Age Discrimination in Employment Act, amended by the Older Workers' Benefit Protection Act (ADEA) and the Americans with Disabilities Act (ADA) (see Chapter 2). The Equal Employment Opportunity Commission (EEOC) is responsible for enforcing these various laws.

As noted, these antidiscrimination laws apply not only during the hiring processes but also during the entirety of the employment relationship, including considerations for such matters as transfer, promotion, layoff, and termination from employment, as well as job advertisement, recruitment, testing, use of the employer's facilities, training, benefits and leaves of absence. These laws generally prohibit not only intentional discrimination against employees but also practices that unintentionally have disparate impacts upon protected classes of employees. Many antidiscrimination laws apply to employers' actions affecting not only their employees but also to independent contractors performing services on an employer's behalves as well.

IN PLAIN ENGLISH

Disparate impact is a technical legal term used in labor and employment law referring to practices in employment, housing, and other areas that negatively affect one particular group of individuals more than another. The affected individuals must be of a protected class—for example, racial minorities or disabled individuals. This is true even though the rules themselves appear to be unbiased.

These laws make clear that employers may not legally retaliate against employees or applicants for employment who file discrimination complaints against the employer. If an employer is found to have unlawfully discriminated, it could be liable for lost wages and punitive and other damages, including attorneys' fees.

Many states, as well as some cities and counties, have also passed laws that reiterate and expand upon the federal government's protections against unlawful discrimination in employment. These local laws are often even more protective of employee rights than their federal counterparts. Additionally, some categories of employment discrimination not covered by federal law, such as those prohibiting employer discrimination based on sexual orientation, such as toward members of the LGBTQ+ community, may be covered by state or local laws.

Title VII

Title VII prohibits discrimination based on race, color, religion, sex, or national origin. With regard to religious discrimination, employers generally may not treat employees or applicants either less or more favorably because of their religious beliefs or practices. Employees cannot be forced to participate or not participate in a religious activity as a condition of employment. Employers must also reasonably accommodate their employees' sincerely held religious beliefs and permit them to engage in religious expression while at work if employees generally are permitted to engage in other personal expressions while in the workplace. This law also requires the employer take steps to prevent religious harassment of their employees, not only by other employees and management but also by its vendors and even customers or clients. Title VII prohibits:

- National-origin discrimination including discrimination based on foreign accents and English fluency, as well as English-only rules, although there are exceptions if they are necessary for the safe or efficient operation of the business.
- Race-based discrimination including discrimination based on skin color, hair texture, and facial features, as well as harassment and segregation. It also includes discrimination based on a person's marriage to or association with those of a different race.
- Sex-based discrimination including pregnancy, birth, and related medical conditions, as well as sexual harassment.
  BREAKING NEWS ALERT. On June 15, 2020, in *Bostock v. Clayton County, Georgia*, the United States Supreme Court in a 6–3 decision announced a landmark ruling concerning Title VII's prohibition against employment discrimination based upon "sex." The Supreme Court majority opinion ruled that included within Title VII's general prohibition

outlawing discrimination based upon "sex" is discrimination against people who are homosexual or transgender. As noted earlier throughout this book, Title VII of the Civil Rights Act of 1964 has major application to employers both during the interview and hiring processes as well as once employees have been hired and are working for employers. Therefore, all of the earlier admonitions and recommendations discussing the phrase "sex discrimination" in employment, now apply with equal force to persons who are gay or transgender. For more complete information employees and employers may wish to seek legal counsel for advice concerning how the United States Supreme Court's latest ruling in this important area affects the employment relationship.

The Equal Pay Act (EPA)

The Equal Pay Act, part of the Fair Labor Standards Act of 1938, as amended (FLSA), also prohibits sex-based discrimination in pay. It prohibits sex-based wage discrimination among persons in the same establishment who perform work under similar working conditions. Virtually all employers are subject to the EPA.

More information about Title VII and the EPA may be found at the following EEOC website: www.eeoc.gov.

Anti–Sexual Harassment

One of the legal obligations of all business owners is to create a nondiscriminatory work environment. Especially in this highly sensitive era of #MeToo, employer policies should be established prohibiting any discriminatory language (i.e., ethnic jokes or racial slurs) or other offensive language or activities, including sexual harassment.

Sexual harassment is one form of illegal sex discrimination, though harassment based on race and certain other characteristics also violates Title VII. There are two basic forms of sexual harassment in the workplace, (a) "quid pro quo" sexual harassment, and (b) "hostile environment" sexual harassment. "Quid pro quo" sexual harassment refers to either a harasser asking for sexual favors in exchange for some advantage in the workplace or a harasser penalizing another person for rejecting their sexual advances. "Hostile environment" sexual harassment, on the other hand, is more generalized in scope and occurs when a harasser creates or permits a hostile work environment concerning an employee's gender through language, activities, and/or conduct.

IN PLAIN ENGLISH

Quid pro quo is a Latin term used in law to define an exchange of goods or services, in which one transfer is dependent upon the other. For example, exchanging sex for a promotion.

An employer is subject to vicarious liability to victims of sexual harassment due to its creation of a hostile work environment. For example, a restaurant owner will be found financially responsible for the actions and language of its supervisor that results in an employee's injury, harm, or damage. If a supervisor has harassed or permitted harassment of an employee by a coworker, customer, client, or vendor, and this situation has led to the victim's termination, relocation, or other negative consequences, the employer will be held liable for the discriminatory sexual actions of its supervisor. To avoid this form of liability, an employer must exercise reasonable care to prevent and promptly correct any harassment behaviors that are reported or otherwise become known to it. On the other hand, an employee who has experienced sexual harassment is obligated to take advantage of all preventive programs or policies offered by the employer. There is a host of training and other resources available to employers wishing to learn more about sexual harassment. Employers are also advised to consult an experienced attorney or their state employment division for further information on this dynamic and rapidly growing area of law (see also Chapter 7).

IN PLAIN ENGLISH

Reasonable care is a technical legal term that defines the duty owed in a particular situation.

Many states have enacted anti-harassment laws as well. California, for example, requires employers with fifty or more employees to provide certain sexual harassment training and education to supervisory employees. Details on California's sexual harassment laws may be obtained at www.dfeh.ca.gov.

More information on sexual harassment is also available at the EEOC's website: www.eeoc.gov.

The Age Discrimination in Employment Act (ADEA)

Federal age antidiscrimination laws apply to employers of twenty or more employees, as well as to government entities and unions. These laws provide that persons forty years old or older may not be discriminated against due to their age in connection with any term, condition, or privilege of employment, including hiring, firing, layoffs, job compensation, benefits, job training, assignments, and promotions.

More information concerning age discrimination in employment is available at the following EEOC website: www.eeoc.gov.

Disabilities Discrimination

The Americans with Disabilities Act (ADA) prohibits discrimination against disabled persons in public accommodations, transportation, telecommunications, and employment. The ADA applies to employers who employ fifteen or more employees. "An individual with a disability" under the ADA means a person who has a physical or mental impairment that substantially limits one or more major life activities, has a record of such an impairment, or who is regarded as having such an impairment. Under the ADA, a qualified individual with a disability is someone who, with or without reasonable accommodation, can perform the essential functions of the job.

Reasonable accommodation must be made so that that a disabled job applicant or employee can perform the necessary and essential work of the position. Reasonable accommodations include making existing employee facilities readily accessible to and usable by disabled employees, including the acquisition or modification of equipment or devices, job restructuring, and modifying work schedules.

A business is not required to provide reasonable accommodations, however, if it will result in an undue hardship. "Undue hardship" under the ADA refers to an action requiring significant difficulty or expense when considered in light of factors such as the employer's size and financial resources.

Under the ADA, complex rules apply to medical examinations and inquiries, so you should contact an experienced attorney for more information if you plan to make such inquiries or require any physical examinations of applicants for employment.

For more information concerning the ADA, refer to www.ada.gov. Many states also have laws that are comparable to or more restrictive than the ADA. You should check with an attorney in your state or its employment division to determine whether your state has this type of legislation and whether your business would be covered by it.

Zero-Tolerance ("One and Done") Policies

A zero-tolerance policy, requiring immediate termination from employment for all acts of discrimination, incentivizes employees to be compliant with discrimination policies and best protect an employer from costly discrimination claims. A well-written employee handbook containing policies against sexual harassment, offensive behaviors, and the like is a good starting point (see Chapter 6). An employee handbook's discrimination policy will apply to behavior, as well as oral and written (including electronic) communications. It will also include procedures that provide employees with a way to confidentially report problems regarding offensive or harassing behavior and will direct management on how to investigate and resolve the issues. The process should include an employee appeals procedure for any adverse findings. The complaint and appeals procedures should direct an employee to contact someone other than the employee's immediate supervisor, such as a designated EEOC compliance specialist. This is because the immediate supervisor may be the person responsible for such alleged misconduct.

Employees should also be advised that both the complaints and appeals need to be in writing so that there can be no misunderstandings, although the first step is often verbal. A well-drafted antidiscrimination policy will state that the employer will, whenever possible, provide complaining employees and witnesses reasonable confidentiality. It should, however, be made clear that there can be no guarantee of confidentiality, because it may become necessary for management to disclose the identity and testimony of relevant parties in the event of a formal legal action.

It is also essential that employers provide employees with ongoing education with respect to employment relations, including harassment and discrimination, because this is a dynamic area of the law.

Physical Safety—OSHA: Workplace and Accessibility Standards

While no manufacturer would intentionally injure an employee, it may nevertheless be engaged in an industry or using processes that involves hazardous activities. It is not uncommon for manufacturers to use toxic materials. Employees of such manufacturers are often unaware of potential hazards that may result from their use of toxic materials while working. It is essential for employers to research the potentially toxic effects of all substances used in its manufacturing process and resulting products. Occupational Safety and Health Administration (OSHA) regulations require that all employers with hazardous chemicals in their workplaces provide labels and Material Safety Data Sheets (MSDS) for their exposed workers and train them to handle the chemicals appropriately. More information on this subject may be found at OSHA's website: http://www.osha.gov/SLTC/hazardcommunications/index.html.

In short, there is a regulatory duty to advise and train employees with respect to hazardous substances in the workplace.

Congress and federal administrative agencies are active in the field of regulation of hazardous substances. Employers should also be aware that state workers' compensation agencies and OSHA may have specific rules regarding an employer's particular enterprise or industry. It is critical to obtain a lawyer's assistance in determining whether any of these regulatory requirements apply to an employer's particular manufacturing process or business. The labor department for the state in which the employer operates may also be able to provide information regarding applicable workplace regulations.

If an employment contract is used, a paragraph containing the required disclosures regarding hazardous substances and the employee's acknowledgment of the known risks should be incorporated into the contract; see Chapter 3. A similar statement should also be included in any employee handbook; see Chapter 6.

While these documents may not provide a defense to an employee's workers' compensation claim, they would at minimum sensitize employees to the need for caution in working with toxic materials. Needless to say, employers should take all precautions possible to protect the health and safety of their valuable employees.

The Family Medical Leave Act (FMLA)

The Family and Medical Leave Act of 1993 (FMLA) allows employees to take up to twelve weeks of unpaid leave each year for certain family or medical reasons if they have worked for the employer for a year and meet certain other eligibility requirements. FMLA must be followed by private-sector employers who employ fifty or more employees during the current or preceding calendar year and who are engaged in interstate commerce or any activity affecting commerce.

An eligible employee may take their twelve-week leave due to the birth and care of their newborn, a foster child being placed with the employee, to care for a spouse, child, or parent with a serious health condition, or to take care of the employee's own serious health condition. FMLA defines "serious health condition" as an illness, injury, impairment, or physical or mental condition that brings about a period of incapacity and/or requires intensive and continual medical treatment. It specifically includes prenatal care.

When the worker returns to the job, the job may be the exact job that the employee left or it may be an equivalent job—with equivalent duties, pay, benefits, and the like. The only employees to which this would not apply are "key" employees, whose absence from their positions will cause "substantial and grievous economic injury" to the employer.

There are certain notice requirements, as well as rules for requiring medical certification of the need for leave. Further information can be found at the Department of Labor's website: www.dol.gov.

Many states have supplemental leave acts. Employers should consult with an attorney in their state as well as its state employment division.

THE US CONSTITUTION

Application of the US Constitution is generally limited to situations involving some form of "state action." As a result, actions involving purely public-sector employers are not subject to the US Constitutional protections, whereas employees of federal, state, city, and county government entities are protected. Exceptions to the rule can occur, such as when a private-sector employer is acting as an agent of the government.

IN PLAIN ENGLISH

Employment by government entities has been legally defined in numerous cases as a property right, which is protected by the US Constitution and by the constitutions of the vast majority of states as well.

Pursuant to the US Constitution, in both the federal and public sectors employee privacy and reputation interests arise from the First, Fourth, Fifth, Ninth, and Fourteenth Amendments. First Amendment issues arise in cases involving (1) adverse employment actions such as discipline or discharge due to employees' exercise of their political affiliations or beliefs, (2) employees' employment status being adversely affected due to their engaging in spoken, written, or other forms of expression, (3) challenges to state statutes limiting the right of government employees to engage in partisan political activities, and (4) adverse employment actions due to employees engaging in private conduct that is viewed by employers as immoral or improper.

Fourth Amendment issues arise where federal and public-sector employees are subjected to unreasonable searches and seizures in their workplace, usually in the context of a government investigation into possible criminal violations.

Fifth Amendment issues stem from government officials seeking to compel employees to disclose information. Courts have concluded that as an employer, government officials can compel an employee to disclose information as a condition of maintaining employment so long as those disclosures cannot be used in subsequent criminal prosecutions of those employees by either state or federal authorities. It is, however, unconstitutional for the state to require as a condition of employment that a public employee agree to waive the privilege against self-incrimination. Where an employee refuses to answer questions that are focused specifically, directly, and narrowly on performance of his official duties, the privilege against self-incrimination does not bar the employee's dismissal and the employee cannot insist on a grant of immunity from prosecution as a condition for answering those questions.

Ninth Amendment issues arise infrequently in limited cases involving potential privacy issues over rights retained by the people.

Finally, Fourteenth Amendment issues apply to due process requirements, such as initially being advised of the content of pending charges and provided copies of any documents in support of the charges. Also, the employee must be given an opportunity to respond, before depriving a public employee of any property right in the employee's continued employment.

COMMON-LAW TORT LIABILITIES APPLICABLE TO AN EMPLOYER'S WORKPLACE

Every person possesses certain inherent rights protected by common law that also become applicable within the context of their employment relationship with an employer. When one of these common-law interests becomes damaged due to an employer's action, a "tort" has been committed against the employee and the employer may be liable for damages unless its actions were justified or excusable. Torts may be either intentional or negligent.

IN PLAIN ENGLISH

A *tort* is defined as a wrongful act or violation of a right that may result in liability.

IN PLAIN ENGLISH

Common law is defined as law that is based on prior cases and court decisions rather than on legislation such as federal and state statutes.

IN PLAIN ENGLISH

An *intentional tort* is one in which the person committing the wrongful act knowingly does it. For example, purposely assaulting another individual by punching that person. A *negligent tort* is one in which an individual carelessly injures another. It involves situations in which the individual's action falls below the acceptable standard and it does not require intent. For example, a driver would be liable for negligence when the driver speeds on an icy road and as a result is unable to avoided an accident. It would also include situations where a surgeon carelessly omits to remove a surgical apparatus when completing a procedure or an attorney does not timely file a required document.

It should be kept in mind in these instances that there are strong financial incentives for plaintiffs to seek to prevail on causes of action "sounding in tort." Where plaintiffs prevail in establishing a tort has been committed by an employer, a potential award by a court may include special damages such as lost wages, general damages such as pain and suffering resulting from the injury sustained, and punitive damages. Because punitive damages are designed to punish the employer due to wrongdoings committed against its employees, they may greatly exceed the amount of special and general damages awarded to the plaintiff.

Privacy

Privacy rights may be found in one of the following two forms: (a) privacy rights concerning employee information collected by employers during the employment relationship including matters such as how that information was (1) obtained, (2) maintained, (3) utilized, and (4) disclosed to third parties; and (b) privacy rights concerning employee behavior while either on or off duty.

Defamation of Character

The common-law tort of defamation of character occurs whenever an employer communicates untrue information concerning an employee that causes that employee to suffer ridicule, hatred, or contempt. Most commonly, communicating an unfavorable performance evaluation or the reason for termination of employment may create liability for the employer if it is untrue and causes harm to the employee's character. Defamation may occur when the information is either communicated in writing (libel) or when it is communicated orally (slander).

An employer may defend acts of defamation on the grounds that a conditional privilege exists to communicate employee information for legitimate business purposes. A conditional privilege may be lost, however, when an employer communicates information known to be false or communicates information with a reckless disregard for its truth or falsity. The conditional privilege may also be lost should an employer publish information more broadly than necessary for a legitimate business purpose or for some purpose that is beyond the interest the privilege serves to protect.

Employer communications to the media concerning employee information that involve matters of public interest may be conditionally privileged as well.

Employers have been found liable for defamation of character in many cases such as when:

- An employer falsely accused an employee of having AIDS and terminated the individual's employment;

- A supervisor stated to other employees that a female employee had infected him with an STD, characterized her as a prostitute, and searched through her personal belongings;
- An employer communicated that an employee had been terminated for theft without verifying that the employee was actually stealing;
- An employer terminated an employee for poor work performance without conducting a proper investigation of substandard performance claims against the employee;
- An employer treated an employee as if the employee was dishonest by firing that employee, accompanying the individual to that person's office to pack up the discharged employee's personal belongings in full view of other employees, and then escorting the discharged employee off its premises;
- An employer terminated an employee based on a coworker's statement that the employee was selling incentive items at a yard sale without allowing the employee to provide the accused employee's side of the story or examining the employer's records to determine whether the employee had reported the employee's activities on the day of the yard sale.

Defamation of Character When Conducting Reference Checks

A common area that gives rise to defamation of character claims is when a former employer is asked to provide a reference by a former employee due to the employee's application for employment elsewhere. When confronted with this potential situation, an employer must proceed cautiously to avoid becoming liable for defamation of character. The dilemmas posed to both the former employer and the prospective employer in this frequent situation are many. First, the prospective employer that seeks a reference from a former employer may be found liable due to negligent hiring should it fail to check the applicant's references, particularly if the new position entails risks to others. Second, the former employer who is asked to provide a reference may be found liable if it fails to disclose information necessary for the applicant's future licensure by a regulatory agency following employment. Third, the former employer that provides information to a prospective employer may be found liable if the reference contains any defamatory information that harms the applicant's future employment opportunities.

IN PLAIN ENGLISH

There have been cases in which employers have been held liable for not checking the references of an individual who was a convicted sexual predator, and once hired was permitted to take care of children. The new employer failed to perform a background check before the individual was hired. The Boy Scouts of America has recently filed for bankruptcy protection because of the numerous lawsuits filed against it for similar problems.

Employers are customarily advised to only provide the following information when asked about a former employee: the employee's date of hire, date of separation, position held, and possibly salary. If the former employee wishes the former employer to provide additional information then the former employee should be required to sign a release providing that the employee will not hold the former employer liable for any information contained in the reference. It should be cautioned, however, that such a waiver may not serve as a valid defense should the former employer be found to have intentionally defamed the applicant in the reference.

IN PLAIN ENGLISH

The release that many former employers use provides that the former employee authorizes the former employer to provide prospective employers with a complete and accurate description of the former employee's work while employed by the former employer. This document should be prepared by an attorney and it should provide the former employer with protection for accurate and truthful statements that relate to the former employee's conduct, skill, and ability while working for the former employer. This underscores the importance of having a complete and accurate employee file that would be available for reference.

Where references are provided in good faith and without malice or reckless disregard of the truth, a qualified privilege may shield both former and prospective employers from liability, because providing references and checking them carefully is responsible conduct of former and prospective employers committed in furtherance of protecting a public interest.

Invasion of Privacy

Both state legislatures and the courts have been active in limiting employers' intrusions into private areas of their employees' lives. The goal of these efforts is to (1) control employers' use of collected information that is irrelevant, incomplete, or inaccurate, for purposes of its making employment decisions including hiring, promotion, compensation, and termination from employment, and (2) overseeing use of that information by third parties. The information concerning employees that is the focus of these intrusions into employees' private area are (a) speech, (b) beliefs, (c) personal information, (d) associations with others, and (e) lifestyles.

Courts have found the following four types of unlawful invasions of privacy for which damages may be awarded against employers:

- Intrusion in an area where a reasonable privacy expectation exists, which courts have found in a variety of areas of employees' lives;
- Appropriation of an employee's name or likeness, done for an employer's commercial advantage;
- Publicity given to an employee's private life where employment information is disclosed that would be highly offensive to a reasonable person and it is not a legitimate public concern; and
- Publicity casting an employee in a false light that would be objectionable to a reasonable person.

Court decisions finding employers liable for damages in the area of invasion of privacy include, for example, the following:

- Employer letters regarding employee activities that were distributed more widely than was necessary;
- Displaying at plant safety meetings photographs depicting an employee's "unsightly wound" on numerous occasions;
- Reading an employee's personal mail;

- Interrogating an employee concerning dating an employee of a competitor;
- Harassing an employee for an interracial relationship;
- Conducting an improper locker search;
- Conducting an employee strip search;
- A supervisor yelling at an employee during a workplace altercation that the employee's spouse had been having sexual relationships with certain people;
- Terminating employment for refusing to identify coworkers who used drugs after pledging confidentiality;
- Disclosing an employee's mastectomy to numerous coworkers;
- Searching a long-haul driver's motel room without the driver's consent for a missing permit book where there was an expectation of privacy and no business was transacted in the motel room; and
- Subjecting an African American store clerk to daily searches for stolen merchandise.

Emerging issues in the area of employee privacy are found in employees' use of technology including computers, cell phones, and GPS devices. Employers who provide such technology to employees for their business use, who in turn consent to their being monitored by their employers, have been found to be operating within their legitimate business interests. When doing so, however, employers must still comply with the Federal Wiretap Act and Stored Communications Act. Furthermore, public-sector employers, such as those in law enforcement, have been found to possess greater rights in monitoring technology used by their employees than have private-sector employers in this emerging area of law.

False Imprisonment

Employers commit the tort of false imprisonment due to the unwarranted detention of an employee for any length of time when the employee is deprived of personal liberty to leave and is aware of the fact that the employee cannot do so. For example, in one case liability was found to exist for employer when a security-services owner joined a security guard in detaining and interrogating a grocery store clerk suspected of theft from a market. The security guard positioned himself between the store clerk and the only door to the room as he advised the grocery store clerk he would decide whether she would be going to jail that evening. The clerk was allowed to receive only one telephone call during her interrogation. The market's owner also acquiesced in the clerk's restraint and continued the interrogation begun earlier by the security guard over a three-hour period.

Intentional Infliction of Emotional Distress

An employer may be held liable for the intentional infliction of emotional distress when (1) its conduct is extreme and outrageous, (2) it acted with an intent to cause emotional distress or with substantial certainty distress would result from its conduct, and (3) severe emotional distress did result from its conduct.

Fraudulent Misrepresentation

An employer commits fraudulent misrepresentation when it makes a misrepresentation of fact, opinion, intention, or law for purposes of inducing an employee to act upon it and the employee suffers a loss as a result of doing so.

Intentional Interference with Third-Party Contractual Relations

Employers may be liable for intentional interference with third-party contractual relations when (1) a prospective or existing contractual relationship exists between an employee and a third party, (2) the employer acts for the purpose of causing the specific type of harm at issue to the employee, (3) the employer's action is without a privilege, and (4) actual harm to the employee results.

Malicious Prosecution

This tort may be committed by either an employer or an employee. It requires that (1) a legal action be initiated by either an employer or an employee against the other, (2) the result of the legal action was unfavorable to the party initiating it, (3) the party initiating the legal action lacked probable cause to bring the action in the first place, and (4) the legal action was initiated with malice and resulted in compensable harm.

Abuse of Process

The tort of abuse of process, like its malicious prosecution cousin, can be committed by either an employer or an employee. In order to prevail, it must be established (1) the defendant entertained an ulterior motive to use the legal process for something other than what it was designed to be used for, and (2) that a willful act was committed by the defendant in its use of the legal process that was improper in the regular conduct of the proceeding.

Blacklisting

The tort of blacklisting is a difficult case to prevail upon. Blacklisting involves an allegation that a former employer of the employee is preventing or attempting to prevent the employee from obtaining future employment. An essential element of the tort, however, is proof the employer acted with malice. Because an employer has a qualified privilege to discuss a former employee's work performance, courts afford a former employer latitude in what it may say to an applicant's prospective employer even when the information provided consists of a false assessment of the employee's overall suitability for the position. In providing references, while a former employer may provide a prospective employer with an overall assessment of its former employee that is negative, it may be difficult for a plaintiff to distinguish between whether the former employer's expressed assessment was its opinion, which is covered by a qualified privilege as discussed above, or was actually false information that was maliciously communicated to a prospective employer.

IN PLAIN ENGLISH

Blacklisting is the action of creating a list of individuals to be avoided or distrusted by those who create the list. A blacklist can list people to be discriminated against, refused employment, or censured.

EMPLOYMENT CONTRACTS

Determining whether someone is an employee or an independent contractor is not always easy. One of the reasons the characterization is important is that employers are responsible for income-tax withholding, Social Security, workers' compensation, and the like, whereas one who hires an independent contractor is not (see Chapter 14).

Another reason the distinction between employees and independent contractors is so important is that it defines how the employment relationship may end. If an individual is working for someone as an independent contractor, the contract between that person and the employer will govern the respective rights of the parties upon termination. On the other hand, if the individual is an employee, care must be taken not to become responsible for a wrongful termination when dismissing the individual.

WRONGFUL TERMINATION

Historically, an employee who was not under any form of an employment contract was employed "at will" and could thus be terminated for any reason whatsoever. Presently, absent an employment contract or collective bargaining agreement, an employee's job can be terminated for (a) the right reason, (b) for no reason, but (c) cannot be terminated for the wrong reason. The wrong reason, for example, includes when an employee's job was terminated for refusing to commit perjury when testifying before a legislative committee. Courts found a public policy exception exists in those instances and the employee was entitled to recover damages against the employer for wrongful termination of the employee's employment. In essence, the public policy exception of having individuals testify honestly before the legislature weighed more heavily in the courts' judgment than the employer's right to control the employee's conduct by ordering the employee to commit perjury while in the employment relationship.

In recent years courts have become increasingly protective of the rights of employees who are at-will. In a 1983 case, *Novosel* v. *Nationwide Insurance Company*, the US Circuit Court of Appeals for the Third Circuit held the power to hire and fire could not be used to dictate an employee's political activity in the form of a refusal to lobby the state legislature on his employer's behalf. The court thus concluded that even a nongovernmental entity, such as a private employer in this instance, is limited by the US Constitution in its power to discharge an employee for the reason stated. The court, in essence, held that one's right to exercise consitutionally protected free speech outweighed the employer's right to control an employee's conduct in this instance.

Wrongful termination cases generally fall into certain categories. Employers may not legally terminate an employee for:

- refusing to commit an unlawful act, such as committing perjury or refusing to participate in illegal price-fixing schemes;

- performing a public obligation, such as serving on a jury or military reserve service;
- exercising a statutory right, such as filing a workers' compensation claim; or,
- refusing to engage in employment discrimination.

Some courts appear to go quite far in holding that an employer cannot discharge an employee unless there is just cause for termination of employment. A number of states have considered the adoption of legislation that would restrict the employer's right to terminate an employee's job to only cases where there was just cause to do so. Most states have laws that contain specific prohibitions on the termination of employment for whistleblowing, (i.e., cases in which employees notify government authorities of wrongful acts committed by employers, such as tax evasion).

PROGRESSIVE DISCIPLINE

Employers who use performance evaluations to improve their employees' work performance may wish to consider also using what is known as "progressive discipline." With progressive discipline, the employer begins the disciplinary process by orally warning the employee that a problem exists with work performance. Should sustained improvement in the employee's work performance not be found, the employer progressively imposes increasingly severe disciplinary measures until termination from employment becomes the employer's only remaining option. The underlying philosophy of progressive discipline is that both employer and employee have invested considerable time, effort, and resources into an employee's future employment. Rather than abruptly reacting to areas of inadequate work performance by immediately terminating the employment relationship on the first instance of an employee's failure to perform satisfactorily, the employer may wish to first attempt to rehabilitate the employee's performance by instructing the employee on what the employee has done wrong and mildly disciplining the employee with a warning that any future transgression will be met with increasingly severe discipline. Of course, some forms of misconduct are so egregious, such as theft, that no form of progressive discipline should be required.

ISSUES RELATING TO THE COVID-19 PANDEMIC

As noted earlier, just as this book was about to go to print, the COVID-19 pandemic hit the United States and wreaked havoc on its economy. Employees were suddenly laid off, furloughed, and terminated from their employment. Millions of workers, suddenly without employment, filed claims for unemployment insurance benefits en masse, overwhelming the state agencies which administer these programs. After several weeks following the initial impact of COVID-19, however, state and local government officials began to lift orders requiring shutdown of businesses and employers began to consider resumption of their operations. In some industries and services, however, employees considered to be "essential employees" continued working for employers who perform services considered essential to the continued health, safety and well-being of the nation despite the serious and deadly health threats posed by continuing to work in an environment at risk due to exposure of COVID-19 from coworkers and the public being served.

An employer's operations are thus impacted in four essential areas of law affected by the COVID-19 pandemic: (1) The health and safety of employees in the workplace as regulated by OSHA and its regulations; (2) an employer's duty to provide a workplace for its employees that is free from discrimination and harassment due to various factors as regulated by various EEO laws and regulations; (3) an employer's duty to bargain in good faith with unions where applicable as regulated by the NLRA and the NLRB concerning those matters in the workplace which are mandatory subjects of bargaining; and finally (4) the Families First Coronavirus Response Act ("FFCRA"), new federal legislation providing for employee paid leave rights. Each of the foregoing four areas of developing law will now be discussed.

While these areas of employment law are just developing and much will continue to be said and done to continue to keep employers and employees up to the minute as the COVID-19 pandemic phenomenon evolves and laws emerge, we provide the following guidance gleaned largely from official governmental sources.

OSHA AND COVID-19

OSHA's General Duty Clause, Section 5(a)(1), requires employers to provide their employees with a workplace free from recognized hazards likely to cause death or serious physical harm. Employers who have not prepared for pandemic events such as COVID-19 should immediately prepare themselves and their workers as far in advance as possible of potentially worsening outbreak conditions. Lack of continuity planning can result in a cascade of failures as employers attempt to address challenges of COVID-19 with insufficient resources and workers who might not be adequately trained for jobs performed under pandemic conditions.

Develop an Infectious Disease Preparedness and Response Plan

Plans should consider and address the level(s) of risk associated with various worksites and job tasks workers perform at those sites. Such considerations may include:

- Where, how, and from what sources of COVID-19 workers might be exposed;
- Nonoccupational risk factors at home and in community settings;
- Workers' individual risk factors (e.g., older age; presence of chronic medical conditions, including immunocompromising conditions and pregnancy); and
- Controls necessary to address those risks;

Following Federal, State, and Local Recommendations

Follow federal, state and local recommendations regarding development of contingency plans for situations that may arise as a result of outbreaks, such as:

- Increased rates of worker absenteeism;
- The need for social distancing, staggered work shifts, downsizing operations, delivering services remotely, and other exposure-reducing measures;
- Options for conducting essential operations with a reduced workforce, including cross-training workers across different jobs in order to continue operations or deliver surge services; and
- Interrupted supply chains or delayed deliveries.

Prepare to Implement Basic Infection Prevention Measures:

- Promote frequent and thorough handwashing;
- Encourage workers to stay home if they are sick;
- Encourage respiratory etiquette, including covering coughs and sneezes;
- Provide customers and the public with tissues and trash receptacles;
- Employers should explore whether they can establish policies and practices, such as flexible worksites (e.g., telecommuting) and flexible work hours (e.g., staggered shifts), to increase the physical distance among employees and between employees and others;
- Discourage workers from using other workers' phones, desks, offices, or other work tools and equipment, whenever possible; and
- Maintain regular housekeeping practices, including routine cleaning and disinfecting of surfaces, equipment, and other elements of the work environment.

Develop Policies and Procedures for Prompt Identification and Isolation of Sick People, if Appropriate:

- Prompt identification and isolation of potentially infectious individuals is a critical step in protecting workers, customers, visitors, and others at a worksite;
- Employers should inform and encourage employees to self-monitor for signs and symptoms of COVID-19 if they suspect possible exposure;
- Employers should develop policies and procedures for employees to report when they are sick or experiencing symptoms of COVID-19;
- Wherever appropriate, employers should develop policies and procedures for immediately isolating people who have signs and/or symptoms of COVID-19, and train workers to implement them;
- Take steps to limit spread of the respiratory secretions of a person who may have COVID-19, provide a face mask,

if feasible and available, and ask the person to wear it, if tolerated;
- If possible, isolate people suspected of having COVID-19 separately from those with confirmed cases of the virus to prevent further transmission;
- Restrict the number of personnel entering isolation areas; and
- Protect workers in close contact with (i.e., within 6 feet of) a sick person or who have prolonged/repeated contact with such persons by using additional engineering and administrative controls, safe work practices, and personal protective equipment ("PPE").

Develop, Implement, and Communicate about Workplace Flexibilities and Protections:

- Actively encourage sick employees to stay home;
- Ensure that sick leave policies are flexible and consistent with public health guidance and that employees are aware of these policies;
- Talk with companies that provide your business with contract or temporary employees about the importance of sick employees staying home and encourage them to develop nonpunitive leave policies;
- Do not require a health-care provider's note for employees who are sick with acute respiratory illness to validate their illness or to return to work, as health-care providers' offices and medical facilities may be extremely busy and not able to provide such documentation in a timely way;
- Maintain flexible policies that permit employees to stay home to care for a sick family member;
- Recognize that workers with ill family members may need to stay home to care for them;
- Be aware of workers' concerns about pay, leave, safety, health, and other issues that may arise during infectious disease outbreaks; and

- Work with insurance companies (e.g., those providing employee health benefits) and state and local health agencies to provide information to workers and customers about medical care in the event of a COVID-19 outbreak.

Implement Workplace Controls

During a COVID-19 outbreak, whenever it may not be possible to eliminate the hazard, the most effective protection measures are (listed from most effective to least effective): engineering controls; administrative controls; safe work practices (a type of administrative control);, and PPE. In most cases, a combination of control measures will be necessary to protect workers from exposure to COVID-19.

Engineering Controls

Engineering controls for COVID-19 include:

- Installing high-efficiency air filters;
- Increasing ventilation rates in the work environment;
- Installing physical barriers, such as clear plastic "sneeze guards";
- Installing a drive-through window for customer service; and
- Specialized negative pressure ventilation in some settings, such as for aerosol-generating procedures (e.g., airborne infection isolation rooms in health-care settings and specialized autopsy suites in mortuary settings).

Administrative Controls

Examples of administrative controls for COVID-19 include:

- Encouraging sick workers to stay at home;
- Minimizing contact among workers, clients, and customers by replacing face-to-face meetings with virtual communications and implementing telework, if feasible;
- Establishing alternating days or extra shifts that reduce the total number of employees in a facility at a given time,

allowing them to maintain distance from one another while maintaining a full onsite workweek;

- Discontinuing nonessential travel to locations with ongoing COVID-19 outbreaks;
- Developing emergency communications plans, including a forum for answering workers' concerns and Internet-based communications, if feasible;
- Providing workers with up-to-date education and training on COVID-19 risk factors and protective behaviors (e.g., cough etiquette and care of PPE); and
- Training workers who need to use PPE how to put it on, use/wear it, and take it off correctly, including in the context of their current and potential duties.

Safe Work Practices

Examples of safe work practices for COVID-19 include:

- Providing resources and a work environment that promotes personal hygiene. For example, provide tissues, no-touch trash cans, hand soap, alcohol-based hand rubs containing at least 60 percent alcohol, disinfectants, and disposable towels for workers to clean their work surfaces;
- Requiring regular handwashing or using alcohol-based hand rubs. Workers should always wash hands when they are visibly soiled and after removing any PPE; and
- Post handwashing signs in restrooms.

Personal Protective Equipment (PPE)

Examples of PPE include: gloves, goggles, face shields, face masks, and respiratory protection, whenever appropriate.

All types of PPE must be:

- Selected based upon the hazard to the worker;
- Properly fitted and periodically refitted, as applicable (e.g., respirators); consistently and properly worn when required, regularly inspected, maintained, and replaced, as necessary; and

- Properly removed, cleaned, and stored or disposed of, as applicable, to avoid contamination of self, others, or the environment.

Employers are obligated to provide their workers, without cost to them, with PPE needed to keep them safe while performing their jobs.

Follow Existing OSHA Standards

Existing OSHA standards may apply to protecting workers from exposure to and infection with COVID-19.

While there is no specific OSHA standard covering COVID-19 exposure, some OSHA requirements may apply to preventing occupational exposure to COVID-19. Among the most relevant are:

- OSHA's PPE standards (in general industry, 29 CFR 1910 Subpart I), which require using gloves, eye and face protection, and respiratory protection; and
- The General Duty Clause, Section 5(a)(1) of OSHA of 1970, 29 USC 654(a)(1), which requires employers to furnish to each worker "employment and a place of employment, which are free from recognized hazards that are causing or are likely to cause death or serious physical harm."

In addition to the foregoing safety standards concerning workers on the job during the COVID-19 pandemic, employers must be aware of other EEO rules applicable to the workplace which have been impacted by COVID-19 also gleaned from regulatory publications.

EEOC AND COVID-19

As a starting point, the laws enforced by the EEOC do not hinder employers from following the COVID-19 guidance from the Centers for Disease Control and Prevention ("CDC") and from state or local public health authorities

It should preliminarily be noted, however, that wage and hour issues, the FLSA, the FMLA, OSHA, unemployment compensation and the newly enacted Families First Coronavirus Response Act discussed later in this chapter are governed by the U.S. Department of Labor and not the EEOC. Questions regarding these laws should be directed to the U.S. Department of Labor, whose website is www.dol.gov. The following guidance provided by EEOC is current as of March 27, 2020.

The COVID-19 pandemic permits an employer to take the temperature of employees who are coming into the workplace. Employers may also ask all employees who will be physically entering the workplace if they have COVID-19, or symptoms associated with COVID-19, or ask if they have been tested for COVID-19. Symptoms associated with COVID-19 include, for example, cough, sore throat, fever, chills, and shortness of breath.

An employer may exclude from the workplace those workers with COVID-19, or symptoms associated with COVID-19, because, as EEOC has stated, their presence would pose a direct threat to the health or safety of their coworkers. For those employees who are teleworking, however, because they are not physically interacting with coworkers, the employer would generally not be permitted to ask the foregoing questions.

The ADA, discussed earlier in this book, allows employers to bar an employee from physical presence in the workplace if they refuse to answer questions about whether they have symptoms associated with COVID-19, or has been tested for COVID-19, as well as the ability to bar the employee's presence if they refuse to have his temperature taken. Employers may wish to ask the reasons for the employee's refusal, however, because the employer may be able to provide information or reassurances that they are taking these steps to promote the safety of everyone in the workplace.

If an employer wishes to ask only a particular employee to answer such questions, or to have that employee's temperature taken, the ADA requires the employer to have a reasonable belief based on objective evidence that this employee might have COVID-19. If an employer notices that an employee has a persistent, hacking cough, it could ask about the cough, whether the employee has been to a doctor due to the symptom and whether the employee knows if they have or might have COVID-19. The reason these types of questions are permissible now is because this type of cough is one of the symptoms associated with COVID-19. On the other hand, if an employer notices that an employee seems distracted, then that would be an insufficient basis to ask whether the employee has COVID-19.

From a public health perspective, only asking an employee about his contact with family members unnecessarily limits the possible extent of an employee's potential exposure to COVID-19. A better question from a public health and workforce management perspective is whether an individual has had contact with anyone who the employee knows has been diagnosed with COVID-19, or who may have symptoms associated with the disease. From EEOC's perspective, this general question is sounder. The Genetic Information Nondiscrimination Act or GINA, prohibits employers from asking employees medical questions about family members.

The ADA requires an employer keep all medical information about employees confidential, even if that information is not about a disability. Clearly, here, the information that an employee has symptoms of, or a diagnosis of, COVID-19, is medical information. But the fact that this is medical information does not prevent the manager from reporting to appropriate employer officials so that they can take actions consistent with guidance from the CDC and other public health authorities.

Exactly who in the organization needs to know the identity of the employee will depend on each workplace and why a specific official needs this information. Employers should make every effort to limit the number of people who get to know the name of the employee.

Certainly, a designated representative of the employer may interview the employee to get a list of people with whom the employee possibly had contact with through the workplace, so that the employer can then take action to notify those who may have come into contact with the employee. However, this does not require disclosing the employee's name. Also remember that all employer officials who are designated as needing to know the identity of an employee should be specifically instructed that they must maintain the confidentiality of this information.

ADA confidentiality does not prevent an employee with information concerning symptoms by a coworker from communicating this information to his supervisor. In other words, it is not an ADA confidentiality violation for such an employee to inform his supervisor about a coworker's symptoms.

If staff needs to know how to contact the employee who is self-quarantining due to COVID-19 symptoms, and that employee continues to work even though not present in the workplace, disclosure to the employee's coworkers of the employer's need to contact the teleworking employee is permissible so long as the employer does not disclose why the employee is teleworking. Also, if the employee was on leave rather than teleworking because they have COVID-19 or symptoms associated with the disease, or any other medical condition, then of course too an employer cannot disclose the reason for the leave, just the fact that the individual is on leave.

Can employers tell the workforce the name of the employee with COVID-19? Again, no. The ADA does not permit such a broad disclosure of the medical condition of a specific employee. More importantly, this broad disclosure is not recommended by the CDC. The CDC specifically advises employers to maintain confidentiality of people with confirmed COVID-19.

The ADA requirement that medical information be kept confidential includes a requirement that it be stored separately from regular personnel files. If a manager or supervisor receives medical information involving COVID-19, or any other medical information, while teleworking, and is able to follow an employer's existing confidentiality protocols while working remotely, the supervisor has to do so. But to the extent that is not feasible, the supervisor still must safeguard this information to the greatest extent possible until the supervisor can properly store it. This means that paper notepads, laptops, or other devices should not be left where others can see them.

Similarly, documentation must not be stored electronically where others would have access. And in fact, a manager may even wish to use initials or another code to further ensure confidentiality of the name of an employee.

Does the ADA permit employers to notify public health authorities if the employer learns an employee has COVID-19? The answer is yes. The ADA permits this notification to public health authorities because, as the EEOC explained in its updated Pandemic publication, COVID-19 at this time poses a direct threat both to individuals with the disease and those they come into contact with.

The Age Discrimination in Employment Act prohibits employment discrimination against workers aged 40 and over. If the reason for an action is older age, over age 40, the law would not permit employers to bar older workers from the workplace, to require them to telework, or to place them on involuntary leave.

The Age Discrimination in Employment Act does not itself have an accommodation provision like the Americans with Disabilities Act. However, if an employer is allowing other comparable workers to telework, it should make sure it is not treating older workers differently based on their age.

Pregnant employees are protected under Title VII of the Civil Rights Act. Employment actions based on pregnancy are employment actions based on sex, so decisions about layoffs or furloughs should not be based on pregnancy.

Title VII as amended by the Pregnancy Discrimination Act states that "women affected by pregnancy shall be treated the same for all employment related purposes as other persons not so affected but similar in their ability or inability to work." Therefore, a pregnant worker should not be denied a needed adjustment that the employer provides to other employees for other reasons but who are similar in their ability or inability to work. In addition, note that pregnancy-related medical conditions sometimes can be ADA disabilities, and if that is the case, they may trigger ADA accommodation rights. However, it should be noted that pregnancy itself is not an ADA disability.

Title VII of the Civil Rights Act prohibits all employment discrimination based on national origin. It does not matter if it is linked to the current COVID-19 pandemic. Employers may wish to remind workers in these difficult times about policies on workplace harassment, and emphasize the broad nature of the prohibition against harassment—meaning that policies include a prohibition on any harassment based on national origin, among other bases, even if the harassment is linked to fear about the virus.

The EEOC advises as follows at this time—This is a very new virus and while medical experts are learning more about it, there is still much that is unknown.

Therefore, it is unclear at this time whether COVID-19 is or could be a disability under the ADA. Regardless of whether COVID-19 is or could be a disability, it should be remembered that an employer may bar an employee with the disease from entering the workplace at this time because of direct threat. Employers should continue to take actions involving persons with COVID-19, or who may have COVID-19, based on the most current guidance available from the CDC and other public health authorities.

The CDC has identified a number of medical conditions—including, for example, chronic lung disease and serious heart conditions—as potentially putting individuals at higher risk. Therefore, this is clearly a request for reasonable accommodation, meaning it is a request for a change in the workplace due to a medical condition. Because the ADA would not require an accommodation where the employee has no disability, the employer may verify that the employee does have a disability, as well as verifying that the accommodation is needed because the particular disability may put the individual at higher risk. There could also be situations where accommodations are requested because a current disability is exacerbated by the current situation.

Again, the employer can verify the existence of the disability and discuss both why an accommodation is needed and the type of accommodation that would meet the employee's health concerns. In either situation, and as with any requests for reasonable accommodation, an employer may also consider whether a reasonable accommodation would pose an undue hardship, meaning the employer may assess whether a specific form of accommodation would pose significant expense or difficulty. Under the current circumstances, for employers seeking documentation from a health-care provider to support the employee's request, they should remember that because of the health crisis many doctors may have difficulty responding quickly. There may be other ways to verify the existence of a disability. For example, a health insurance record or a prescription may document the existence of the disability. If the employer is waiting to receive documentation, it may want to provide the accommodation on a temporary basis. This could be particularly critical where the request is for telework or leave from an employee whose disability puts them at higher risk for COVID-19.

The employee only has a right to reasonable accommodation for his own disability. If an employee does not have a disability but seeks reasonable accommodation due to a member of their household's disability, the ADA does not require reasonable accommodation for the employee. However, the employer should consider if it is treating the employee differently than other employees with a similar need before it responds to the request.

The interactive process refers to the process an employer and employee should use to fully discuss a request for accommodation so that the employer obtains necessary information to make an informed decision. In the current situation, some requests may need an employer's prompt attention, such as those employees who have disabilities putting them at higher risk. Employers may provide requested accommodations on a temporary basis (for example, one or two weeks) while the employer is discussing the request more fully with the employee or waiting to receive medical documentation. Given the current circumstances, employers and employees should try to be as flexible and creative as possible. There may be accommodations that are not ideal but will meet an employee's needs, at least on a short-term basis. For federal agencies, the current COVID-19 crisis constitutes an extenuating circumstance that can justify exceeding the normal time lines they must follow in processing requests for and providing reasonable accommodations.

So as a practical matter, given the circumstances that have led to the need for telework, employers and employees should both be creative and flexible about what can be done where an employee needs a reasonable accommodation for telework at home in these circumstances. If possible, providing interim accommodations might be appropriate while an employer discusses a request with the employee or is waiting for additional information.

Any time an employee requests a reasonable accommodation, the employer is entitled to understand the disability-related limitation that necessitates an accommodation. If there is no disability-related limitation that requires teleworking, then of course the employer does not have to provide telework as an accommodation. Or if there is a disability-related limitation, but the employer can effectively address the need with another form of reasonable accommodation at the workplace, then the employer can choose that alternative to telework.

To the extent that an employer is permitting telework to employees because of COVID-19 and is choosing to excuse an employee from performing one or more essential functions, then a request—after the COVID-19 crisis has ended—to continue telework as a reasonable accommodation does not have to be granted if it requires continuing to excuse the employee from performing an essential function. This is because the ADA never requires an employer to eliminate an essential function as an accommodation for an individual with a disability.

Assuming all the requirements for such a reasonable accommodation are satisfied, the temporary telework experience could be relevant to considering a renewed request for accommodation. In this situation, for example, the period of providing telework because of the COVID-19 pandemic could serve as a trial period that showed whether or not this employee with a disability could satisfactorily perform all essential functions while working remotely, and the employer should consider any new requests in light of this information. But as with all accommodation requests, the employee and the employer should engage in a flexible, cooperative interactive process if this issue does arise.

THE DUTY TO BARGAIN CONCERNING MANDATORY SUBJECTS OF BARGAINING

As discussed in Chapter 5: "Collective Bargaining Agreement," in those instances where an employer's employees are represented by a union, the employer is required, pursuant to the NLRA, to bargain in good faith with it concerning wages, hours and other terms and conditions of employment. Under a long line of precedential decisions, employers under such circumstances must bargain with unions on such matters as workplace safety for employees, scheduling of hours such as alternative work shifts and wages and benefits paid which might be impacted by any changes in the workplace due to COVID-19.

While it is still too early to know, the duty to bargain may itself be impacted by the emergency nature of the COVID-19 pandemic. Whenever possible, however, employers would be well-advised in the practical interests of time and conservation of resources, to work collaboratively with its union seeking solutions to problems posed as workers return to the workplace. In this regard, it will initially be necessary for employers, when implementing changes in the workplace, to meet the threat of COVID-19 by (1) performing risk assessments and implement protection plans, (2) train workers on limiting virus spread, including recognizing COVID-19 symptoms and staying home when symptoms are present, (3) implementing individual control measures and screening, (4) implement disinfecting protocols, and (5) implementing physical distancing guidelines. When implementing the foregoing steps, each industry must be assessed individually in consultation with the state where the workplace is located. Employers should therefore engage and negotiate whenever possible with their unions and memorialize all agreements in writing in the form of COVID-19 Pandemic Side Letters to their collective bargaining agreements that spell out best practices for workers' safety and provide workers with a safe work environment consistent with CDC recommendations.

IN PLAIN ENGLISH

Some hand sanitizers have been determined to be dangerous to the public. You should check the Food and Drug Administration's ("FDA") website in order to determine whether any of the hand sanitizers you currently have available or intend to purchase are on that list.

Some areas where bargaining may be required include PPE (which must be provided without charge to employees) including masks, gloves, hand sanitizer, handwashing stations and time off to wash hands, gowns, plastic protective face shields, Plexiglas protective workstation shields and deep cleaning supplies. A second area is social distancing standards including enclosed office spaces, standards for working in such diverse areas as schools, libraries and public facilities, stores and retail outlets, outdoor construction and other outdoor occupations.

Changes in operations in retail, manufacturing and office work settings might include bargaining concerning staggered work shifts, cafeteria or lunch/rest breaks including seating rules, rules concerning use of restroom and cleaning, elevators and staircases use, lobbies and other shared areas, parking areas whether enclosed or open, and shared use of offices.

The laws protecting equal pay for equal work continue to apply, thus precluding two-tier wage structures in response to COVID-19.

Whether a business is a retailer where employees must interact with customers in a store, a manufacturing operation, or an office, there are numerous, well-thought-out measures that should be taken throughout its operations which will minimize the risks to workers associated with COVID-19. Some of these measures may be relatively inexpensive and commonsensical, such as washing hands, while others may be more expensive such modifying the workplace's heating, ventilation, and air-conditioning system. The key to solutions regarding each of these areas is gathering as much information concerning how to minimize spread of COVID-19 and well-thought-out planning concerning each of the affected area in the employer's operations. Because employees who must perform work functions within the employer's plant or facility possess a great deal of knowledge concerning how work duties are performed and may possibly offer suggestions on how measures may be taken in the interests of protecting their own health and safety, it makes sense for employers to confer with their unions for both practical as well as legally required reasons before implementing changes in the workplace in response to COVID-19.

FAMILIES FIRST CORONAVIRUS RESPONSE ACT ("FFCRA")

Generally, FFCRA provides that employees of covered employers are eligible for:

- *Two weeks (up to 80 hours) of* ***paid sick leave*** *at the employee's regular* rate of pay where the employee is unable to work because the employee is quarantined (pursuant to Federal, State, or local government order or advice of a health-care provider), and/or experiencing COVID-19 symptoms and seeking a medical diagnosis; or

- *Two weeks (up to 80 hours) of* ***paid sick leave*** *at two-thirds the employee's regular rate of pay* because the employee is unable to work because of a bona fide need to care for an individual subject to quarantine (pursuant to Federal, State, or local government order or advice of a health-care provider), or to care for a child (under 18 years of age) whose school or child-care provider is closed or unavailable for reasons related to COVID-19, and/or the employee is experiencing a substantially similar condition as specified by the Secretary of Health and Human Services, in consultation with the Secretaries of the Treasury and Labor; and
- *Up to an additional 10 weeks of* ***paid expanded family and medical leave*** *at two-thirds the employee's regular rate of pay* where an employee, who has been employed for at least 30 calendar days, is unable to work due to a bona fide need for leave to care for a child whose school or childcare provider is closed or unavailable for reasons related to COVID-19.

CONCLUSION

Care must always be taken to avoid violating employees' rights of dignity, privacy, and reputation in the workplace. Employer liability for violations of various federal and state laws concerning discrimination in the workplace, the commission of torts against employees in the workplace, and wrongful termination of the employment relationship in violation of public policy can result in catastrophic financial consequences to employers. When in doubt, an employer should prudently contact an attorney before taking actions affecting employees' employment. In this dynamic field of law, as with others, a relatively small measure of preventive legal counseling can avoid a very large award of damages following time-consuming and emotionally draining litigation.

CHAPTER 10

Ownership of Work Created by Employees

INTRODUCTION

When an individual is employed for the purpose of creating or developing a product, providing a service, or selling, it is important to determine whether the employer or the employee owns or controls the work product involved. In this chapter we will discuss the relationship between employers and employees with respect to tangible items such as merchandise and intangibles such as patents, trademarks, and copyrights.

TANGIBLE PROPERTY ITEMS

When an employee creates tangible items while employed, such as automobile parts, computer components, textiles, or any other form of merchandise, the item created belongs to the employer. Often companies allow employees to purchase samples of the merchandise created for significant discounts with the understanding that the employee will not resell those samples in competition with the employer. Many companies actually have employee stores in which the samples are offered for sale. Of course, if an employee complies with the employers' rules regarding samples, the relationship will remain positive. If, on the other hand, employees violate those rules, then serious consequences can result. It is important for the rules regarding products to be clearly spelled out either in the employee handbook, online on the employer's employee website, or if an employee store has been established, then in that store.

INTANGIBLE PROPERTY ITEMS

Patents

Many businesses involve situations in which employees develop products that are new and innovative. If the invention is novel and desirable, then it may be patentable. In this event, the question is whether the patent belongs to the employee or the employer.

To begin with, it is important to determine whether an invention is novel and, if so, whether it can be patented. This should be determined by consulting with a patent attorney or a patent agent. The difference between patent attorneys and agents is that a patent attorney is a lawyer who has obtained a special license to assist with the writing and filing of patents with the US Patent and Trademark Office (USPTO). That person can also assist with other legal matters as well. A patent agent is not an attorney and can only assist in obtaining a patent. Patent agents are customarily less expensive than patent attorneys, but they have a more limited scope of practice.

In the United States, a patent can only be applied for by an individual. The individual can assign the patent or its rights to a company, but a company cannot itself apply for a patent. For this reason, it is a good idea to have a written agreement between the employer and employee making it clear that any patentable invention created by the employee during the term of employment will belong to the employer. If there is no such agreement, then the question is whether the employer owns the invention when it is created during the term of the employment. If the employee created the invention outside of work, will the invention belong to the employer or will it remain the property of the employee? Unfortunately, there are a number of additional problems that can and do arise with respect to these types of arrangements. To begin with, if an employee had developed the invention before the employment commenced but only disclosed it after being employed, would that be covered by the agreement? If the employee developed the invention at home, on vacation, during a leave, or on paid holiday, does the invention belong to the employer? If the employee develops the invention but does not disclose it until the employee terminates employment, will the invention still belong to the employer? These are some of the questions that should be considered when writing a contract between the employer and employee with respect to patentable inventions. As you can see, the issues are complex and technical and can involve huge sums of money. For these reasons, it is very important for both employers and employees to clearly understand the relationship between them with respect to patentable inventions, and it is very important for an experienced attorney to be involved in preparing the agreement that deals with this subject.

Copyrights

Another form of intangible property is copyright. Copyright applies to art, music, literature, software, and combinations of these, such as audiovisual works. In fact, any original work of authorship that is put into some tangible form is copyrightable. Copyright applies to all forms of creative work. Under copyright law, if a work is created by an employee within the scope of the individual's employment, then the copyright in that work belongs to the employer. If, on the other hand, the work is created outside the scope of employment or by an independent contractor, then the copyright remains the property of the individual who created the work unless both parties agree otherwise. There is a doctrine under copyright law known as the "work for hire" doctrine that states that if the parties agree in writing that the copyright in the work will belong to the person ordering or commissioning the work rather than the contractor creating the work and if the work falls into nine enumerated categories, then the copyright will belong to the person commissioning or ordering the work. The nine enumerated categories are: 1) a contribution to a collective work; 2) a part of a motion picture or other audiovisual work; 3) a translation; 4) a supplementary work; 5) a compilation; 6) an instructional text; 7) a test; 8) answer material for a test; or 9) an atlas.

If the parties did not initially set up the appropriate arrangement for a work for hire, they can still accomplish the same end result by having the independent contractor assign or license the copyright to the party commissioning or ordering the work. The difference between an assignment and a license is that an assignment transfers the rights to the other party whereas a license only permits the other party to use the rights. There are a host of variations of these types of transfer, so it is important for you to work with an experienced intellectual property lawyer with respect to these arrangements.

Because virtually every individual and every business deals with copyright in some form, it is very important to understand your rights and enlist the aid of a competent attorney. Examples of copyrightable materials that you likely have include photographs, writing such as letters, poems, articles, books, and the like, all forms of music, and even some texts you sent to family members, friends, or colleagues may be copyrightable.

Both employers and employees likely have copyrightable material they have created which may be important to them. It is important to determine whether the items remain the property of the individual who created the item or whether it belongs to someone else. In addition, the mere fact that an item is accessible on the web, in the library, or even in your possession, does not mean that you may copy, display, or use that item without restriction. Downloading software on your computer without obtaining permission from the appropriate party could subject you to serious consequences including damages and, in some cases, even criminal sanctions. For these reasons, you should work with an experienced attorney whenever copyright issues arise.

Trademarks

Any name, symbol, logo, or combination of these items that is used to identify the source or sponsorship of a product or services defined as a trademark. The difference between a trademark and copyright is that trademarks are product or service identifiers, whereas copyrights protect creative works, and in order for something to be copyrightable it must be substantial. A single word is not copyrightable, though it can be a trademark.

The most valuable asset a business likely has is its good name. The business name, if used to identify the business in interstate or foreign commerce, is protected by the trademark laws of the United States. Additional protection can be obtained for the business trademark by having it registered with the US Patent and Trademark Office. This registration is only effective in the United States. If registration of a trademark is desired in other countries, the United States is party to a multinational treaty known as the Madrid Accord, which enables registration of trademarks in 105 countries as of the date of this writing through the US Trademark Office.

Protectable Trademarks

In order for a trademark to be protectable it must be distinctive and not generic. Generic and descriptive names are not considered distinctive enough to be granted trademark status. A generic word merely identifies the product for what it is. Thus, the use of the name *Beer* to identify a brand of beer is generic and would not be accepted as a trademark. Similarly, a descriptive name only characterizes the attributes or qualities of the product. For example, using the name *Raisin Bran* to identify a cereal is merely descriptive of the product's ingredients and might have difficulty gaining trademark status.

Generic words are never afforded trademark protection. Descriptive trademarks, however, may be protected in limited circumstances. A descriptive mark may be protected if the proprietor of the mark can prove that it has acquired a secondary meaning. Secondary meaning will exist when the public no longer connects the words of the trademark with the literal, dictionary meaning, but rather with a unique product. For example, the descriptive term TV Guide also has a secondary meaning as the (registered) trademark of a particular publication that contains television program listings and topical articles about the industry.

Some trademarks, even though they are considered distinctive, are nevertheless prohibited by statute or public policy. Obscene or scandalous trademarks are generally denied trademark protection. Trademarks that are deemed deceptive and misleading, such as the mark Idaho Potatoes to identify potatoes produced in some area other than Idaho, are also denied protection.

Protecting a Trademark

In order to secure trademark protection, it is not sufficient merely to adopt a distinctive mark. The trademark must be used in the ordinary course of trade or used in commerce. The use requirement is fundamental to trademark law and is necessary for common-law protection, as well as federal and state registration.

Common law is the body of law developed from court decisions rather than from state or federal statutes. Federal or state registration of a trademark has certain advantages but is not necessary. This will be discussed more fully later in this chapter. Common-law protection will suffice and has the benefit of not requiring any interaction with governmental agencies.

A trademark is deemed to be used when it has been placed in any manner on the product, its containers or displays associated with it, or on any of the tags or labels affixed to the product. Thus, it is not always necessary that the trademark actually be physically affixed to the goods. As long as the trademark is associated with the product at the point of sale and in such a way that the product can be readily identified as coming from a particular manufacturer or source, the trademark may be protected. It should be noted, however, that the mere listing of a trademark in a catalog, the ordering of labels bearing the trademark, the use of the trademark on invoices, or the exhibition of trademarked goods at a trade show alone may not be sufficient in and of themselves to constitute use, because the use of the trademark was not associated with the point of sale.

IN PLAIN ENGLISH

To ensure trademark protection, the trademark proprietor is well advised to physically affix the trademark to the product. In this way, the product is certain to bear the trademark when it is sold. Proper use of a service mark is accomplished by identifying the service by the mark in advertising, signs, brochures, and the like.

Confusingly Similar

Common law protects the trademark proprietor against someone else subsequently using a trademark that is confusingly similar. This raises the question of when trademarks are considered confusingly similar. Generally, trademarks will be confusing if they are similar in sound or appearance, particularly if the trademarks are affixed to similar products or if products are marketed throughout the same or similar geographic areas.

On the other hand, if two products bearing similar trademarks are not related or are marketed in different geographic areas, there may not be any infringement. Thus, a business that distributes its products solely in the Northwest could probably adopt and use a trademark already used by a business distributing its product solely in the state of Maine, provided the mark of the Northwest business does not adversely affect the value of the trademark used by the Maine company.

Moreover, a Northwest toy manufacturer could probably adopt and use a trademark used by a Northwest chain saw manufacturer. In these situations, there may be no infringement, because it is not likely that the use of the mark by the toy manufacturer would confuse chain saw purchasers. Here again, appropriation of another's trademark may be wrongful if the use, even by a noncompeting business, would dilute the value of the mark to the original owner. (Remedies for trademark infringement will be discussed later in this chapter.)

Federal Registration

The trademark proprietor can procure greater protection under federal or state statutes than under the common law. The federal statute governing trademarks is known as the Lanham Act of 1946, which has been amended and updated from time to time. It is not the function of the Lanham Act to grant trademark rights, because those are secured by the common-law principles discussed above but, rather, to provide a central clearinghouse for existing trademarks via registration.

In 1989, the Trademark Law Revision Act of 1988 (TLRA) became effective and made substantive changes to the previous trademark laws. In addition, the trademark law was amended in 1996 to add a federal antidilution provision. Though the Lanham Act provides much of the skeleton of trademark law, these amendments add the needed detail to make trademark law a more complete body of law. Unfortunately, the Supreme Court weakened the antidilution provision in 2005, and, as a result, legislation has been enacted by Congress to clarify and strengthen this form of protection.

Prior to enactment of the TLRA, a mark could be registered only upon actual use in interstate commerce. This requirement was satisfied when an applicant sold a few units of the product bearing the trademark in an interstate transaction. A mark could essentially be reserved for later use by making a token use at the time of application. The minimum token use requirement allowed the registering of trademarks that might never be used and possibly prevented other proprietors from legitimately using the mark. This judicially sanctioned practice also clogged the federal register with unused marks.

Under the TLRA, token use is no longer permitted. Actual use of the mark is required in order for a trademark to be registered. In addition, the revised law allows for the filing of an application for a trademark based on a bona fide intention to use that mark in the future. This reserves and protects a mark for a limited time and to a limited extent prior to its being used in commerce. If the mark is not actually used within a certain time period, the trademark registration will be denied.

There are two official registers for trademarks: the Principal Register and the Supplemental Register. Marks registered on the Principal Register enjoy all of the benefits of the trademark law. Marks registered on the Supplemental Register do not enjoy all of those benefits. The following sections about how to register a trademark apply to the Principal Register. (A separate section included later in this chapter describes what the Supplemental Register covers and how it may be used.)

Applications Based on Actual Use

The use requirement is met if the mark is protected as a common-law trademark. Once the proprietor has established a mark's actual use in commerce, the mark can be registered by filing an application with the US Patent and Trademark Office (USPTO). This process entails filling out an application, sending in a drawing of the mark, including specimens of the mark used in commerce, and paying the required fee. (The filing fee is constantly changing, though there is a reduced fee for those who file online and agree to prosecute the entire registration through an online procedure. For current information, see www.uspto.gov. As of the date of publication, the fee for electronic registration ranges between $225 and $400 per mark for a single class.)

If the examining officer at the USPTO accepts the application, the trademark will appear shortly thereafter in the Official Gazette. Anyone who believes that they would be injured by the issuance of the registration has thirty days to file a written notice stating the reasons for opposition. If nobody objects or if the objections are found to be without merit, a certificate of registration will be issued.

Applications Based on Intent-to-Use

Under the TLRA, a right to a particular mark can be preserved for future use through an intent-to-use provision. This does not remove the requirement of actual use in commerce, which is still necessary for registration of the mark.

Protection of a mark for future use can be accomplished by filing an application based on the applicant's bona fide intent to use the mark in commerce. An intent-to-use registration should not be requested merely for the purpose of attempting to reserve a mark. The statute does not explicitly define bona fide intent, but the good faith of the applicant will be determined from the circumstances surrounding the application and the applicant's conduct with respect to the mark. The history behind the statute's enactment suggests that the applicant's conduct concerning the intent-to-use the mark will be measured against standards accepted in the trade or business.

Opposition

If the intent-to-use application satisfies the requirements of the USPTO regulations, it will receive approval for publication in the Official Gazette. Upon such publication, a thirty-day period for opposition to registration of the mark begins to run. This period is similar to that accorded applications for registration of marks that are in actual use. Those applications that go unopposed receive a notice of allowance. The date the notice is issued is very important because the reservation of the mark is limited to a period of six months from the date of allowance, during which time actual use of the mark in commerce must begin or the trademark application will lapse.

Extensions

If an applicant fails to commence using the mark in commerce within the allowable six-month period, it is possible to obtain an extension for another six months. This extension is automatic upon application and payment of fee only if submitted before the original six-month period expires. Four additional six-month extensions are also possible but require, in addition to application and fee submission before expiration of the then current six-month period, approval by the USPTO upon a showing of good cause why such extension should be granted. In no event shall the period between the date of allowance and the commencement of use of the mark in commerce be permitted to exceed thirty-six months.

In making a request for extension, the applicant must include the following:

- a verified statement of continued bona fide intent to use the mark in commerce;
- the specification as to which classification(s) of goods and services the intent continues to apply; and
- the required fee (currently $150 per extension per classification of goods or services).

Application forms may be obtained by calling the USPTO at (800) 786–9199 or from its website at www.uspto.gov.

Statement of Use

Once actual use of the mark in commerce has occurred, the applicant must file a verified statement of use. If everything is in order, the mark will be registered for the goods or services that the statement of use indicates. The Commissioner for Trademarks shall notify an applicant as to whether a statement of use has been accepted or refused. An applicant will be allowed to amend the statement of use if the mark was not used on all the goods initially identified.

Constructive Use

An important concept found in the Lanham Act and improved by later amendments is that of constructive use. This concept, which has been called the cornerstone of the intent-to-use method, also applies to use-based applications as well. When an application to register a mark is filed under the doctrine of constructive use, filing constitutes use of the mark as of the filing date. Thus, when the application to register is filed, a right of priority to exclusive use of the mark is created throughout the United States. This is true only if the mark is filed for registration on the Principal Register. The constructive use doctrine does not apply to domestic (or foreign) applications on the Supplemental Register.

This doctrine gives applicants a strong incentive to file for registration as early as possible. The constructive use statute provides priority filing protection, and thereby prevents others from acquiring the mark by simply using it before the intent-to-use applicant does. Constructive use greatly reduces disputes as to which party has priority, thus saving costs and limiting uncertainty in infringement or opposition proceedings.

Exceptions

Exceptions to the priority right of use are marks used prior to the applicant's filing date, intent-to-use applications filed prior to the applicant's filing date, and use-based applications registered prior to the applicant's filing date. Applications for registration filed by foreign applicants are also excepted if the foreign application was filed prior to the constructive use application.

Assignments

The current law generally prohibits assignment of intent-to-use applications, thereby preventing applications for marks being filed by individuals for the sole purpose of selling them. However, an intent-to-use application may be assigned to the applicant's business.

Benefits of Registration

Registering your mark provides you many benefits. First, registration enables a proprietor to use the "®" symbol or the phrase "registered trademark" in conjunction with the mark. This may well deter others from using the mark. Proprietors of marks that have not been registered are prohibited from using the above symbols with their marks. Commonly, "TM" for trademark or "TM" for service mark is used in conjunction with an unregistered mark during the application period. These designations have no official status, but they do provide notice to others that the user is claiming a property right in the mark.

Second, registration on the Principal Register is evidence of the validity of the registration, the registrant's ownership of the mark, and the exclusive right to use the mark on identified goods in commerce.

Finally, a registered trademark that has been in continuous use for a period of five consecutive years may become incontestable. By registering the trademark, the proprietor may secure rights superior to those of a prior but unregistered user, but only if the original user does not object to the registrant's use within five years.

Duration

Under the trademark law, registration remains in effect for a period of ten years. It may be renewed in additional ten-year increments by filing an application for renewal during the six months prior to the expiration of the existing ten-year term.

Supplemental Register

Supplemental Register applications may be made directly if the applicant is sure that registration on the Principal Register is unlikely or in response to the USPTO's final refusal to register the mark on the Principal Register. This registration provides protection for individuals capable of distinguishing their marks from those of others, but whose marks do not comply with the requirements for registration on the Principal Register. Marks for the Supplemental Register are not published for, or subject to, opposition. They are, however, published as registered in the Official Gazette. If a person believes that they will be damaged by the registration of another's mark on the Supplemental Register, that person may, at any time, petition for cancellation of the registration.

Applications filed on the Supplemental Register cannot be based on intent-to-use and do not enjoy the benefits of constructive use. Under the Lanham Act, an application filed on the Supplemental Register had to be in lawful use for a year prior to the filing of the application.

Loss of Protection

A use or intent-to-use is a prerequisite to trademark protection. It should be noted that some forms of use might result in the loss of a trademark. A number of well-known trademarks such as Aspirin, Thermos, and Escalator have been lost as a result of improper usage. Trademark protection is lost because the mark is used in some capacity other than as an adjective modifying a noun. When a trademark is used as a noun or a verb, it no longer functions to identify the source of the product, but rather becomes the name of the product itself. At that point, the mark becomes generic and is not subject to protection.

Abandonment of a mark will also result in loss of protection. A trademark is deemed abandoned when it has not been used for two years and there is no intent to resume its use. Token use will not be sufficient to avoid abandonment. To avoid abandonment, the proprietor does not have to use the mark in interstate commerce in the ordinary course of trade or business, but the mark should be used in intrastate commerce.

Infringement

A trademark that is in use and has been infringed allows the trademark proprietor to sue the infringing party either for monetary damages or for an injunction prohibiting the infringing use, or sometimes for both. Monetary damages may be measured either by the plaintiff's losses resulting from the infringement or by the defendant's profits. In certain exceptional circumstances where the defendant's conduct is willful and flagrant, the plaintiff might also be entitled to exemplary damages equal to three times the actual damages and/or attorneys' fees.

The relevant sections under the Lanham Act provide for remedies for infringement on marks that actually are in use. This effectively precludes an intent-to-use applicant from suing for infringement because use has not been made of the mark. The law permits anyone who feels that they will be damaged by acts that are likely to cause confusion, mistake, or deception as to the origin, sponsorship, or approval of the complainant's goods or services with those of another to sue for unfair competition. Under the act, all remedies available for infringement actions are also available for actions of unfair competition.

Antidilution

In 1996, the federal trademark law was amended to provide special protection to famous marks. If you believe a famous mark is involved, either because your mark is famous or because you would like to use the famous mark of another, you should first discuss the situation with an experienced intellectual property attorney in order to avoid becoming involved in an expensive dispute.

International Protection

As of the date of this writing, there is no multinational treaty to which the United States belongs providing international trademark protection. The European Union has established a pan-European trademark registration for its member nations, but the United States is not a party to that treaty.

In 2003, the United States became a party to the Madrid Accord, which is the closest that this country has come to providing its citizens with international trademark protection. Under the Madrid Accord, Americans can apply for trademark protection in 105 countries as of the date of this writing by filing the appropriate application and paying the required fees to the United States Patent and Trademark Office. It is, thus, no longer necessary for U.S. companies to hire specialists in every country in which trademark registration is desired. Under the current arrangement, the application filed with the U.S. Patent and Trademark Office can identify the member countries in which registration is sought and the class of goods or services to be covered. The cost savings for using this process is significant and the convenience provides U.S. businesses with a more efficient method of obtaining foreign trademark registrations in the Madrid Accord member nations. It should be noted that the number of countries party to the Madrid Accord continues to increase. The fees required for registration are set by each country, in its own currency, and, as a result, are constantly in flux. In order to determine the actual fee at any time, an applicant should check the online registry, which contains a fee meter based on the number of countries, the classes in which a mark is to be registered, and the countries' currency exchange rates. For a current listing of participating countries, as well as the fees charged and application process, see www.wipo.int/madrid.

State Registration

Trademarks can also be registered under state law. The trademark proprietor may file with the appropriate state officer a trademark application, along with documentation similar to that required by the Lanham Act. State law protection of a trademark does not extend beyond the borders of the state. The number of specimens of the mark needed to complete registration may vary from state to state and the registration fee may also be different. Protection under state law can be broader than that found under federal laws. Remedies available under state law are also very likely to be different from those found under the federal statute. If a conflict arises between federal and state trademark law, it is important to remember that under the supremacy clause of the US Constitution, federal law will supersede state law.

Using an Attorney

Registration can be quite beneficial to a business that has invested time, money, and energy in developing a reputation for quality work. Procuring trademark protection on either the state or federal level may require a considerable amount of time and skill. In this regard, an attorney may prove invaluable. An attorney can, first of all, determine if the benefits to be derived from registration justify the expenses. The total cost of trademark registration usually runs about $1,500, not counting any artist's fees for drawings. Second, an attorney can research trademark databases to determine if there are any conflicting marks. Finally, an attorney can complete the application and deal with any problems that may occur while it is being processed for registration.

If you are interested in contacting attorneys who specialize in trademark work, you can conduct an online search for trademark attorneys in your area or ask your state bar association for some recommendations.

Trade Secrets

Another form of protection, known as trade secret law, allows exploitation of a particular innovation and may afford even greater protection than copyright or patent laws, which were already discussed in this chapter. A trade secret may be loosely defined as anything that has not been revealed and could give you a competitive advantage. The secret should cover something that you actually use in your business and that you take some reasonable steps to protect. A trade secret may be lost if the owner fails to either identify it or take reasonable steps to protect it. Otherwise, the trade secret protection is perpetual. In fact, one of the most famous trade secrets is the recipe for Coca-Cola, which is more than 125 years old. Attempts to misappropriate Coca-Cola company trade secrets are currently being prosecuted under both federal and state trade secret laws.

Patent or Padlock Dilemma

The determination of whether patent or trade secret protection is most appropriate is sometimes referred to as the patent or padlock dilemma. You cannot obtain both kinds of protection, because achieving one will render the other impossible. The patent-versus-padlock decision must be made within one year after disclosure. This is because, as discussed above, the patent laws provide that a patent can be obtained only when the invention in question has not been in public use or on sale for more than one year before application is made. Furthermore, use by the inventor for commercial purposes, even in secret, is considered a disclosure within the meaning of the patent law. Thus, during the first year, the inventor must decide how the innovation will be protected. If trade secret protection is selected and no patent application is filed, then patent protection is probably lost forever.

Selecting a patent will destroy trade secret protection once the patent is issued, because the patent application must contain a full description of precisely what was invented. Thus, it is impossible to get both a patent and to keep some aspect of the invention secret. In order to determine which of these methods of protection should be elected, consult an attorney or patent agent who specializes in intellectual property.

Trade Secret Protection

All that is necessary for something to be protectable as a trade secret is the following:

- it gives you a competitive advantage;
- it will, in fact, be treated as a secret by you; and
- it is not generally known in your industry or business.

The fundamental question of trade secret law is—what is protectable? The way you use knowledge and information, the specific portions of information you have grouped together, and the mere assembly of information itself may all be trade secrets even if everything you consider important for your secrets is publicly available information. For example, if there are numerous methods for producing a particular dye and you have selected one of them, the mere fact that you have selected this method may itself be a trade secret. The identity of your suppliers may be a trade secret, even if they are all listed online. The fact that you have done business with these people and found them to be reputable and responsive to you may make the list of their names a trade secret.

Many trade secrets will be embodied in some form of document. One of the first things you should do is to mark any paper, photograph, or the like, "confidential." You should also take steps to prevent demonstrations of your trade secret, such as manufacturing methods. Taking these steps will not create trade secret protection. However, the fact that an effort has been made to identify the materials and methods you consider secret will aid you in establishing that you treated them as a trade secret should litigation ever occur.

Protecting a Trade Secret

In this area, a little thought and cleverness will go a long way toward giving you the protection of the trade secret laws.

Physical Security

First, you should have some degree of physical security. It has been said that physical security is 90 percent common sense and 10 percent true protection. You should restrict the access to the area in which the trade secret is used. Some precaution should be taken to prevent visitors from peering into the manufacturing area where the secret process, formula, or technique is employed. The credentials of delivery and service persons should be examined. Employee access to trade secret information should be on a need-to-know basis. Employees should not be granted automatic free access to the material you desire to keep as a trade secret. Extra care should be taken with laptops, cell phones, tablets, and the like, because if they are lost or stolen, a tremendous amount of data is at risk of disclosure.

Employee Access

As noted, documents, pictures, or sketches containing trade secrets should be clearly labeled. A procedure should be established for controlled employee access to the documents. For instance, one person could be responsible for granting access to them and a sign-in/sign-out process could be instituted for those permitted access to the documents. Employees should realize that violation of an employer's trade secret protection can and often will result in serious consequences.

Fragmenting Information

If possible, the information that you consider to be a trade secret should be fragmented. This means no one employee should have possession of the entire secret. Thus, no one person will have sufficient information to hurt you.

Confidentiality Agreements

It is also a good idea to have employees sign a confidentiality or nondisclosure agreement when hired. An attorney who deals with intellectual property can prepare agreements for use within your business. Employees should have these agreements reviewed by an experienced attorney before they are signed, because the individual will be agreeing to restrictions that must be adhered to or serious consequences may result.

If it ever becomes important for you to reveal a secret to an outsider, such as when someone desires to purchase the right to exploit your innovation through a licensing arrangement, a different form of confidentiality agreement is in order. These agreements generally provide that in exchange for disclosure of the confidential trade secret information, the party receiving such information will keep it in confidence and will not use or disclose it without the express written permission of the person making the disclosure. Again, your intellectual property lawyer can prepare such an agreement for you.

Vague Labeling

Another method of protecting your trade secret is to engage in some vague labeling. For example, if your trade secret consists of a unique mixture for a glaze, then instead of having the components of the glaze bear their true names, you should label them "Ingredient A," "Ingredient B," "Ingredient C," etc. Then, if an employee quits or if a stranger happens into your office, all they will learn is that by mixing some portion of A with some portion of B, combined with some portion of C, the desired result will be achieved. This will not be very useful information. Similarly, if the trade secret is the temperature at which a glaze is fired, instead of actually marking the thermometer, you may wish to have the original temperature marks removed and replaced by colored zones.

IN PLAIN ENGLISH

If you are publishing in or contributing to industry or trade journals, take care not to reveal trade secrets. Occasionally, manufacturers or their employees inadvertently disclose valuable information in an attempt to impress their colleagues.

Misappropriating Trade Secrets

In order to avoid the charge that you are stealing someone else's trade secret, you should question employees who come to work for you from a competitor. If there is any possibility of a new employee using the competitor's trade secret information, the new employee should meet with the former employer and get written permission to use the information while working for you. Similarly, employees should be careful not to disclose or use the trade secrets of employers either when going out on their own or when starting a new job.

Trade secrets have been deemed so important that in the mid-1990s, the US Congress passed a federal law making it a crime to misappropriate another's trade secret. It was felt that if the United States is to retain its technological competitive edge, the government must assist industry with this form of protection. Since its enactment, there have been several high-profile cases underscoring both the importance of trade secrets and the federal government's efforts in helping to protect them.

Trade secret laws may be the only protection available for your business secrets. Care should therefore be taken to restrict access to the information and to treat the information as truly secret. Contractual arrangements both with employees and outsiders are quite useful. These, coupled with your common sense in the day-to-day operation of your business, will go a long way toward protecting your intellectual property. Employees must also be aware of the importance of trade secrets and they should not use or reveal them without obtaining appropriate permission from the owner of the trade secret or serious consequences may result.

Other Intangibles: URLs and Passwords

Since the early 1990s, when personal computers became popular and the Internet became widely available to individuals, there have been questions regarding the extent of legal and intellectual property protection in cyberspace. This is discussed more fully in the next chapter.

CHAPTER 11

The Internet

PROTECTING BUSINESS PROPERTY

The Internet's popularity has raised significant questions regarding the extent of legal and intellectual property protection in cyberspace. One of the earliest cases involved the Church of Scientology and raised the question of whether US copyright laws and state trade secret laws are enforceable in cyberspace. In that case, several former church members were sued for posting copyrighted material online that they had received in confidence.

The court held that these traditional forms of intellectual property protection were, indeed, applicable in cyberspace. In addition, it was held that the Internet service provider (ISP) could also be exposed to liability for merely permitting the infringing material to appear online. As elsewhere, one who facilitates or aids in the commission of an infringing act may be liable as a contributory infringer. Congress later changed this situation for ISPs who do not have control over the content of the material posted.

The Church of Scientology also claimed that the wrongdoers misappropriated the church's trade secrets and sought an injunction to have the offending material removed from the Internet. The court rejected this argument, pointing out that once information is posted in cyberspace, it is no longer secret, and the injunction was denied. However, if a protected trade secret is posted on a website in violation of an agreement or in breach of one's duty to the owner of the protected information, then the act of posting would be wrongful and the perpetrator would likely be liable for the improper activity.

PROTECTING CONSUMER INFORMATION

Consumer protection on the Internet is now regulated by the Federal Trade Commission (FTC). This is a federal agency was created in 1914 for the purpose of protecting individuals from consumer fraud and to promote commerce. The FTC now regulates the Internet for Americans. It prohibits unfair and misleading solicitations from being posted on the web. Employers should comply with the FTC requirements or serious consequences will result. Employees should also comply with the FTC rules, which apply to them because they can also be subjected to serious penalties for violating the FTC rules. It is therefore important for you to be sure that you are aware of the FTC rules with respect to your online activities, and if you have any concerns, you should consult an experienced attorney for assistance.

DOMAIN NAMES

Characterization of website names has also presented some vexing problems. It is unclear whether a domain name is merely an address (uniform resource locator (URL)) used for the purpose of locating the site or whether that name may be characterized as a trademark. In addition, the problem is compounded by the fact that, while there is only one World Wide Web, each trademark is distinguished by the classification of goods or services it covers. Under the federal trademark law, there are thirty-four international classes of goods and twelve international classes of services.

Example: The American Bar Association, commonly referred to as the ABA, wished to register its acronym as its domain name. It was not able to do so, because the American Booksellers Association—also commonly known as the ABA—had already registered www.aba.org.

Domain names were originally registered with Network Solutions. Today, there are a number of different registrars. Competition for domain name registration is fierce. Prices for securing a domain name have become far more competitive. Generally, domain names are registered on a first-come, first-served basis. Many businesses or websites can assist you in obtaining a domain name.

Initially, there were five top-level domain name categories for US-based registrants: *.com* for commerce; *.org* for organizations; *.gov* for government; *.mil* for military; and *.edu* for educational institutions. These suffixes were supposed to be made available only to those who qualified for their use. As the availability of popular domain names shrank, it became necessary to create additional opportunities by creating new suffixes, such as *.pro* for professionals, *.biz* for businesses, *.fm* for radio, and the process continues. In fact, the number of suffixes is becoming rather large, though the initial five are still the most popular. In addition to all of the US designators, many other countries have distinctive suffixes, as well, such as *.uk* for the United Kingdom, *.ru* for Russia, etc.

Disputes

There are several methods for resolving domain name disputes. These include litigation in federal district court, reliance on the anti-cybersquatting legislation, and the online arbitration process using the procedure established by ICANN. (The Internet Corporation for Assigned Names and Numbers offer numerous resources at its website www.icann.org.) The anti-cybersquatting legislation is intended to prevent so-called cybersquatters from obtaining an inventory of domain name registrations for the purpose of reselling them to those who are likely to have a better right to that name as a URL. A lawyer specializing in online intellectual property issues should be consulted when these issues arise.

WEBSITES

The purpose of a domain name is to attract attention to a website, and today virtually every business and many individuals have their own website. Initially, the creation of a website was quite difficult and only experienced professionals were able to assist with their creation. Today, there are websites such as WordPress, which are available for anyone to create a website, though more complex sites may still need the assistance of professionals. Employers may wish to work with specialists in order to have their sites contain more "bells and whistles." That specialist can either be hired as an employee or retained as an independent contractor. Employees who are interested in creating their own individual sites can also work with professionals, though it is likely that the professional would only be hired as a consultant. Individuals, on the other hand, will not have to spend a great deal in order to have an appealing site. You should decide whether you wish to create and maintain your own website, or whether you would be willing to enlist the aid of a professional to assist with the creation or maintenance of your site.

This is an extraordinarily dynamic area that evolves and expands on a regular basis. Conducting some online research and determining your objectives are important. Creative individuals may enjoy the challenge involved in developing a spectacular site and maintaining it, though there is a cost involved in either money or time and you will need to determine whether you are willing to invest either or both.

Trademarked Business Names

Generally speaking, obtaining a trademark registration for a business name will also provide leverage in both obtaining and keeping the business name as a domain name. (See Chapter 10 for a more complete discussion of trademarks.) Thus, for example, Nike would likely have success in either obtaining the URL nike.com or in defending that URL against another potential registrant of that domain name because the Nike business name is a registered trademark. As noted in the chapter on trademarks, it is possible today to register trademarks in 105 countries throughout the world pursuant to the Madrid Protocol through the US Patent and Trademark Office. One of the principal reasons for this expanded opportunity to obtain international trademark protection was the expanded use of trademarks in commerce online.

Under some circumstances, using a business name as a domain name may be considered adequate for purposes of trademark registration. A number of cases have dealt with trademark issues in cyberspace. In those cases, the applicability of federal trademark law and the question as to which jurisdiction was proper for purposes of litigating the wrongdoing were considered. While the issues have not been definitively resolved, the trend appears to be in favor of extending trademark laws to cyberspace and holding infringers liable wherever their infringing activity can be accessed.

In a landmark case, an enterprising individual residing in Illinois decided to register a number of popular business names as website domain names. When the business owners who had previously registered those names as trademarks attempted to register their company names as domain names, they were told that they were too late. The entrepreneurial registrant then offered to sell these companies the domain names for their own registered trademarks. The companies filed suit in federal court in California, alleging that the appropriation of the protected trademarks as domain names by one who lacks authority from the trademark owner is an infringement. The court agreed and stated that this outrageous conduct would result in liability.

Framing

A number of other issues have generated Web-based litigation. When Total News, Inc., decided to provide Web surfers with the ability to compare data from several news sources, such as the *Washington Post* and CNN, problems arose. The other services filed suit, complaining that the visual presentation of their material was framed within the host's name and that their protected material was, thereby, being retransmitted without their permission. The case was settled, with Total News agreeing to refrain from framing the protected material, and the plaintiffs agreeing to grant Total News licenses to link directly to their sites. Later cases have judicially established that framing is unlawful and can be legally redressed.

IN PLAIN ENGLISH

Framing is a situation in which a website pulls information onto its site from another website by using a link or picture.

Linking

In the Total News case, the question of linking, where one may jump from one site to another by simply clicking on an identifying icon or phrase, was raised but not resolved. More recent cases have established that hyperlinking is not an infringement.

IN PLAIN ENGLISH

A hyperlink is a device in which one can jump from one website to another by clicking on an icon or text

INTERNET ADVERTISING

The Internet has become the most popular and most effective method for advertising today. Historically, advertising was accomplished in magazines, newspapers, radio, or television. Of course, the cost of those forms of advertising was quite high, and the audience was quite limited.

Today, advertising on a business or individual's own site, or on sites such as Google, Avvo, Craigslist, Angie's List, or the like, the information is disseminated throughout the world and the cost is minimal and, in some instances, nonexistent. You will have to decide whether you wish to increase your visibility by paying something for the increased exposure or whether you are willing to really rely on your information attracting the attention you desire. Working with an experienced individual can be very helpful in making these decisions.

Key Words

One of the more controversial practices that has occurred in recent years is the sale by search engines, such as Google, of the right to use the name of a competitor for the purpose of deflecting business. Some courts have held that this practice is unlawful passing off, whereas others have condoned it. Thus far the cases have been primarily against the search engines themselves, but it is likely that disgruntled business owners will seek to hold the advertiser liable as well.

Audits

Some intellectual property practitioners suggest that an attorney who has expertise in working with websites be requested to conduct a so-called Internet traffic and Web-content audit. This would include evaluating whether the appropriate permissions to display material have been obtained. For example, if copyrighted material is to be used, has the copyright owner granted permission for the work to be displayed on the web? If testimonials are to be displayed, then it is important to get written permission from the individual providing the testimonial.

Liability Insurance

Internet advertisers also need to determine whether their existing liability insurance covers their activity online. Losses resulting from a crashed website are probably not covered in a traditional policy. Similarly, errors and omissions insurance should be considered for situations where your Web designer creates a site that contains infringing work or defames someone.

International Concerns

Because websites are, by definition, worldwide, it is important to determine whether your site, the content of which is legal in the United States, may subject you to liability elsewhere. For example, comparative advertising is generally permissible and fairly common in the United States. Other countries, such as South Africa, are far more restrictive in what they permit in a comparative advertising spread.

In addition, activities that are legal in the United States can nonetheless subject a website owner to liability abroad.

Example: When Yahoo! permitted auction sales of Nazi memorabilia, it was sued in France by the Union of Jewish Students and the International League Against Racism and Anti-Semitism for violating French law that prohibits such activities. The court was not sympathetic to Yahoo!'s position that it could not technologically isolate France from the rest of the world with respect to its online auctions. In fact, the judge believed the plaintiffs' expert, who said that technology was available to create such a block. The online auction house was found guilty and fined for its activities in France. Yahoo! then filed suit in the United States for the purpose of preventing enforcement of the judgment.

The problem is clear—one who engages in Internet activity has, by definition, established a worldwide presence and must, therefore, comply with worldwide laws—a difficult process even for multimillion-dollar companies like Yahoo!.

SERVER PROTECTION

One significant risk in maintaining a website is that it may serve as a window to your company's computer system. There are some safeguards that should be taken in order to prevent improper access and protect a business's valuable trade secrets.

IN PLAIN ENGLISH

If your business hosts its site on its own server that is networked with your other business computers, hackers could gain access to your entire system and all of your data.

Information you deem to be confidential and sensitive should be encrypted. That is, it should be available only through use of special software. Similarly, your system should always be protected by a password and that word should not be obvious or simple. In addition, it should be changed frequently. More and more systems are using firewalls, which are electronic blocks preventing access to all but those who have the proper key. Many businesses have been created for the purpose of developing and installing computer security devices or software. You should consult with an expert when designing your website in order to take advantage of the latest technology.

EMAIL

The popularity of the World Wide Web has been paralleled by the expanded use of email. Communications within a business are commonplace and efficient. Internal, paperless transmissions of important messages throughout an office or plant help facilitate the day-to-day operations in many businesses. In addition, more and more businesses are developing intranets. These are websites available only to a defined network, such as a company's employees.

Because of the widespread use of internal email, business handbooks and policy statements should deal with the proper use of email, as well as other related computer issues. For instance, it has been held that repeated transmission of sexually explicit or racially offensive email messages by one employee to another may be deemed harassment and, if not controlled by the employer, may render the employer liable as well.

External use of email is also quite common, enabling business users to communicate quickly with customers, clients, suppliers, and the like. Here, too, security is an issue to consider to make sure that the transmission is safe from uninvited inquisitors. Once again, there are a variety of vehicles available for security, such as encryption.

CHAPTER 12

Private Employment vs. Public Employment

In this chapter, we will be discussing the differences for individuals working in the private and public sectors, as well as working for nonprofit organizations. There are employment pros and cons for individuals to consider, which we will discuss below. We will also discuss the ways constitutional protections impact employment in the different sectors.

PRIVATE-SECTOR EMPLOYMENT

Some positions in the private sector can afford greater professional growth. This, of course, is dependent upon the type of position and the company for which you work. Private employers are able to put greater restrictions upon their employees (such as speech restrictions, expression restrictions, etc.) than the government.

Working for Larger Private Businesses

Advantages

Generally, working for larger private businesses has a number of incentives. The room for professional growth is greater than in comparable positions in small businesses and the government. Employees working with these types of companies often have higher earning potential and more room for upward mobility within the company. Many times, larger corporations provide employees with the opportunity to specialize in the work they do, so employees develop a very specific skill set. Frequently, larger companies are also able to provide their employees with larger benefit packages than smaller businesses and nonprofit organizations. Larger companies also generally provide greater stability for their employees than nonprofit organizations or smaller businesses because of the larger economic resources these businesses have.

Disadvantages

As mentioned above, the skill sets of employees can be very specialized in order to be more efficient. While this can be an advantage in working for a larger company, it can also be limiting in the breadth of skills developed by employees. Additionally, working for a large corporation can mean working longer hours, because the bottom line is especially important to these types of companies. Some employees in this type of company may also feel as if they are merely a "cog in a machine," because there are so many other employees serving similar functions. Another problem is that the hours worked by these employees may be longer than employees in the public sectors performing a comparable job.

Legal aspects of working for a larger company

Many federal employment laws and regulations apply to businesses depending upon how many employees the business has, varying from businesses with fifteen or more employees (for the Americans with Disabilities Act and Title VII of the Civil Rights Act) to businesses with a hundred or more employees (for the Employer Information Report EEO-1 and the Workers Adjustment and Retraining Notification Act). See Appendix B. Certain federal laws apply to all employers regardless of the number of employees, including the Equal Pay Act, Fair Labor Standards Act, Occupational Safety and Health Act, Immigration Reform and Control Act, and the Employee Retirement Income Security Act. Another protection available for all employees regardless of company size is protection for "whistleblowers," individuals who identify and complain about legal problems. It should be noted that most states have additional laws and regulations to protect employees. For this reason, it is important for you to determine what state laws are available in the state where you are employed. This information should be available online by googling "Employment law in (your state)."

Working for Nonprofit Organizations

A nonprofit organization is an organization that is created by state law and does not have owners. Instead, a nonprofit organization is, as the name implies, created so that it does not realize a profit, but nevertheless provides benefit to society or specified groups. A nonprofit organization customarily accounts to the state attorney general and is regulated by state law. Most nonprofits are exempt from federal taxes and state tax. Working for a nonprofit organization can be a rewarding experience if the mission of the organization strikes a chord with your values. However, there are some considerations that you should take into account if you are planning to work for a nonprofit.

Advantages

Many individuals who work for a nonprofit do so because of the mission attached to the organization. This can be a draw for people who hope to make an impact on their community or who have a drive to solve a perceived problem in society. For these types of individuals, the reward in making a difference can make up for the disadvantages in working for a nonprofit listed below.

Additionally, nonprofits frequently give their employees the opportunity for greater professional growth because their employees often juggle more projects than their counterparts in the other sectors. For this reason, these employees tend to gain hands-on experience rather quickly. Because many nonprofits are structured in the same way as business entities, the experience gained in working for them is transferrable to a for-profit organization at a later time.

Disadvantages

Nonprofit organizations are not structured to make a profit (as is clear in the name); therefore, the future for a nonprofit organization, particularly a newly formed nonprofit, can be uncertain. As a result of this, many nonprofit employees are overworked and earn less than they would in a comparable position in the business or government sectors. Nonprofits also have specific bureaucratic requirements to maintain their funding, which can make the job more difficult for employees. Because of these factors, nonprofit employees often burn out more quickly than employees in other situations. Additionally, because of the financial nature of nonprofit organizations, an important aspect of working for a nonprofit is the necessary fundraising to keep the organization operational. Of course, the vast majority of nonprofits are structured so that donations made to them are tax-deductible. This benefit is frequently used as an incentive and specialists are frequently employed to assist nonprofits in their fundraising activities.

Legal aspects of a nonprofit

As mentioned above, there can be federal and state laws and regulations specific to nonprofits that can apply for actually running a nonprofit organization. With regard to employment laws, the same laws listed the previous section apply. If you are founding a nonprofit organization or work for a nonprofit organization and have questions, you should work with an experienced attorney to explore your options and be sure that you are complying with state and federal law. You may also wish to consult *The Law (In Plain English) for Nonprofit Organizations.*

Working for Small Businesses

Advantages

There are numerous advantages in working for a small business. These include the ability to obtain broader opportunities, because, with fewer employees, everyone must perform several tasks. In addition, employees of small businesses have the potential to "grow" as the business grows, and most small business employees personalize their job. Small businesses often have a familylike atmosphere so that employees in those businesses tend to be more engaged by their work.

Disadvantages

Unfortunately, small businesses are often undercapitalized and, therefore, employees may earn less for the work they perform. Because small businesses have fewer employees, the hours worked may be longer and the working conditions may not be as appealing. The benefits available for employees of small businesses may also be leaner than those available for employees in larger businesses or the government. Despite these issues, many individuals prefer to start their careers by working for small businesses, because there is a greater potential for personal and professional growth.

Legal Aspect of Working for a Small Business

As noted above, many of the protections afforded to individuals by federal and state law are dependent upon the number of employees working for a business. If the company you work for does not meet the minimum numbers required by these laws, the company does not have to provide those protections.

PUBLIC-SECTOR EMPLOYMENT

Constitutional Rights of Federal, State, and Municipal Employees

The US Constitution and state constitutions application to employment is limited to those employees in the "public sector" including federal, state and municipal employees unless some form of state action is involved in private-sector employment. Public employers are required to follow all federal laws, and state and municipal employers are required to follow all state laws in their respective state. Constitutional rights are applicable to public-sector employees' privacy, termination from employment as a deprivation of a property right in the form of employment, and rights of free speech and association.

Free Speech and Public Employment

Public employees are not afforded total free speech protection in the scope of their employment, though the government cannot prohibit speech to the same extent as private employers. The US Supreme Court has evaluated the free speech rights of several types of public employees, including teachers, law enforcement officials, and public officials. A two-step analysis was adopted by the court for determining whether a public employee's speech is protected. The first step is to determine whether the employee was speaking as a private citizen. If the employee was not speaking as a private citizen, then the second step is to determine whether the governmental entity has a sufficient reason to treat its employee differently than it treats members of the general public. Examples of this are military members being prohibited from making political statements while in uniform and governmental employees (such as assistant district attorneys) using their platform to criticize elected officials.

Advantages

The advantages of public employment are the fact that there is job security because the government is not likely to go out of business. In addition, the benefits provided by government employment are extraordinarily broad, including numerous days off, medical benefits, pension benefits, educational benefits, and numerous other benefits depending upon which branch of the government and which level of the government is the employer. Another benefit is the fact that most government employees have very stable and fixed hours, which rarely, if ever, change. Government employees can be terminated for cause, but, unlike private employees, they are rarely, if ever, terminated without cause.

Disadvantages

The disadvantages for working for the government are the fact that the opportunities are limited, because salaries are scheduled and not based on increased profit. In addition, requirements for positions and promotions are fixed by formulas and an employee's potential for job growth is limited. Salaries are frequently capped, and government employees are limited in their potential financial growth. Government employees rarely, if ever, have the ability to be independent, and they are required to follow fairly strict guidelines for their positions. Despite these issues, many individuals are willing to exchange the stable position afforded by public employment for the others that may be available in the private sector. This is particularly true for individuals with young families, with medical problems, and individuals who are nearing retirement.

In this chapter, we discussed some of the pros and cons of working in small businesses, large businesses, nonprofit organizations, and for the government. We have also identified some of the numerous federal and state laws that apply to these employment situations. It is important for you to understand these differences and use the information provided in this chapter to assist you in selecting a position when appropriate, either to begin employment or change positions. It is also important for you to be aware of the laws that apply to your position if problems arise. Certainly, it is essential for you to work with an experienced attorney if and when you encounter any employment problems. In fact, the earlier you commence working with a lawyer in an employment-related dispute, the more likely you are to obtain the maximum benefit available to you.

CHAPTER 13

The Virtual Office & Reopening After COVID-19

The vast majority of employment relationships are centered around offices, factories, or shops. Yet this is not the only way that employment relationships can be structured. Many employees work outside of the traditional business environment. For example, For example, even traditional positions such as salespeople sometimes work from remote locations. In this chapter, we will discuss employment situations that are structured so that the employee is working from a remote location.

Employees the world over would like to work from home, but many businesses shy away from allowing telecommuting in their place of work. Maybe it's because they are afraid of losing control over employees, or maybe it's because they don't know enough about telecommuting as a benefit. Telecommuting can improve the overall efficiency and quality of a business, as well as make it more eco-friendly.

INCREASED PRODUCTIVITY

Contrary to what many business executives believe, research has shown that telecommuting actually increases productivity among workers. There seems to be an idea around telecommuting that involves pj's, missed deadlines, and a general careless attitude. This idea, though, is a major misconception. In fact, a Stanford University study of call center employees who worked from home showed an increase in productivity by 13 percent. Improved productivity leads to more efficient operations, which allows a company to be more environmentally friendly.

HIGHER RETENTION RATES

Finding and recruiting quality staff is not for the faint of heart. It drains resources, time, and energy. With telecommuting, employees are satisfied and are more likely to stay with a company long-term. Employees who are allowed to work remotely are happier than those who aren't. This level of employee happiness can save a significant amount of money in the long run by reducing costly employee turnover.

COMPETITIVE EDGE

Because of the difficult process of recruiting, businesses need an edge over the competition in order to hire and keep exceptional talent. That's exactly what telecommuting offers. Even if a company cannot provide the highest salary in an area, or the best health insurance, letting potential job candidates know that the business is open to telecommuting as a benefit increases the odds of hiring the best person. Flexibility for workers to work where they prefer to work is critical to retention, which is a driver of a business' competitive advantage.

ENVIRONMENTAL FRIENDLINESS

More telecommuting means fewer vehicles on the road. The Consumer Electronics Association conducted a study that found telecommuting preserves enough energy to send power to a million homes in the United States for a whole year. Offering telecommuting is an easy way to reduce a company's carbon footprint, as well as the carbon footprint of employees in addition to reducing commuting costs. One day of telecommuting would be equal to saving twelve hours of electricity use of an average household.

COST-EFFECTIVENESS

Believe it or not, employees aren't the only people who see telecommuting as a benefit financially. Employers save on things like office supplies, office space, and other overhead costs. In fact, it has been estimated that companies save approximately $11,000 per year for each telecommuting employee.

With the perks listed here, it's not hard to see telecommuting as a benefit to employers and employees. Although it's a change to the traditional employment structure, incorporating telecommuting will have a huge impact and likely benefit both employers and employees.

MOBILE WORK

Some employees, by virtue of the work they do, are required to operate outside the workplace. This would include situations such as tow truck operators, construction workers and craftspeople such as electricians, plumbers, and carpenters, repair technicians such as individuals who maintain refrigerators and washing machines, landscapers, and the host of other individuals who deliver their product or service to the consumer.

These may be employees or independent contractors (a discussion of this subject can be found in Chapter 14). The characterization of the individual's relationship to the employer is important for a number of reasons, such as liability, responsibility, control, and the like. It is also important to establish appropriate guidelines for both the employer and the employee and for an employer and an independent contractor in situations such as these, because many problems can and do arise in these employment relationships on a day-to-day basis.

It is important for the employer and the individual employed to have a clear understanding of their relationship in order to avoid potential disputes. It is also important for both parties to understand their obligations as well as liabilities so that appropriate safeguards can be established. Working with experienced attorneys before the hiring is established and throughout the ongoing employment relationship will be beneficial for both parties.

COMMUNICATION DEVICES

In addition to situations in considering decentralizing a business' structure, many companies have employees who traditionally work outside the normal office environment, such as outside or traveling salespeople. These individuals communicate with their mangers in a variety of ways, such as cell phones, computers, tablets, and virtually every other new form of remote communication.

Issues involving devices such as these frequently do arise. For example, if an employee uses a communication device while operating a vehicle and an accident occurs, will the employer be responsible?

The answer to this question depends on a number of factors. First, who purchased or owns the device, employer or employee? Second, did the employer have a rule regarding use of the communication device while operating a vehicle and, if so, was that rule contained in the employee handbook, contract, or merely understood by the parties? Third, was the employee actually operating the device for purposes of employment or for personal purposes when the incident occurred?

These are all technical legal questions that will need to be evaluated by an experienced attorney in order to determine the employee or employer is responsible for a wrongful act. Because the exposure can be very significant for both employers and employees, it is important for there to be clear, unambiguous rules regarding these issues in place before a problem arises.

If an employee commits a wrongful act such as having an accident, breaching a contract, or intentionally injuring another person and that wrongful act is committed within the scope of employment, then the employer will be liable for the wrongful act and the employee will also be liable for the wrongful act. This liability will be imposed even if the wrongful act occurs outside the traditional business environment so long as the act was within the scope of employment. Determining whether a wrongful act occurs within the scope of employment is a very technical legal process and it is essential for businesses involved in this type of dispute to work with attorneys. It is also important for employees who find themselves in this type of problem to work with experienced attorneys as well. Employee handbooks, discussed in Chapter 6, and employment contracts, discussed in Chapter 3, should address these subjects.

IN PLAIN ENGLISH

Scope of employment is defined thoroughly in the preceding chapter. It can generally be considered as covering everything traditionally associated with that kind of employment, whether authorized or not.

TOOLS AND EQUIPMENT

When the employment relationship is in the employer's location, the vast majority of tools, equipment, furniture, and supplies are provided by and are the property of the employer. There are some situations in which the norms of the business are different. Machinists and mechanics in many businesses are required to provide many of their own hand tools. Some professionals provide their own furniture, books, and computers. Physicians, for example, who work for hospitals or clinics customarily provide some of their own equipment. The rules vary from business to business, industry to industry, and profession to profession. It is important to determine whether the employer or employee owns the employment-related device, because responsibility for that device can be an important factor when a problem arise. The cost of maintaining and repairing the device, replacing it if necessary, and legal responsibility for its operation can be significant and contested if not appropriately established. For these reasons, it is essential to have documentation regarding these issues in an employment contract or employee handbook.

COVID-19 REOPENING

In early 2020, the COVID-19 pandemic struck the united states. At that time, the vast majority of states began issuing emergency shelter-in-place orders and at some point, the president issued an executive order addressing the same problem. By early May more Americans died from the pandemic than were killed during the Vietnam War. This country was virtually shut down.

The governors of many states determined that it was in the best interest of their respective states to begin to reopen. As states begin to reopen, their economies, employers and employees alike are concerned about the safety risks.

Obviously, the risks vary greatly from one workplace to another. Some states will issue rules or guidelines for reopening. While this book cannot go into the specifics for each type of business in each location There are some issues that virtually all employers should address.

Liability

It is important that the employer feel confident that it can reopen safely. There has been talk of enacting laws giving employers immunity from any

COVID-19 related claims, but as of the date of this publication, no such law has been enacted.

If an employer reopens for business without an immunity law in place, it may be sued by those who claim the employer's actions contributed to the deaths and injuries of themselves or their loved ones from COVID-19, so it's important for the employer to be able to establish that it made the workplace as safe as reasonably possible for employees and for visitors, including independent contractors and customers.

Further, if work-related activity results in probable exposure to the virus, workers' compensation may cover any COVID-19 related illness or death. Depending on the employer's jurisdiction, there may even be a presumption that the worker contracted the virus on the job. It is, therefore, vital that for the employer to maintain evidence of the safety measures taken in order to rebut that presumption.

Remember that federal law requires nearly all employers to provide their employees with a workplace free from recognized hazards likely to cause death or serious bodily harm. Employers may have additional obligations to employees under contract or state law.

Screening Employees

It is crucial for the employer to determine if it plans to screen employees for COVID-19 symptoms

For example, will employees' temperatures be taken before entering onto the work premises or otherwise beginning work? According to the CDC, a temperature of 100.4 degrees or higher is an indication of a possible COVID-19 infection.

The employer must determine whether it will require each employee to complete a questionnaire that lists each of the symptoms before that employee enters the workplace. The CDC says symptoms include cough, shortness of breath or difficulty breathing, fever, chills, muscle pain, sore throat, new loss of taste or smell, nausea, vomiting, and diarrhea.

If employees are screened, the employer will need to create a protocol for when and how screening is done and what to do if someone is found to have a fever or other possible COVID-19 symptoms.

Testing

The employer must also determine whether it will test employees for COVID-19 or for antibodies.

If so, will the employer must test everyone or only people who have (or for antibody testing, have had) symptoms indicative of a possible COVID-19 infection. Though it should be noted that an important consideration will be the simple ability to obtain the necessary number of tests.

If the employer chooses to test, it must establish a written protocol for responding to a positive test result. The protocol should include workplace contact tracing, any required reporting to government entities, disclosure to coworkers, and conditions for a return to work.

Privacy Concerns

It is also crucial to take into consideration any privacy concerns if testing or screening of employees is undertaken The EEOC has taken the position that employee medical information related to the pandemic is confidential medical information.

The employer should, therefore, draft a detailed written plan for how you'll handle and keep confidential any health information you gather.

Wage and Hour Laws

There is also a question of whether an employer must pay employees for time they spend being screened or tested. At the time of this publication, some states require it; others make it optional.

Discrimination Claims

If the employer chooses to not test or screen all of your employees, it must create a written policy describing who will be tested or screened, based on nondiscriminatory business reasons.

Examples include testing employees who have frequent interaction with customers or who are required by the nature of their positions to have more frequent contact with each other than other employees.

Telework and Scheduling

Should the employer continue to have all those who can work remotely do so, there are some important considerations to keep in mind. Some states have already indicated that those employees will be the last who are legally permitted to return to the workplace.

The employer must consider whether it can put employees on rotating schedules to ensure social distancing. Or whether it is possible to put employees on flexible schedules so they avoid peak commute times on public transit.

Given that many employees have families, the employer must also determine if there is a way it can allow employees with a lack of childcare due to school and daycare closures to continue to work from home or work part-time.

Training and Enforcement

If employees are not properly trained and the employer's protocols are not enforced, the employer may well be liable for resulting illnesses.

The employer will need to train its employees to ensure that they are aware of any new health and safety protocols.

The employer will also need to determine how it will discipline employees who do not comply with the new safety protocols. The employer should have a written policy concerning this issue. At a minimum, it should notify employees in advance that they may be disciplined (up to and including possible termination of employment) for failure to comply.

Refusal to Work

It might also be helpful for the employer to determine ahead of time how it respond if an employee refuses to perform certain assignments due to safety concerns or doesn't want to return to work at all because of concerns about COVID-19 in the workplace.

Safety Measures

Some of the safety measures the employer should consider include: '

Requiring personal protective equipment (PPE) for employees and visitors

Ensuring adequate social distancing (do you need signs or floor markings showing the appropriate distance?)

Physical barriers in areas where social distancing is not possible

Cleaning and disinfecting protocols

Reminders about the need for frequent handwashing

Providing hand sanitizer at convenient locations.

Be sure to regularly check federal and state OSHA guidelines for your particular industry to make sure the workplace is in full compliance with the latest health and safety requirements.

Remember too, that amid all these safety concerns and the new legal protections for employees that apply only during the pandemic (e.g., paid sick leave), the employer must continue to comply with the same employment-related laws it always has. This includes wage and hour laws, paid sick leave, family leave, antidiscrimination laws, laws against retaliation, and workers' compensation obligations. Those laws are discussed elsewhere in this book. Because everything related to the pandemic and reopening is changing on a regular basis, it is important to continuously update oneself regarding the rules for reopening and working remotely.

CHAPTER 14

Independent Contractors vs. Employees Statutes

There comes a time in the life of almost every business when it is necessary to get help, be it brain or brawn. The help most commonly needed first is the bookkeeper or accountant who can handle taxes, billing, and the like. When things get a little hectic around the shop or office, the employer might then hire someone to help with the packing or running errands. If selling is necessary for a business, an employer may engage the services of a salesperson or a manufacturer's representative. If this salesperson is really good, the business will soon have to hire more employees to keep up with the demand.

INDEPENDENT CONTRACTORS

Someone hired on a onetime or job-by-job basis is called an independent contractor. Although paid for their services by the hiring firm or individual, contractors remain their own bosses and may even employ others to actually do the work.

If you occasionally give products to a friend to sell on consignment, the friend is probably an independent contractor. If you hire a bookkeeper or accountant once or twice a year to go over your business records, that person too is an independent contractor. The fact that the person is independent and not your employee means that you do not have to pay Social Security taxes, withhold income taxes, obtain a workers' compensation policy, or comply with the myriad rules imposed on employers.

More importantly, the employer is generally not liable for injuries to a third party resulting from the independent contractor's negligence or wrongful acts even while working for the business. However, there are situations where, despite the employer's innocence, an independent contractor can render a business legally responsible for their wrongful acts. Such situations fall into the following three basic categories:

1. If an employer is careless in hiring an independent contractor and a careful investigation would have disclosed facts to indicate that the contractor was not qualified, the employer may be liable when the independent contractor fails to properly perform the job and a third person is injured.
2. If a job is so dangerous as to be characterized as ultrahazardous or inherently dangerous (both legal terms) and is to be performed for the employer's benefit, then regardless of who performs the work, the employer will remain legally responsible for any injuries that occur during the performance of the work. A fireworks displayer, for example, cannot escape liability by having fuses lit or rockets aimed by independent contractors.
3. An employer may be required by law to perform certain tasks for the health and safety of the community.

These responsibilities are said to be nondelegable—that is, an employer cannot delegate them and, thus, escape liability for their improper performance. If, therefore, a nondelegable duty is performed by an independent contractor, the employer will remain responsible for any injury that results.

A good example of a nondelegable duty is the law (common in many states) that homeowners and storekeepers are responsible for keeping their sidewalks free of dangerous obstacles. If a homeowner hires an independent contractor to fulfill this obligation by removing ice during the winter, the homeowner is still legally liable if someone is injured on the slippery sidewalk even if the accident resulted from the contractor's carelessness.

If you are the individual who is hired as an independent contractor, then you should be sure that you will be responsible for your own Social Security taxes, medical insurance, and the like. In fact, you will be considered your own independent business and you must be aware of these obligations when you offer your services.

It is important to distinguish between employees and independent contractors for purposes of liability, obligations, and control. The distinction between these two categories of individuals is not always clear, and there are federal laws, state laws, and court cases that contain tests for determining these distinctions. Perhaps the most important test, which is contained to some extent in the vast majority of laws and cases, is the control test. If the employer is able to control the individual's conduct, then it is likely that the individual is an employee and not an independent contractor.

A good way to think about this distinction is to consider the difference between having construction on your building performed by a general contractor rather than having a salesperson assist by hammering a nail into a wall for the purpose of hanging a picture. The general contractor is independent and is hired to complete the job contracted for. The salesperson, on the other hand, is an employee and subject to the employer's control. Similarly, in hair salons, customarily the individuals who work on patrons' hair are independent contractors who have their own independent business and lease the space they use. Typically, they are not employees of the salon in which they are located. In fact, they set their own schedule, make their own appointments, and are responsible for their own expenses. They may obtain some services from the salon in which they are located other than the space. For example, the rent they pay may include, among other things, a receptionist and a cleaning service.

EMPLOYEES

The second capacity in which someone can work for a business is as an employee. This category includes anyone whose work the employer exercises direct control over—helpers, apprentices, salespeople who represent the business alone, a bookkeeper who is a full-time member of the staff, and so forth. The formation of this relationship entails nothing more than an agreement on the employer's side to hire someone and an agreement by that person to work. Although a written contract is generally not necessary, it is suggested that employment terms be put down in writing so that there are no misunderstandings later (see Chapter 3 for in-depth discussion of employment contracts).

Liability

Unlike the situation where an independent contractor is hired, a business is vicariously liable for the negligence and, sometimes, even the intentional wrongdoing of an employee when the employee is acting on the business' behalf. This means that if an employee is on the job and is involved in an automobile accident that is their fault, the business and the employee are both legally liable. An employer would be wise to be extremely careful when hiring and to contact the employer's insurance agent to obtain sufficient insurance coverage for the additional exposure.

Other Considerations in Hiring

There are other issues a business should consider when hiring an employee, most of which fall into the realm of accounting or bookkeeping responsibilities. An employer should, therefore, consult with an accountant or bookkeeper regarding such items as the following:

- A workers' compensation policy for employees in the event of on-the-job injury or occupational illness. State laws vary on the minimum number of employees that trigger this very important requirement. The workers' compensation laws of many states provide that an employer who has failed to obtain or keep in force required workers' compensation insurance will be strictly liable even in the absence of negligence for on-the-job injury or illness. This includes not only medical expenses, but also damages for pain and suffering, lost earning potential, and other damages that are a consequence of on-the-job injuries or illnesses.
- Withholding taxes (federal, state, and local). Here, too, the laws vary, and an employer must find out what is required in their locale. Employers are required to withhold employees' federal taxes, and failure to do so will expose the employer to liability for that amount plus interest and penalties.
- Social Security (FICA). There are some exemptions from this body of social legislation. Contact your nearby Social Security office to determine how these exemptions may affect you.
- Unemployment insurance (both federal and state). These also include certain technical requirements for subcontractors and the like.
- Health and safety regulations (both federal and state).

- Municipal taxes for specific programs such as schools or public transportation.
- Employee benefits such as insurance coverage (medical, dental, prepaid legal), retirement benefits, memberships, and parking.
- Union requirements, if you or your employees are subject to union contracts. See Chapter 4 for more information about unions.
- Wage and hour laws (both federal and state). These include minimum wage and overtime requirements. In some states, the law also regulates holidays and vacations, as well as the method of paying employees during employment and upon termination.

As already noted, the requirements of these laws may vary dramatically from state to state. You are well advised to discuss them with your lawyer, accountant, and bookkeeper. In addition, you should find out if any other forms of employment legislation, such as licensing requirements, apply to you, your employees, or your business.

Hazards in the Workplace

While few manufacturers would intentionally injure a fellow human being, you may nevertheless find yourself in an industry or using a process that involves hazardous activities. It is not uncommon to use toxic materials. Employees are often not aware of the potential hazard that may result from the toxic materials. It is essential to research the potentially toxic effects of all substances used in the production process or product you are involved with. Occupational Safety and Health Administration (OSHA) regulations require that all employers with hazardous chemicals in their workplaces provide labels and Safety Data Sheets (SDS) for their exposed workers and train them to handle the chemicals appropriately. (More information on this can be found at the OSHA website at www.osha.gov/SLTC/hazardcommunications/index.html.) In other words, there is a regulatory duty to advise and train employees with respect to hazardous substances in the workplace.

If you are an employee, it is important that you pay attention to the training that is provided to you. Additionally, if you do not receive appropriate training it should be requested.

Congress and federal administrative agencies are active in the field of regulation of hazardous substances. You should also be aware that your state workers' compensation agency and OSHA may have specific rules regarding your specific type of industry. It is critical to obtain a lawyer's assistance in determining whether any of these regulations apply to you. Your state's labor department may also be able to give you information regarding applicable workplace regulations.

If an employment contract is used, a paragraph containing the required disclosure regarding hazardous substances and the employee's acknowledgment of the known risks should be incorporated in the contract. A similar statement should also be included in any employment handbook. See Chapter 6 for a discussion of employee handbooks.

While these documents would not provide a defense to a workers' compensation claim, they would sensitize employees to the need for caution in working with the toxic materials. Needless to say, a business should take all precautions possible to protect the health and safety of its employees.

Discrimination

Business owners must comply with numerous antidiscrimination laws, including the Civil Rights Act, the Equal Pay Act, the Age Discrimination in Employment Act (amended by the Older Workers Benefit Protection Act), and the Americans with Disabilities Act. The Equal Employment Opportunity Commission (EEOC) is responsible for enforcement of these laws. Antidiscrimination laws apply not only during the hiring processes but also during the employment itself, including considerations for transfer, promotion, layoff, and termination, as well as job advertisements, recruitment, testing, use of company facilities, training, benefits, and leave. These laws generally prohibit not only intentional discrimination but also practices that have the effect of discrimination. Note that many antidiscrimination laws apply to independent contractors as well as to employees.

These laws make it clear that management may not legally retaliate against employees or job applicants who file discrimination charges against them. If a business is found to have unlawfully discriminated, then that business will likely be liable for lost wages and punitive and other damages, including attorneys' fees.

Many states, as well as some cities and counties, have also passed laws that reiterate and expand the federal government's protection against discrimination. These laws are often more protective of employees than the federal law. In addition, some categories not covered by federal law, including those with respect to sexual orientation and gender identity, may be covered by state or local law.

Civil Rights Act

The Civil Rights Act prohibits discrimination based on race, color, religion, sex, or national origin.

With regard to religious discrimination, employers generally may not treat employees or applicants less or more favorably because of their religious beliefs or practices. Employees cannot be forced to participate or not participate in a religious activity as a condition of employment. Employers must reasonably accommodate employees' sincerely held religious beliefs and permit employees to engage in religious expression if employees are permitted to engage in other personal expressions at work. This law also requires the employer to take steps to prevent religious harassment of their employees, not only by other employees and management but also by vendors and customers.

National-origin discrimination includes discrimination based on foreign accents and English fluency, as well as English-only rules, though there are exceptions if they are necessary for the safe or efficient operation of the business.

Race-based discrimination includes discrimination based on skin color, hair texture, and facial features, as well as harassment and segregation. It also includes discrimination based on a person's marriage to or association with those of a different race.

The prohibitions against sex-based discrimination encompass pregnancy, birth, and related medical conditions, as well as sexual harassment.

The Equal Pay Act (part of the Fair Labor Standards Act of 1938, as amended) also prohibits sex-based discrimination; it prohibits sex-based wage discrimination among persons in the same establishment who are performing under similar working conditions. Virtually all employers are subject to this act.

More information about the Civil Rights Act and the Equal Pay Act can be obtained at the EEOC's website, www.eeoc.gov.

Harassment

One of the legal obligations of all business owners is to create a nondiscriminatory work environment. A policy should be established prohibiting any discriminatory language (i.e., ethnic jokes or racial slurs) or other offensive language or activities.

Sexual harassment is one form of illegal discrimination, though harassment based on race and certain other characteristics also violates the Civil Rights Act. There are two basic types of sexual harassment: quid pro quo and that of a hostile environment. Quid pro quo refers to either a harasser asking for sexual favors in exchange for some advantage in the workplace or a harasser penalizing another person for rejecting their sexual advances. A hostile environment, on the other hand, is more generalized in that the harasser creates or permits a hostile work environment through language, activities, and/or conduct.

IN PLAIN ENGLISH

Quid pro quo is Latin for "this for that," which, in this context, suggests an exchange of sexual favors for some form of employment compensation.

An employer is subject to vicarious liability for a hostile work environment; for example, restaurant management will be responsible for the actions and language of a supervisor that results in an employee's injury, harm, or damage. If a supervisor has harassed or permitted harassment of an employee, and this situation has led to that employee's termination, relocation, or the like, the employer will be held liable for the discriminatory sexual actions of its supervisor. To avoid this form of liability, the employer must exercise reasonable care to prevent and promptly correct any harassment behaviors that are reported or otherwise become known to it, and the employee who was harassed must have taken advantage of all preventive programs or policies provided by the employer. There are many training and other resources available to business owners. Check with your business attorney or state employment division.

Many states have anti-harassment policies as well. For example, California requires employers with fifty or more employees to provide certain sexual harassment training and education to supervisory employees. Details of the California sexual harassment laws can be obtained at www.dfeh.ca.gov.

More information on sexual harassment is available at the EEOC website (www.eeoc.gov).

Age Discrimination

Federal age antidiscrimination laws apply to employers of twenty or more employees, as well as to government and union offices. These laws provide that persons forty years old or older may not be discriminated against due to their age in connection with any term, condition, or privilege of employment, including hiring, firing, layoffs, job compensation, benefits, job training, assignments and tasks, and promotions.

More information on age discrimination is available at www.eeoc.gov.

Disabilities Discrimination

The Americans with Disabilities Act (ADA) prohibits discrimination against disabled persons in public accommodations, transportation, telecommunications, and employment. This act applies to those who employ fifteen or more individuals. "An individual with a disability" means a person who has a physical or mental impairment that substantially limits one or more major life activities, has a record of such an impairment, or who is regarded as having such an impairment. A qualified individual with a disability is someone who, with or without reasonable accommodation, can perform the essential functions of the job.

Reasonable accommodation must be made so that that a disabled job applicant or employee can perform the necessary and essential work of the job position. Reasonable accommodations include making existing employee facilities readily accessible to and usable by disabled employees, including the acquisition or modification of equipment or devices, job restructuring, and modifying work schedules.

A business is not required to provide reasonable accommodations if it will result in an undue hardship. "Undue hardship" under the Americans with Disabilities Act refers to an action requiring significant difficulty or expense when considered in light of factors such as the employer's size and financial resources.

Under the ADA, complex rules apply to medical examinations and inquiries, so a business should contact an attorney for more information if it plan to make such inquiries or require any physical examinations.

For more information concerning the Americans with Disabilities Act, see www.ada.gov. Many states have laws that are comparable to or more restrictive than the ADA. You should check with your business attorney or state employment division to determine whether your state has such legislation.

Zero-Tolerance Policies

A zero-tolerance standard will best protect an employer from discrimination claims. An employee handbook containing policies against sexual harassment, offensive behaviors, and the like is a good starting point. A well-drafted discrimination policy will apply to behavior and oral and written (including electronic) communications. It will include procedures that provide employees with a way to confidentially report problems regarding offensive or harassing behavior and will direct management on how to investigate and resolve the issues. The process should include an employee appeals process for any adverse findings. The complaint and appeals procedures should direct an employee to contact someone other than the employee's immediate supervisor, because that supervisor may be the one responsible for such conduct.

Employees should be advised that both the complaints and appeals need to be put in writing so that there can be no misunderstandings, though the first step is often verbal. A well-drafted policy will state that the employer will, whenever possible, provide complaining employees and witnesses reasonable confidentiality, but it should be made clear that there can be no assurance of confidentiality, because it may become necessary for management to disclose the identity and testimony of relevant parties in any legal proceeding.

It is also essential for employers to provide employees with ongoing education with respect to employment relations, including harassment and discrimination issues.

The Family Medical Leave Act

The Family and Medical Leave Act of 1993 (FMLA) allows employees to take up to twelve weeks of unpaid leave each year for certain family or medical reasons if they have worked for the employer for a year and meet certain other eligibility requirements. FMLA must be followed by private-sector employers who employ fifty or more employees during the current or preceding calendar year and who are engaged in interstate commerce or any activity affecting commerce.

An eligible employee may take their twelve-week leave due to the birth and care of their newborn, a foster child being placed with the employee, to care for a spouse, child, or parent with a serious health condition, or to take care of the employee's own serious health condition. FMLA defines "serious health condition" as an illness, injury, impairment, or physical or mental condition that brings about a period of incapacity and/or requires intensive and continual medical treatment, and specifically includes prenatal care.

When the worker returns to the job, the job may be the exact job that the employee left or it may be an equivalent job—with equivalent duties, pay, benefits, and the like. The only employees to which this would not apply are "key" employees whose absence from their positions will cause "substantial and grievous economic injury" to the employer.

There are certain notice requirements, as well as rules for requiring medical certification of the need for leave. Further information can be found at www.dol.gov.

Many states have supplemental leave acts. Check with your business attorney or state employment division.

CHAPTER 15

Discipline and Termination of the Employment Relationship

INTRODUCTION

In earlier chapters of this book we have discussed how the employment relationship begins, including but not limited to (a) advertising for an open position with the employer, (b) interviewing candidates who submit applications for employment, and (c) hiring employees. We have furthermore examined the employment relationship once it has begun including (a) "onboarding" of new employees, (b) uniform enforcement of practices and rules to ensure employees are provided a safe workplace, free from all forms of unlawful discrimination and harassment, and (c) providing continual guidance and training to employees throughout the employment relationship by use of a well-drafted employee handbook, periodic performance reviews, and refresher training.

Like everything involving the "Human Condition," however, where there is a beginning and a middle, there must inevitably be an end. In this chapter we shall therefore discuss termination of the employment relationship, whether by means of an employee's voluntary resignation or by an employer's action terminating employment.

THE PROBATIONARY PERIOD

Following an employee's initial hire, most employers require the employee undergo a uniformly applied probationary period of review. During the probationary period, which varies among employers from three months to a year, the employee undergoes periodic and timely reviews of performance and receives written evaluations rating work performance in specific areas of the job. This can include meeting grooming standards, attendance, attitude, and competence in performing the essential duties of the position for which the employee has been hired, as well as a general overall assessment of whether the employee's performance is meeting or is below expectations. During the probationary period, the employer's written standards should clearly explain to the employee that the probationary period provides an opportunity for the employer to assess whether the employee is meeting its expectations and provides guidance to the employee concerning any areas that are found to be deficient and thus require improvement.

Whenever there is a probationary period, the employer should be careful to explain, preferably in a well-written employee handbook, that should the employee successfully pass his probationary period the employee will then become a "regular" or "full-time" employee. It is, however, very important to avoid ever advising the probationary employee will become a "permanent employee," because use of the latter phrase may imply to the employee, and ultimately to a court of law if ever challenged, that the employee has a lawfully vested right to continued employment once the employee has passed probation. Additionally, if there is an evaluation of the employee's performance when the probationary period nears completion, it should be conducted objectively. When evaluations become pro forma and the evaluator, who is usually the employee's supervisor and has worked closely with the employee, is less than candid and objective in the assessment, problems can and will arise, because the employee may thereafter argue the employee's satisfactory performance evaluations are evidence that a subsequent decision terminating employment must have been unlawfully motivated by something other than alleged poor work performance.

IN PLAIN ENGLISH

Pro forma is Latin phrase used in law used to describe a practice or action that is performed as a courtesy or satisfies minimum requirements. It is often considered a mere formality.

DISTINCTIONS BETWEEN FEDERAL, PUBLIC, AND PRIVATE EMPLOYMENT

The rules concerning both (a) issuance of progressive discipline and (b) termination of employment are derived from various laws governing the employment relationship in the following sectors.

The Federal Sector

If the employer is a federal government agency, such as Department of Defense, Department of Homeland Security, Department of Treasury, or Social Security Administration, it operates within the "federal sector" and the employment relationship between the government agency and its employees is governed pursuant to federal laws and executive orders designed for that purpose.

The federal law governing the employment relationship in the federal sectors is the Federal Service Labor-Management and Employee Relations Law, which created several new agencies such as the Office of Personnel Management, the Merit Systems Protection Board, the Federal Labor Relations Authority, and Federal Service Impasse Panel. This law loosely parallels the provisions of the National Labor Relations Act (NLRA) regarding establishing bargaining units, election of unions to represent bargaining units, negotiating collective bargaining agreements, and establishing unfair labor practices and a process for their adjudication.

The Public Sector

On the other hand, when the employer is a state government entity such as Department of Motor Vehicles, Highway Patrol, Department of Corrections, or a public university, it is within the "public sector" and the employment relationship between that state employer and its employees is governed by specific state laws designed to regulate that employment relationship. Similarly, if the employer is a local governmental entity such as a city, county, school district, or special district providing water, sewer, or fire protection services, it is also in the "public sector," but the relationship between the local governmental employer and its employees is governed by separate state laws, and in some instances local ordinances, specifically written to cover their employment relationships with its employees. Once again, the various state laws loosely parallel the NLRA.

The Private Sector

Finally, all other employers that do not operate in either the federal or public sectors are in the "private sector." The relationship between private-sector employers and their employees are also governed in part by various federal, state, and local laws applicable to specific aspects of the employment relationship such as occupational safety (OSHA), minimum wage and overtime pay (FLSA), discrimination in employment (Title VII, CRA of 1964), and collective bargaining (NLRA). The employment relationship between such private-sector employers and their respective workforces may furthermore be conducted pursuant to individual employment contracts with employees (see Chapter 3), or by means of collective bargaining agreements with unions (see Chapter 5).

DISCIPLINE AND DISCHARGE IN THE PRIVATE SECTOR

Collective Bargaining Agreements

In the private sector, employees are provided the right under the National Labor Relations Act (NLRA) to organize, join, and be represented for purposes of engaging in collective bargaining and enforcement of agreements by a union of their own choosing. In collective bargaining employment relationships, employees are grouped into bargaining units along with other employees who share a "community of interest" regarding their employment relationship with their employer. Those employees, through freely conducted elections, vote whether to be represented by a particular union for purposes of determining their wages, hours, and terms and conditions of employment. The union, if approved by a majority of the bargaining unit members, then meets at the negotiating table with the employer and negotiates a written collective bargaining agreement, which includes the members' wages, hours, and other terms and conditions of employment. See Chapter 5 for more detail on this topic.

"Just Cause" Discipline and Discharge Under Collective Bargaining Agreements

From an employee's perspective, among the many advantages of collective bargaining agreements is that they provide a strong measure of protection for employees who are disciplined or discharged from employment by an employer. Under a collective bargaining agreement, an employer may only terminate an employee's employment on limited grounds rather than for virtually any reason whatsoever, as is the case when employees are employed "at will." Employers with collective bargaining agreements may nevertheless terminate employment for a broad range of employee misconduct, including such offenses as theft, insubordination, discrimination against coworkers, sexual harassment, and violence in the workplace. Most collective bargaining agreements provide that such terminations may only be for "just cause." While "just cause" is a very broad term of art used in most collective bargaining agreements, it generally means the employer cannot terminate an employee for arbitrary, capricious, or discriminatory reasons. As sometimes summarized, discharge must "be for just cause and not just because."

IN PLAIN ENGLISH

The employer is required to prove that the termination was justified if the termination is challenged by the union, or the employee may be reinstated or awarded damages for a wrongful discharge or both.

Collective bargaining agreements customarily provide that employers, with certain exceptions, must first seek to rehabilitate an employee's workplace behavior through the administration of progressive discipline. This is sometimes referred to as the employer's obligation to "salvage and not savage" the employment relationship before terminating an employee's employment. Progressive discipline thus requires the rehabilitation process begins by providing an employee with either a written or a verbal warning placing the employee on notice that the employee's work performance is deficient in some specified area. Should that first level of discipline fail to correct the problem, the employer is then obligated pursuant to progressive discipline to escalate the level of discipline to a disciplinary suspension without pay and final warning. Only if a disciplinary suspension and final warning still fail to get the employee's attention and cause the employee to correct the unsatisfactory conduct may the employer then move to the final step of termination. As mentioned earlier, however, there are certain well-accepted exceptions that apply in instances when the misconduct is so egregious that progressive discipline requirements are not applicable. Examples of recognized misconduct justifying summary discharge are theft, flagrant insubordination, and violence in the workplace. Where, for example, it is concluded an employee has engaged in theft of the employer's or a coworker's property, requirements of progressive discipline are not followed on the grounds that theft is so egregious and destructive of the employment relationship that no form of progressive discipline can ever hope to restore the level of trust essential to the employer-employee relationship.

Further precedent under the just cause clause of collective bargaining agreements provides that employees must first be advised of their employer's expected standards of conduct before they may be disciplined for a violation. This principle of just cause reasons that unless the employer first advises the employee of what it expects the employee to do or refrain from doing while in the workplace, the employee cannot be expected to conform the employee's behavior to the employer's standards. Once again, however, there are certain exceptions to the notice requirement of just cause. One such exception includes where the misconduct at issue is so commonly recognized as inappropriate in the workplace that no reasonable employee could possibly not have understood even in the absence of a specific employer rule that the conduct would constitute grounds for discipline. Some examples of these areas of misconduct where specific notice is not required include fighting on the job and theft.

Yet, another protection provided to employees before discipline may be imposed consistent with just cause requirements is that the employer is required to conduct a fair and impartial investigation. The basis for this requirement is recognition that once an employer has taken steps to terminate an employee's employment, its position has usually become hardened and no level of subsequent review during the grievance procedure in the collective bargaining agreement will likely convince the employer to withdraw or modify its discipline. Also, even though the employee may be successful in ultimately overturning the discipline through arbitration and employment restored and back pay awarded, the imposition of a discharge during the interim will undoubtedly be economically and emotionally devastating to the employee and the employee's family. In the interests of preventing such an injustice, just cause requires employers first conduct full and fair investigations into alleged misconduct by employees as a measure to prevent economic and emotional harm to a wrongfully accused employee.

Grievance Procedures and Arbitration under Collective Bargaining Agreements

Collective bargaining agreements usually provide for a "grievance procedure" pursuant to which the employee and/or the union may initiate grievances. A grievance is a kind of complaint, alleging that the employer has violated some term of the collective bargaining agreement that includes a clause providing there must be just cause for disciplining or terminating an employee's employment.

Finally, should the employer and the union be unable to resolve a grievance by informally meeting to discuss the issues presented at the initial steps of the grievance procedure, the union has the right to invoke arbitration and present the grievance, such as the termination of an employee's employment, to a neutral arbitrator. The arbitrator must be jointly selected by the employer and the union, and will hear evidence presented by both parties to the dispute in a hearing similar to a court trial. The arbitrator then makes a final and binding decision in the matter.

Private-Sector Employment in the Absence of Collective Bargaining Agreements

In the private sector, if the employees of an employer have not exercised their right pursuant to the NLRA to organize into a union, they are still afforded some limited protections from certain actions by employers. These protections include the Fair Labor Standards Act (FLSA) regarding pay and overtime, Title VII regarding discrimination in employment, Occupational Safety and Health Act (OSHA) regarding safety, and Age Discrimination in Employment Act (ADEA) regarding age discrimination against persons forty years of age or older (see Chapter 9). Of course, other than the administrative agencies that oversee these various laws at both the federal and state levels, which may be somewhat bureaucratic and slow to react, no one is available to step in and represent an employee who has a claim under those laws free of charge. Because employers' pockets are relatively deeper than those of an employee, employers will often engage the services of lawyer to represent their interests whenever disputes arise. The employee, on the other hand, who may have just lost the job and is without a paycheck, must decide whether to likewise engage the services of an attorney to represent the employee. Retention of counsel under these circumstances may, as a matter of economic reality, be simply unaffordable.

IN PLAIN ENGLISH

Attorneys are compensated in a variety of different ways. The most common are by receiving payment for the work performed on an hourly basis. In this situation the attorney will write down the work performed, the time spent on that work (usually in six-minute increments), and the client will be billed for that work. Another common method of compensating an attorney is for the attorney to agree to accept a percentage of the recovery as full compensation for the work performed. In this situation the attorney will only be paid if there is a recovery. This is referred to as a contingent fee arrangement. It is highly unlikely that an attorney would agree to a contingent fee arrangement in which liability is unclear. Typical examples of contingent fee cases are cases in which an individual in injured in an automobile accident when the other party is responsible for rear-ending the injured party. In this type of case, liability is clear and the only remaining question is the extent of damage for which recovery is available. In employment cases attorneys commonly accept contingent fee arrangements when there is clear violation of law with respect to compensation. Attorneys will rarely if ever agree to contingent fee arrangements for other types of employment related claims.

The Doctrine of Employment "At Will"

Absent the protections to employees afforded by collective bargaining agreements that provide that discipline and discharge may only be for just cause, private-sector employees may be discharged from employment "at will." This simply means an employee may be discharged by the employer without notice for any reason, or even no reason at all, so long as it is not for a wrong reason such as a violation of federal or state law. A wrong reason would include, for example, a termination due to a person's religion, race, or gender, all of which are prohibited by Title VII of the Civil Rights Act of 1964, or due to the employee engaging in protected activities in the formation of a union under the NLRA.

The doctrine of "at will" employment was created by the courts during America's industrial revolution in keeping with a laissez-faire attitude, which believed both employers and employees alike benefited from an employment relationship that was unencumbered by any expectations it would continue for an indefinite period of time. The judicially created doctrine of at-will employment, however, began to slowly change in the late twentieth century as limited public policy exceptions to it were also created by the courts in response to certain situations where employees were terminated from employment due to their actions that the courts concluded should be protected by "public policy" considerations.

The Public Policy Exception to Doctrine of Employment at Will

In nearly all states courts have recognized exceptions to the doctrine of employment at will when employees are discharged due to their actions that enhance or promote clearly defined public policies for which protection should be provided. The right of employees to seek redress for civil damages caused to them from an employer's commission of a tort due to termination of the employment relationship on the grounds that they engaged in actions that enhance public policies has thus become known as the "public policy exception." Public policy exceptions generally fall within one of the following four categories where an employee has been terminated after the employee's: (1) refusal to act in an *unlawful* manner; (2) attempt to perform a *statutorily prescribed duty;* (3) exercise of a right the *law specifically confers* on the employee; or (4) *report of unlawful* or *improper* employer conduct, known as "whistleblowing." Note that each of the foregoing public policy exceptions to at-will employment is firmly grounded on some *legal* theory. The courts have refrained from creating exceptions based on what they subjectively believe enhances some undefined public policy. Also, remember that unlike terminations arising under collective bargaining agreements where the employer must bear the burden of proof when challenged by a union, in a civil action alleging an employer has breached a public policy exception, it is the employee's obligation to prove an exception applies. Finally, courts have not uniformly adopted each of the foregoing exceptions discussed in this section in every jurisdiction. There are also many subtle distinctions among the courts concerning how these exceptions are to be legally applied. An employee contemplating taking legal action against an employer following their termination on the grounds of a public policy exception would therefore be well advised to proceed cautiously and seek advice from an attorney in their state.

Several examples where terminations from employment have been overturned by the courts due to an employee's *refusal to act unlawfully* include (a) an employee's refusal to violate mandatory staff-child ratios at a day-care center, (b) an employee's refusal to drive a truck that did not possess a lawfully required safety inspection certificate, (c) an employee's refusing to drive a truck when the driver did not possess a required commercial driver's license, (d) an employee's refusing to engage in an illegal price-fixing scheme, and (e) an employee's refusal to perform catheterizations the employee was neither trained nor licensed to perform.

Other examples where terminations from employment have been overturned when an employee has *performed statutorily prescribed duties* include (a) an employee's refusing to obey an employer's order to be excused from jury duty, and (b) an employee's responding to a subpoena.

Examples where courts have applied the public policy exception to terminations of at-will employees due to the employees' *exercise of rights* specifically *conferred* on the employees *by law* include (a) an employee's filing a workers' compensation claim, (b) an employee's refusing to take a lie detector test in a state prohibiting its administration, (c) an employee's initiating legal action against an employer, and (d) an employee's filing an unemployment compensation claim while the employee was temporarily unemployed.

Finally, where employees have engaged in whistleblowing by reporting their employer's unlawful or improper activities, terminations have been overturned by courts where the employee (a) complained to the employer concerning unlawful labeling of packaged foods, (b) advised the employee's attorney that the employer had submitted false evidence in state bar disciplinary proceeding, and (c) reported that fellow firefighters had downloaded pornography on fire department computers.

Constructive Discharge and Voluntary Quit

Circumstances may arise in the workplace where an employer does not take affirmative steps to formally terminate an employee's employment and the employee resigns from employment. In those instances, the employee may simply cease coming to work at all or may actually tender a formal resignation from employment. Those instances, however, may nevertheless trigger lawsuits alleging wrongful termination from employment under the theory the employee has been "constructively" discharged.

A constructive discharge may occur when conditions in the workplace, which are known to exist by the employer or are even created or exacerbated by an employer, cause an employee to leave their employment. Under such circumstances, courts and administrative agencies have recognized such resignations are not truly voluntary and the employer, by creating or permitting the situation that caused the employee to leave the employment, has constructively discharged the employee. Where such constructive discharges can also be proven to be the result of the employee's actions constituting a public policy exception to employment at will as discussed above, the employer may be liable for damages just as if it had taken affirmative action to terminate the employment relationship.

On the other hand, employees may be found to have "constructively quit" their employment. In these circumstances an employee without notice simply fails to report to duty as scheduled for several successive workdays. While the employee, under such circumstances, may be subject to discharge for just cause due to absenteeism, to avoid triggering various benefits such as severance pay that may become due to the discharged employee, the employer may decline to formally terminate the employee and alternatively presume the employee has constructively quit their employment. Under these circumstances, no such benefits would be owed. An employer faced with such circumstances must proceed with caution, because the foregoing assumption of a constructive quit may be found unreasonable, such as when an employee becomes injured while on the employer's premises or the employer possesses some other information concerning the circumstances surrounding the employee's absence from work, such as the incarceration or hospitalization of the employee or some other similar event or tragedy.

Worker Adjustment and Retraining Notification Act (WARN)

WARN, enacted in 1988, requires businesses that employ one hundred employees or more to provide affected employees or their union representative, as well as state and local government agencies, with sixty days' advance written notification before plant closings or massive layoffs become effective. The general requirement of WARN is that notice be given sixty calendar days prior to the closing or layoff. But WARN's application and an ascertainment of all its requirements are highly technical and complex. WARN's procedures, exemptions, and defenses are therefore beyond the scope of this book. It should be noted, however, that employer liability for its violation can be consequential and should not be ignored. An employer that violates WARN may be required to pay (a) a civil penalty of up to $500 for each day of its violation payable to the appropriate unit of local government that was not notified, (b) back pay to each affected employee for each day of violation, and (c) attorneys' fees to plaintiffs' counsel awarded at the court's discretion. Should issues arise concerning a plant closing or massive layoffs, employers and their affected employees should promptly seek advice from an attorney who is knowledgeable and experienced in this highly technical and detailed area of law.

The Importance of Keeping Accurate Employment Records

Regardless of which laws, regulations, or collective bargaining agreements apply in instances of discipline and discharge, the importance of preparing and maintaining accurate employment records cannot be overemphasized. Because all discipline should be based on an employee's alleged violation of some employer standard or rule, it must be based on a record created that contains an employer's standards. These standards are best memorialized in a written employee handbook, as discussed in Chapter 6 of this book. Employers should take precautions to avoid being placed in the untenable position of having become legally bound to individuals in their employment once the relationship has soured. This potential dilemma can result from language in employee handbooks that might be construed as giving rise to a contractual right of the employee. It is even possible that oral statements made by recruiters or interviewers to candidates for employment could also give rise to contractual employee rights. To avoid this problem, an employer should have a legend placed in its employee handbook that makes it clear in plain and unambiguous language that the material contained in the employee handbook is not an employment contract. It has also become commonplace for employers to require prospective employees to sign a statement making it clear that the employment is strictly "at will" and does not give rise to any contractual right with an employee.

IN PLAIN ENGLISH

Individuals who conduct preemployment interviews should be trained as to what the individual is allowed to discuss during the preemployment interview as well as what the individual is legally prohibited from discussing during that interview. In addition, the individual should be provided with a checklist outlining or listing interview questions, identifying the subject matter to be discussed, and noting subject matter that may not legally be discussed. It is a good idea to have a list of same questions for the interviewer so the preemployment interview will be properly conducted.

As also mentioned in Chapter 7, a written acknowledgment form should be prepared, presented, and signed by the employee when beginning employment. This documents that the employee has read and understands the contents of the employee handbook and acknowledges, consistent with its contents, that it does not establish an employment contract and employment is at-will and can be terminated without advance notice for any reason or for no reason at all. Maintenance of the employee handbook, any revisions to the document, and signed written acknowledgment forms setting forth the above will prove invaluable to the employer if ever faced with a challenge by an employee to its decision to terminate the employment relationship.

The employer should maintain these documents in the employment file along with documentation of any measures of progressive discipline issued to the employee prior to termination from employment. This documentation should establish that the employee has been warned in advance of those areas of employment that are deficient and must be corrected. For similar reasons, records of all performance appraisals should be maintained in order to establish the employee has been placed on notice regarding any areas of performance that the employer has determined are unsatisfactory and require improvement.

When an employee is suspected of wrongdoing in the workplace, the employer should:

- conduct a full and fair investigation;
- document and maintain all records created and used during the course of its investigation including signed interview notes of witness statements, surveillance video and audio recordings, and any physical evidence collected;
- prepare a written summary of the investigator's findings;
- invite the employee to be interviewed and if requested, permit union counsel to attend; and
- prepare a detailed written summation of why the person making the decision to discharge has reached that decision after considering both the employee's side of the story and alternative disciplinary measures.

Unemployment Compensation

The Federal Unemployment Compensation Act (FUCA) is designed to provide unemployment compensation benefits to employees who become unemployed due to no fault of their own. Because unemployment compensation is a joint responsibility of both the federal and state governments, FUCA imposes a payroll tax on employers, which may be reduced to less than 1 percent if the employer is covered by a state unemployment compensation law that meets certain requirements. Because tax rates paid by state law are typically under 5 percent in most states, there is a financial incentive for state participation.

Eligibility requirements for receipt of benefits under FUCA include that the applicant (a) has earned a minimum amount of wages in a job covered by the unemployment compensation tax system during the period prior to becoming unemployed, (b) is currently unemployed, (c) is available and able to work, and (d) has registered at an appropriate government-operated employment service office for referral to prospective employers.

Benefits to eligible applicants are paid from an employer's individual reserve account funded through state unemployment taxes attributable to the employer's employees. Employers who experience relatively fewer benefit claims from former or laid-off employees are taxed at lower rates. Claimants for unemployment compensation may be disqualified under prescribed circumstances such as when they (a) have voluntarily quit employment, (b) their employment was terminated for misconduct that may not be equivalent to termination for "good cause," (c) refused suitable employment, (d) are unemployed due to labor disputes, and (e) receive benefits from other sources such as workers' compensation, severance pay, pay in lieu of termination or layoff notice, or employer-financed retirement benefits.

CONCLUSION

Termination of the employment relationship must be conducted properly or serious consequences can result. This chapter has identified may of the issues employers and employees should consider when the relationship has come to an end. It is important for you, whether an employer or an employee, to be aware of the issues discussed in this chapter. You are urged to consult with an attorney whenever you believe legal issues may be involved.

CHAPTER 16

Dispute Resolution

INTRODUCTION

At some time in the employment relationship a dispute may arise between the employer and the employee. In this chapter we will discuss the variety of methods that are available to resolve an employment dispute. Both the employment handbook in Chapter 6 and the employment contract discussed in Chapter 3 should contain language that addresses dispute resolution.

Whether you handle the matter yourself or have an attorney or other representative, for example a shop steward, work with you is a decision that you should make before the proceeding begins. We recommend that you discuss the proceeding with your attorney or representative in order to determine whether that party's assistance would be beneficial.

MEDIATION

This is a process whereby an individual known as a mediator assists both the employer and the employee in working out an acceptable resolution of the dispute. The mediator is an individual who must be impartial and act like a referee. While mediators are frequently lawyers or retired judges, they do not have to be legal professionals, and there are a number of very prominent mediators who do not have a legal background.

The mediation process may vary, but generally it begins by having both sides prepare a summary of the issues they believe are involved in the dispute. This summary can either be confidential and only provided to the mediator or it can be exchanged with the other party to the mediation depending on what the parties involved in the dispute agree to. The method by which the mediation is conducted varies from mediator to mediator depending upon the experience of the individual conducting the proceeding and the needs of the parties.

The mediation is frequently conducted in an office, and it could be conducted with all three parties (employer, employee, and mediator) in the same room talking it through, or, more commonly, it is conducted with the employer and employee in separate rooms, while the mediator shuttles back and forth between them. The mediator does not decide the dispute; rather, the mediator assists the parties in working out their differences. Mediation may be required by the employment handbook, employment contract, or upon an order from a court, agency, or law.

Customarily the parties to a mediation are provided with a list of possible mediators and the parties must agree to the individual who will serve as mediator. The mediator's sole mission is to assist the parties in settling the dispute. The mediation may continue for several days, and occasionally a mediation can wind up taking longer. In fact, it is not uncommon for there to be "cooling-off periods" between rounds of mediation in order to provide the parties with an opportunity to determine the best way to resolve a dispute.

The mediator is paid by the parties, and customarily it is agreed that each party pay half of the mediator's fee. Mediation should be distinguished from a settlement conference, which is discussed in the next section

SETTLEMENT CONFERENCE

A settlement conference is very much like a mediation but it is customarily conducted by a judge in a legal proceeding. A judge is not paid by the parties; rather, the judge is salaried. Settlement conferences are frequently required by courts as a part of the litigation process, and the judge conducting the settlement conference or the court in which the proceeding is pending will have local rules regarding the documents that must be provided before the conference. Hereto the settlement judge does not take sides in the dispute. The settlement judge merely assists the parties in working out their differences. However, if no settlement is reached, the settlement judge may not discuss the settlement proceedings with anyone else. Those proceedings are confidential.

ARBITRATION

Arbitration is a legal proceeding whereby an individual known as an arbitrator acts like a judge. In some situations, the rules require there to be at least three arbitrators, and the matter is resolved when two of them rule in favor of one of the parties.

Arbitrations can be required by contract or may be required by law in some situations. They can be final, in which event the arbitrator's decision may not be appealed unless the arbitrator has abused their discretion. Other arbitrations that are required in some states as part of the litigation process may be appealed by either party. Arbitration should be distinguished from mediation, because the arbitrator decides the dispute like a judge, whereas a mediator acts as a referee.

IN PLAIN ENGLISH

Abuse of discretion is a legal concept whereby the individual misuses the power and authority that the individual was provided, and as a result the proceeding is considered unfair. This is extraordinarily difficult to establish.

LITIGATION

If the employer or employee feels that a lawsuit is necessary, then suit can be filed in either state or federal court. It is important for an attorney to be involved in litigation, because there are a number of procedural requirements that must be complied with.

Litigation will typically take place in state court, where the state's procedural rules must be followed. Typically, a document called a complaint will be prepared, which will spell out the facts of the dispute and the relief sought. It will be filed in court and served on the other party. The other party will then have a specified period, customarily thirty days, to respond to the complaint, at which time the case will be started. There will then be a period during which both sides request documents from the other side and conduct other forms of discovery, which are allowed by the local rules. This is probably the most time-consuming and expensive portion of the lawsuit, and an attorney should assist with this process. The case can then be resolved by having it summarily decided or it can be tried by a judge or jury.

IN PLAIN ENGLISH

This is a proceeding whereby the parties believe that the issues and legal rules are so clearly in that party's favor that a document explaining the party's position is prepared and filed with the court. A judge will then review that document, conduct a hearing, and determine whether the case or a portion of the case should be resolved in favor of the party who prepared the document. This is referred to as a summary judgment.

At any time in the litigation process, the parties can settle. Litigation is frequently stressful, time-consuming, and expensive. For these reasons the vast majority of disputes are settled before they are ever tried.

Instead of having a case filed in state court, the parties may wish to have their dispute litigated in federal court. In order for a case to be filed in federal court, it must either involve a federal question—for example a federal law must be involved—or the parties must be located in different states and the amount involved in the dispute must exceed $75,000. This is known as diversity jurisdiction and it requires the complainant to be from a state that is different from the state of the parties on the other side. If more than one party is involved, then the attorney must decide whether there is complete diversity before filing a federal lawsuit. The procedural rules in federal court may be different from the rules in state court and the attorney handling the case will likely advise you as to which rules that attorney believes would be beneficial.

IN PLAIN ENGLISH

Complete diversity means that the parties on the complainant side must be from a state or states that are different from any of the parties on the other side of the case. There are complex rules in determining the state a party is from. For example, a corporation that is created in Delaware but has registered offices in numerous other states could be considered to be from all of those states for diversity purposes.

The cost of federal litigation may be higher than state litigation, because the procedural rules are frequently more technical and federal cases may take longer to decide. There are two levels of federal judges, and the parties to a federal lawsuit can decide whether to allow a magistrate judge to handle the case, in which event the case may go faster, or they can choose to have an Article 3 judge, in which event the case is likely to take longer. The attorney involved in the case will likely provide recommendations based on that attorney's experience.

IN PLAIN ENGLISH

Article 3 of the US Constitution provides for the appointment of federal judges, and judges appointed pursuant to that article are referred to as Article 3 judges. They should be distinguished from magistrate judges who are not appointed pursuant to that constitution provision. Instead, individuals apply for the position of magistrate judge and they are hired for a specified period of time in that capacity. A magistrate judge's decision on many issues may be appealed to an Article 3 judge.

ADMINISTRATIVE AGENCIES

There are a number of administrative agencies available when employment disputes arise. For employment disputes involving larger businesses, the National Labor Relations Board (NLRB) is available, and that federal agency has its own dispute resolution process. For NLRB disputes you should work with an attorney.

Another federal agency that is available to assist with disputes involving health and safety is the Occupational Safety Health Administration (OSHA). OSHA does not require the use of attorneys, but it is strongly recommended, because OSHA can impose significate penalties.

Both the NLRB and OSHA investigate the complaints they are provided and both agencies have the ability to impose significant sanctions.

Every state in the United States of America has a state employment agency, and those state agencies have procedures for addressing complaints. In fact, the vast majority of state agencies have websites that provide understandable explanations of the laws and rules for employment in that state. You should consult those websites whenever any issue involving employment arises in your workplace.

CHAPTER 17

Fringe Benefits

INTRODUCTION

The employment relationship not only provides compensation to employees by way of salary, but it may include many additional or fringe benefits as well. In this chapter, we will discuss some of the more common fringe benefits that may be available today. Because technology and the law continue to expand, opportunities frequently change and possible benefits regularly evolve. The items discussed in this chapter are merely a starting point, and employers as well as employees should determine what additional fringe benefits are available on a regular basis. Once a new opportunity is identified, then the parties should determine whether it can be added to the employment relationship, and, if so, how that modification can be worked out.

RETIREMENT PLANS

One of the most important fringe benefits for employees is a retirement plan. These plans provide employees with ongoing support after they retire. A retirement plan is a written savings program. If the plan meets specific rules and regulations, then it is called a qualified plan. This means contributions are tax-deductible to some extent for the person or the business making the investments. Income taxes on the investment earnings are delayed until benefits are paid to participants. A qualified plan is one of the last remaining legal tax shelters available to highly compensated individuals. It may be used to set aside funds for retirement and to attract and retain key employees. If properly structured and invested on a prudent basis with a diversified portfolio of investments, the plan should provide financial security for the individual's retirement.

Since 1982, federal tax laws have allowed unincorporated businesses the same status as corporations with regard to qualified retirement plans. Further, this same legislation eliminated the need for a corporate trustee (who was approved by the Internal Revenue Service), thus allowing the self-employed person to be the trustee of their own plan.

IN PLAIN ENGLISH

When choosing a plan, employers should consider the needs of both the company and the employees.

There are essentially two types of qualified plans—defined benefit and defined contribution.

Defined Benefit Plans

Contributions to a defined benefit plan are determined by a relatively complex formula and are then monitored by an enrolled actuary. The promised benefit is not to exceed the lesser of 100 percent of the employee's annual average income for the three highest-salaried consecutive years or a specified amount that is adjusted annually and dependent on changes in the Consumer Price Index. For the current permissible amount, see the IRS website at www.irs.gov. Excess earnings (investment income greater than the assumptions made by the actuary) are used to reduce the cost of contributions to the plan by the employer.

Advantages

Normally, defined benefit plans are appropriate where the business owner is mature, with less than ten to fifteen working years until retirement. Defined benefit plans are appropriate—and potentially beneficial—for businesses that have enjoyed considerable financial success with limited fluctuations in cash flow. The defined benefit plan can be designed to drain excess funds and allocate them to retirement on behalf of the senior preferred participant (the principal owner). In many instances, this same advantage can be attained through the use of an age-weighted defined contribution plan, such as a profit-sharing or target-benefit plan.

Defined Contribution Plans

In a defined contribution plan, the contribution on behalf of the participant is defined and is usually either a discretionary amount or a percentage of their annual compensation (ignoring compensation in excess of $220,000). The benefit that will be available to the participant at retirement is not defined. Investment earnings increase the retirement benefit for the plan participants, and the longer the period over which investments are accumulated and interest is earned, the greater the amount of benefits that will be available to the participants at retirement.

IN PLAIN ENGLISH

A major difference between a defined contribution plan and a defined benefit plan is who bears the risk of poor investment performance. The employer bears the risk in defined benefit plans, whereas participants bear this risk in defined contribution plans.

Profit-sharing plans, money-purchase plans, and salary savings or reduction plans, such as 401(k)s and SIMPLE plans, are all defined contribution plans, as are Simplified Employee Pension Plans (SEPs) and Employee Stock Ownership Plans (ESOPs).

Profit-Sharing Plans

If the income from a business varies significantly from year to year, a profit-sharing plan may be the most appropriate type of plan to offer employees. Contributions may be determined at or after the end of the tax year. Contributions to the plan can be determined by a vote of a business's management (i.e., managing partners or the board of directors) or by a formula previously designated in the plan's documents. It is no longer required that business entities, such as corporations or certain types of LLCs, actually have a profit in order to make a contribution. The maximum deductible contribution to a profit-sharing plan is now 25 percent of an employee's annual compensation, with each participant's total annual addition limited to $44,000 per year.

Salary Savings/Reduction Plans

These plans, which include 401(k)s, are a variant of profit-sharing plans. Under this type of plan, the employee elects to have a percentage of their gross salary diverted into a qualified plan. Employees can have a choice of saving on a tax-deferred basis or by making after-tax Roth contributions that may eventually qualify for tax-free withdrawal. Depending on the plan, the employer may elect to match all or a portion of the contributions made by the employee. Usually, the amount of the matching contribution has a self-imposed percentage limit.

The main feature of salary savings/reduction plans is that a portion of the cost shifts from the employer to the employee. The business, therefore, makes less of a cash contribution.

A major drawback is the limitation of contributions by highly compensated employees. The maximum contributions allowable continuously change and can be found on the IRS website at www.irs.gov. In addition, owners and highly compensated employees may not be allowed to save the maximum amount if the savings rate of the other employees is too low. They are generally allowed to save about 2 percent of compensation more than the average of the non-highly compensated employees. To avoid being limited by this restriction, you may consider a safe harbor 401(k) plan that requires advance notice to participants and a nonforfeitable employer contribution.

A new approach to dealing with low savings rates of rank-and-file employees is called "automatic enrollment." Instead of being asked how much they want to save, they are informed that they will be saving at a plan-prescribed rate unless they elect otherwise. A year later, the plan's "automatic escalation" feature kicks in to raise their savings rate unless they act. Studies have proven that this "inertia" approach increases the overall savings rate substantially.

Simplified Employee Pension Plans

These plans are often viewed incorrectly as an alternative to the more highly structured qualified plans. The maximum contribution that the employer may contribute per participant to a SEP continues to change and can be found on the IRS website at www.irs.gov. Contributions are based on an equal percentage of annual salary for all employees twenty-one years or older who have performed service for the employer during at least three out of five years and have received a salary specified by the tax laws. You should also consult the IRS website for the current salary range. Although its low maintenance cost is an initial attraction, its simplicity results in a significant inflexibility that many employers are not willing to accept. For example, those whose employment has been terminated must share in any contribution and all contributions are 100 percent vested and nonforfeitable. (Vesting is more thoroughly explained below.)

Simple IRAs

SAR/SEPs (Salary Reduction Simplified Employee Pension Plans) could no longer be created after December 31, 1996. Existing SAR/SEPs were grandfathered in and are allowed to exist until the employer terminates them. A new salary reduction plan called the SIMPLE IRA was introduced to replace the SAR/SEP. This plan is available to employers with up to one hundred employees. Employees are eligible if they earned at least $5,000 during any of the previous two years and are expected to earn at least $5,000 during the current year. These requirements can be reduced or eliminated if the employer waives them. The maximum employee contribution for 2006 is $10,000 for participants under the age of fifty and $12,500 for participants aged fifty or older. The employer is required to match up to 3 percent of the employee compensation. Vesting for the employer contributions is 100 percent and immediate.

Money-Purchase Plans

This type of defined contribution plan has a fixed funding requirement, such as 10 percent of compensation of all eligible participants. It also requires that participants be offered a qualified joint and survivor annuity as a form of benefit distribution. It has the same tax deduction and annual addition limits that apply to profit-sharing plans. Most new plan sponsors choose the profit-sharing plan instead. Many money-purchase plans have been converted to profit-sharing plans.

Employee Stock Ownership Plans

In an ESOP plan, the majority of the assets are shares of stock in the corporate plan sponsor. Generally, ESOPs are not useful for owners of small businesses.

Hybrid Plans

The target-benefit plan is receiving renewed interest as a result of changes in income tax law. This hybrid plan combines the contribution and benefit levels of a defined contribution plan with the recognition for mature employees found in defined benefit plans. Another hybrid, the age-weighted profit-sharing plan (AWPSP), is also available. As with the target-benefit plan, the contributions are weighted or skewed toward senior employees.

Designing and Documenting a Plan

The creation of a qualified plan requires the creation and adoption of a written plan document and trust agreement before the end of the first plan year. A summary plan description must also be drafted to inform participants about the plan. Documentation is available in two forms—prototype documents and individually drafted documents. Each form has its own advantages and limitations. It is, therefore, essential to work with an experienced professional when selecting and establishing a plan.

Employer-Sponsored Plans

Many qualified plans of small businesses are top heavy. This is a special status that results from key employees having more than 60 percent of the plan's benefits. As a result, minimum contribution rules and faster vesting rules apply. The minimum contribution is the lesser of 3 percent of compensation or the highest rate allocated to a key employee. The vesting schedule options are a three-year cliff of a graded schedule of 20 percent per year from the second to the sixth year of employment.

Plans may be combined or stacked in order to more specifically meet the needs of the business. However, this creates a need for separate sets of rules and limitations. Stacking also increases the amount of administrative paperwork and forms, thus driving up the cost of operating and maintaining the plan. Fortunately, the need to stack plans was significantly reduced in 2002 when the deduction limit of profit-sharing plans was raised from 15 percent to 25 percent.

The design features outlined below can be used to limit or reduce the cost of rank-and-file employees in the employer-sponsored plan.

Vesting

A key element of any qualified plan is rewarding long-term service by employees. One method used to limit benefits for employees who have been employed for a relatively short period of time is by a vesting schedule that forfeits all or some of the participant's employer-provided benefits. Vesting means having rights in, which is to say that the employee has the right to all or part of their benefits in the retirement plan.

Currently, there are two primary vesting schedule formulas.

1. Five-year cliff vesting. This schedule does not allow vesting for employees with less than five years of service. Upon

completion of five years of service, the employee is 100 percent vested in all employer-provided benefits. When the plan is top-heavy, the longest permitted cliff vesting schedule is three years.

2. Three-to-seven-year graded vesting. This vesting schedule provides for 20 percent vesting after three years of employment and an additional 20 percent for each subsequent year. After completing seven years of employment, the employee is eligible to receive 100 percent of the employer-provided benefits upon termination of employment. When the plan is top-heavy, the graded schedule must start with the second year of employment rather than the third year.

Minimum Hours

The plan sponsor may limit the participation of employees by permanently excluding those who work fewer than one thousand hours per year and then by limiting each year's contributions to those who have worked at least five hundred hours during the year. This feature is very important for businesses that use temporary employees.

Minimum Age

The plan sponsor may also limit participation of employees through the use of a minimum-age requirement. Current law allows an employer to postpone participation by employees under twenty-one years of age. At the time the employee reaches age twenty-one, they enter the plan and all of their years of employment are counted in the vesting formula.

Unions

Employees that are a part of a collective bargaining unit may be specifically excluded from participation in a qualified plan established by an employer for its nonunion employees, provided that retirement benefits were the subject of good-faith bargaining. (A more extensive discussion of unions is found in Chapter 4 and of collective bargaining agreements in Chapter 5.)

Integration with Social Security

This feature allows the plan sponsor to recognize contributions made on behalf of the employee to Social Security. An integrated plan (also referred to as allowing permitted disparity) has an extra contribution for those whose compensation is greater than the Social Security wage base.

Investments in a Qualified Plan

The primary governing law regarding investments made by a qualified plan comes from the Employee Retirement Income Security Act (ERISA). Under its Prudent Expert Investment Principle, investments should be made with primary consideration given to what an expert, rather than an amateur investor, would do.

There is a plethora of investment opportunities, including stocks, bonds, money market accounts, real estate, and partnership interests. Therefore, it is essential that you confer with a registered investment advisor or certified financial planner to structure your plan investments based on the plan's goals, the economy, and other relevant factors.

HEALTH-CARE PLANS AND THE AFFORDABLE CARE ACT

Another extraordinarily important fringe benefit for employees is a medical plan. These plans can provide employees with the ability to obtain medical assistance for themselves or their families. Employees should determine which plan best serves their needs and those of their families. There are a host of different types of employment medical plans, as described below.

Health Maintenance Organizations (HMOs)

HMOs have a network of doctors, hospitals, and other health-care providers, who have agreed to accept payment at lower than market level to keep costs down for its members. Examples of HMOs are Cigna, Humana, and Kaiser Permanente.

Preferred Provider Organization (PPO)

A PPO is a medical care organization in which medical professionals and facilities provide services to insured individual at a lower cost. These professionals are known as preferred providers. This allows members of PPOs more flexibility in choosing their medical professionals. Examples of PPOs are Blue Cross Blue Shield, Aetna, and United Healthcare.

Health Savings Accounts (HSA)

These plans are used in conjunction with insurance policies that have high deductibles. These accounts have a tax advantage because they are not subject to federal income tax at the time of contribution. If the funds are not spent during the annual term, then those funds can be rolled over into the following year and used in that year. These funds can be used to pay for qualified medical expenses such as dental, vision, and chiropractic care. HSAs allow for insurance premiums to be lower by raising the deductible but still allow employees to seek care without overly worrying about the associated costs. These plans follow the employee; that is when an employee changes jobs, the plan permits the employee to take those benefits to the new job.

Health-care Reimbursement Arrangements (HRA)

An HRA is a benefit in which the employer can reimburse an employee's out-of-pocket medical expenses up to a specified amount. These arrangements cannot be transferred after the employment relationship has ended. Starting in 2020, employers may offer an HRA in lieu of an insurance policy so that employees may purchase, with pretax dollars, their own individual health insurance. Employers that continue to offer traditional group health insurance can offer excepted benefit HRAs to reimburse employees up to $1,800 per year.

Consolidated Omnibus Budget Reconciliation Act (COBRA)

COBRA is a law that requires employer with more than twenty employees to provide employees with the opportunity to continue medical benefits after the employment terminates for a limited period. The employee must pay for these benefits, though it is common for employees to negotiate payment by the employer as part of a severance package.

Because the items discussed in this chapter vary from state to state and from employer to employer, it is essential for both employers and employees to work with experienced insurance agents so that the best arrangement can be adopted. Whether you are an employee or an employer, it is important for you to have the best benefits package available for your needs.

TIME OFF

Another benefit that is typically available is time off. This would include both paid and unpaid time off. The time off could be for specified holidays, sick days, special celebrations such as birthdays, vacation, family leave, and any other specified occasions for employees to have time off. The employee handbook discussed in Chapter 6 and the employment contract discussed in Chapter 3 should identify this benefit, spell out in detail the amount of time off available, whether it is paid, and when employees are entitled to enjoy this benefit.

Some of these items—for example, sick leave—are regulated by both state and federal law. The Family Medical Leave Act (FMLA) deals with serious medical issues and, as of the date of this writing, nine states and the District of Columbia provide for paid sick leave. Those states are Arizona, California, Connecticut, Maryland, Massachusetts, New Jersey, Oregon, Rhode Island, Vermont, and Washington. Because laws frequently change, it is important for you to determine what the rules are in your state.

Another important category is maternity and paternity leave, which may be available for new mothers and new fathers. In some situations, it also available for individuals who adopt children. FMLA provides for twelve weeks of leave, though it is unpaid. Some businesses may provide more by either paying for some or all of the time and some go so far as too extend the period. The employment handbook discussed in Chapter 6 and the employment contract discussed in Chapter 3 should address this benefit.

As of the date of this writing, five states and the District of Columbia require paid maternity and paternity leave. These states are California, New Jersey, New York, Rhode Island, and Washington. The US Congress has been considering legislation on this subject for some time. Because this is a very dynamic area, you should consult with an experienced attorney in order to determine whether your benefits comply with the law and are up to date.

CHAPTER 18

Finding a Lawyer and an Accountant

Most individuals and businesses expect to seek the advice of a lawyer only occasionally, for counseling on important matters such as the decision to incorporate or the purchase of a building. If this is your concept of the attorney's role in your business, you need to reevaluate it. Most small businesses would operate more efficiently and more profitably in the long run if they had a relationship with a business attorney more like that between a family doctor and patient. An ongoing relationship that allows the attorney to get to know the business well enough to engage in preventive legal counseling and to assist in planning makes it possible to solve many problems before they occur.

If your business is small or undercapitalized, you are doubtless anxious to keep operating costs down. You probably do not relish the idea of paying an attorney to get to know your business if you are not involved in an immediate crisis. However, it is a good bet that a visit with a competent business lawyer right now will result in the raising of issues vital to the future of your business. There is good reason why larger, successful businesses employ one or more attorneys full-time as in-house counsel. Ready access to legal advice is something you should not deny your business at any time, for any reason.

An attorney experienced in business law can give you important information regarding the risks unique to your business. Furthermore, a lawyer can advise you regarding your rights and obligations in your relationship with present and future employees, the rules that apply in your state regarding the hiring and firing of employees, permissible collection practices, and so forth. Ignorance of these issues and violation of the rules can result in financially devastating lawsuits and even criminal penalties. Because each state has its own laws covering certain business practices, state laws must be consulted on many areas covered in this book. A competent local business attorney is, therefore, your best source of information on many issues that will arise in the running of your business. Many law firms have attorneys who are licensed in several jurisdictions, and others have relationships with attorneys in other locales.

IN PLAIN ENGLISH

Most legal problems cost more to solve or defend after they arise than it would have cost to prevent their occurrence in the first place. Litigation is notoriously inefficient and expensive. You do not want to sue or to be sued, if you can help it.

Employees who work in union shops generally have access to union attorneys to assist them. If an employee does not work in a union shop it is still a good idea to consider enlisting the aid of an attorney to review employment contracts, assist with estate plans such as drafting wills, trusts, and incorporating employment benefits into those plans, and to be available for other legal problems as they arise.

FINDING A LAWYER

If you do not know any attorneys, ask other businesspeople if they know any good ones. You want either a lawyer who specializes in business or a general practitioner who has many satisfied business clients. Finding the lawyer who is right for you may require that you shop around a bit. Most local and state bar associations have referral services. A good tip is to find out who is in the business law section of the state or local bar association or who has served on special bar committees dealing with law reform. It may also be useful to find out if any articles covering the area of law with which you are concerned have been published in either scholarly journals or continuing-legal-education publications and if the author is available to assist you.

It is a good idea to hire a specialist, or a law firm with a number of specialists, rather than a general practitioner. While it is true that you may pay more per hour for the expert, you will not have to pay for the attorney's learning time. Experience is valuable. In this regard, you may wish to keep in mind that it is uncommon for a lawyer to specialize in business practice and also handle criminal matters. Thus, if you are faced with a criminal prosecution for the death of an employee, then you should be searching for an experienced criminal defense lawyer.

EVALUATING A LAWYER

One method by which you can attempt to evaluate an attorney in regard to representing business clients is by consulting the *Martindale-Hubbell Law Directory* in your local county law library or online at www.martindale.com. While this may be useful, the mere fact that an attorney's name does not appear in the book should not be given too much weight, because there is a significant charge for being included, and some lawyers may have chosen not to pay for the listing. You may also wish to search elsewhere online. Many law firms have established websites. The larger firms usually include extensive information about the firm, its practice areas, and its attorneys. You could also search Google, Yelp, and Avvo for attorney recommendations.

After you have obtained several recommendations for attorneys, it is appropriate for you to talk with them for a short period of time to determine whether you would be comfortable working with them. Do not be afraid to ask about their background, experience, and whether they feel they can help you.

USING A LAWYER

Once you have completed the interview process, select the person who appears to best satisfy your needs. One of the first items you should discuss with your lawyer is the fee structure. You are entitled to an estimate. However, unless you enter into an agreement to the contrary with the attorney, the estimate is just that. Business lawyers generally charge by the hour, though you may be quoted a flat rate for a specific service, such as incorporation or a simple will.

Contact your lawyer whenever you believe a legal question has arisen. Your attorney should aid you in identifying which questions require legal action or advice and which require business decisions. Generally, lawyers will deal only with legal issues, though they may help you to evaluate business problems.

Some attorneys encourage clients to feel comfortable calling at the office during the day or at home in the evening. Other lawyers, however, may resent having their personal time invaded. Some, in fact, do not list their home telephone numbers. You should learn your attorney's preference early on.

The attorney-client relationship is such that you should feel comfortable when confiding in your attorney. This person will not disclose your confidential communications; in fact, a violation of this rule, depending on the circumstances, can be considered an ethical breach that could subject the attorney to professional sanctions.

If you take the time to develop a good working relationship with your attorney, it may well prove to be one of your more valuable business assets.

FINDING AN ACCOUNTANT

In addition to an attorney, most small businesses and individuals will need the services of a competent accountant to aid with tax planning, the filing of periodic reports, and annual tax returns. Finding an accountant with whom you are compatible is similar to finding an attorney. You should ask around and learn which accountants are serving businesses similar to yours. State professional accounting associations may also provide a referral service or point you to a directory of accountants in your area. You should interview prospective accountants to determine whether you feel you can work with them and whether you feel their skills will be compatible with your needs.

Like your attorney, your accountant can provide valuable assistance in planning for the future. It is important to work with professionals you trust and with whom you are able to relate on a professional level.

For an online newsletter that covers many of the issues discussed in this book and updates that information on a regular basis, go to www.dubofflaw.com.

APPENDIX A

Laws Governing Non-compete Agreements by State

STATE	LAWS GOVERNING NON-COMPETE AGREEMENTS	EARLY DISCLOSURE REQUIREMENT
Alabama	Ala. Code §§ 8-1-190-197	No
Alaska	N/A	No
Arizona	ARS § 23–494	No
Arkansas	Ark. Code § 4-75-101	No
California	Cal. Code Ch. 1; 16600—16607	No
Colorado	Colo. Rev. Stat. § 8-2-113; SB18-082	No
Connecticut	Conn. Gen. Stat. § 31-50a; 31-50b; Conn. Public. Act. 351	No
Delaware	6 Del. Code § 2707	No
District of Columbia	D.C. Code § 32–572	No
Florida	Fla. Stat. Ann. §§ 542.335	No
Georgia	Ga. Code §13-8-53	No
Hawaii	Haw. Rev. Stat. § 480–4 (c); §607–14.9	No
Idaho	Idaho Code §§ 44-2701-2704	No

STATE	LAWS GOVERNING NON-COMPETE AGREEMENTS	EARLY DISCLOSURE REQUIREMENT
Illinois	820 ILCS 90; 820 ILCS 17/10; 30 ILCS 500/50–25	No
Indiana	N/A	No
Iowa	N/A	No
Kansas	N/A	No
Kentucky	N/A	No
Louisiana	La. Rev. Stat. Ann. §§ 23:921; La. Rev. Statute 37:1448.1	No
Maine	Title 26, Ch. 7, Sec. 599(b)	No
Maryland	N/A	No
Massachusetts	Mass. Gen. Laws c. 149, § 24L; c.112 §12X; c. 112 §74D; c. 112 § 135c; c. 145 s. 186	Yes
Michigan	Mich. Comp. Laws § 445.774a	No
Minnesota	N/A	No
Mississippi	N/A	No
Missouri	Mo. Stat. Ann. § 431.202	No
Montana	Mont. Code Ann. § 28- 2–703	No
Nebraska	N/A	No
Nevada	Nev. Rev. Stat. § 613.195	No
New Hampshire	Sec. 275:70; Sec. 329:31-a	Yes
New Jersey	N/A	No
New Mexico	NM Stat § 24-1I-2 (2015)	No
New York	NY Labor Law §202-k	No
North Carolina	N.C. Gen. Stat. § 75–4	No
North Dakota	N.D. Cent. Code § 9-08-06	No
Ohio	N/A	No
Oklahoma	15 Okl. St. Ann. § 217–219	No
Oregon	Or. Rev. Stat. § 653.295	Yes
Pennsylvania	N/A	No
Rhode Island	R.I. Gen. Laws §5-37-33	No

STATE	LAWS GOVERNING NON-COMPETE AGREEMENTS	EARLY DISCLOSURE REQUIREMENT
South Carolina	N/A	No
South Dakota	S.D. Chapter 53-9-11	No
Tennessee	Tenn. Code Ann. § 63-1-148	No
Texas	Tex. Bus. & Com. Code §§ 15.50 to 15.52	No
Utah	Utah Code §34-51-101	No
Vermont	Ver. Title 26 Chapter 6	No
Virginia	N/A	No
Washington	Wash. Sec. 49.44.190	No
West Virginia	N/A	No
Wisconsin	Wis. Stat. Ann. § 103.465	No
Wyoming	N/A	No

APPENDIX B

Federal Employment Laws[1]

LAW	BRIEF DESCRIPTION	COVERED EMPLOYERS
Affordable Care Act (ACA)—Employer Shared Responsibility Rules	Requires employers to offer affordable, minimum value health coverage to their full-time employees (and dependent children) to avoid potential penalties.	Employers with 50 or more full-time employees, including full-time equivalent employees.
ACA—Break Time for Nursing Mothers	Requires employers to provide rest breaks and accommodations for employees who are nursing mothers to express breast milk. Virtually all employers are covered, regardless of size.	Employers with fewer than 50 employees may be exempt if they can demonstrate that compliance would impose an undue hardship.
Age Discrimination in Employment Act (ADEA)	Prohibits employers from discriminating against employees or applicants who are age 40 or older based on their age.	Private-sector employers with 20 or more employees and state and local governments.

1 "Which Federal Employment Laws Apply to My Company?" *Clark & Associates*, July 11, 2018, https://www.clarkandassoc.com/2018/07/11/which-federal-employment-laws-apply-to-my-company/.

LAW	BRIEF DESCRIPTION	COVERED EMPLOYERS
Americans with Disabilities Act (ADA)	Prohibits employers from discriminating against qualified individuals with disabilities in all employment practices, such as recruitment, compensation, hiring and firing, job assignments, training, leave and benefits.	All employers with 15 or more employees.
Consolidated Omnibus Budget Reconciliation Act (COBRA)	Requires employer-sponsored group health plans to offer continuation coverage to eligible employees and their dependents when coverage would otherwise be lost due to certain events (for example, a termination of employment).	Private-sector employers with 20 or more employees that sponsor group health plans. Most group health plans sponsored by state and local governments are also covered. Group health plans sponsored by churches are exempt.
Consumer Credit Protection Act (CCPA)	Protects employees from discharge because their wages have been garnished for any one debt and limits the amount of an employee's earnings that may be garnished in any one week.	All employers, regardless of size.
EEO-1 Report	The Employer Information Report EEO-1 (commonly known as the EEO-1 Report) requires employers to submit employment data categorized by race/ethnicity, gender and job category to the EEOC.	Private-sector employers with 100 or more employees. State and local governments, primary and secondary school systems, institutions of higher learning and tax-exempt private membership clubs other than labor organizations are exempt from this reporting requirement.

LAW	BRIEF DESCRIPTION	COVERED EMPLOYERS
Employee Polygraph Protection Act (EPPA)	Prohibits employers from using lie detector tests, either for pre-employment screening or during the course of employment, with certain exceptions.	All employers, regardless of size. Does NOT apply to federal, state, and local governments.
Employee Retirement Income Security Act (ERISA)	Sets minimum standards for employee benefit plans, including retirement plans, such as 401(k) plans, and welfare benefit plans, such as group health plans.	All private-sector employers, regardless of size, that maintain employee benefit plans. Government and church employers are exempt.
Equal Pay Act (EPA)	Employers must provide equal compensation to men and women who perform equal work within the same workplace.	Virtually all employers are covered, regardless of size.
Fair Credit Reporting Act (FCRA)	Establishes legal obligations of employers who use consumer reports (including	All employers, regardless of size.
Fair Labor Standards Act (FLSA)	Establishes minimum wage, overtime, recordkeeping, and child labor standards for employers.	Virtually all employers are covered, regardless of size.
Family and Medical Leave Act (FMLA)	Requires employers to provide eligible employees with unpaid, job-protected leave for specified family and medical reasons.	Private-sector employers with 50 or more employees, public agencies (for example, state and local governments), the federal government, and local educational agencies.
Genetic Information Nondiscrimination Act (GINA)	Prohibits employers from discriminating against employees or applicants based on their genetic information.	All employers with 15 or more employees.

LAW	BRIEF DESCRIPTION	COVERED EMPLOYERS
Immigration Reform and Control Act (IRCA)	Employers are prohibited from hiring and retaining employees who are not authorized to work in the United States. Employers and employees must complete the Form I-9 (Employment Eligibility Verification Form).	All employers, regardless of size.
Jury System Improvements Act	Prohibits employers from discharging or taking certain other actions against an employee summoned to serve as a juror in federal court.	All employers, regardless of size.
Occupational Safety and Health Act (OSH Act)	Requires employers to provide a safe workplace for their employees. Coverage is provided through either the federal Occupational Health and Safety Administration (OSHA) or by an OSHA-approved state job safety and health plan.	Virtually all private-sector employers, regardless of size. Workers at state and local government agencies are NOT covered by federal OSHA but are protected under the OSH Act if they work in states that have OSHA-approved state programs.
Pregnancy Discrimination Act (PDA)	Prohibits workplace discrimination based on pregnancy, childbirth. or related medical conditions.	All employers with 15 or more employees.
Title VII of the Civil Rights Act	Prohibits employers from discriminating in the workplace based on race, color, religion, sex, or national origin.	All employers with 15 or more employees.

LAW	BRIEF DESCRIPTION	COVERED EMPLOYERS
Uniformed Services Employment and Reemployment Rights Act (USERRA)	Prohibits employers from discriminating against individuals on the basis of membership in the uniformed services with regard to any aspect of employment.	All employers, regardless of size.
Worker Adjustment and Retraining Notification (WARN) Act	Employers are required to provide a 60-day advance notice to employees of imminent covered plant closings and covered mass layoffs.	Private-sector employers with 100 or more employees. Regular federal, state, and local government entities that provide public services are NOT covered.

APPENDIX C

Employment At-Will Exceptions by State

STATE	PUBLIC POLICY	IMPLIED CONTRACT	COVENANT OF GOOD FAITH AND FAIR DEALING
Alabama	No	Yes	Yes
Alaska	Yes	Yes	Yes
Arizona	Yes	Yes	Yes
Arkansas	Yes	Yes	No
California	Yes	Yes	Yes
Colorado	Yes	Yes	No
Connecticut	Yes	Yes	No
Delaware	Yes	No	Yes
District of Columbia	Yes	Yes	No
Florida	No	No	No
Georgia	No	No	No
Hawaii	Yes	Yes	No
Idaho	Yes	Yes	Yes
Illinois	Yes	Yes	No
Indiana	Yes	No	No
Iowa	Yes	Yes	No
Kansas	Yes	Yes	No
Kentucky	Yes	Yes	No
Louisiana	No	No	No

STATE	PUBLIC POLICY	IMPLIED CONTRACT	COVENANT OF GOOD FAITH AND FAIR DEALING
Maine	Yes	Yes	No
Maryland	Yes	Yes	No
Massachusetts	Yes	No	Yes
Michigan	Yes	Yes	No
Minnesota	Yes	Yes	No
Mississippi	Yes	Yes	No
Missouri	Yes	No	No
Montana	Yes	No	Yes
Nebraska	No	Yes	Yes
Nevada	Yes	Yes	No
New Hampshire	Yes	Yes	No
New Jersey	Yes	Yes	No
New Mexico	Yes	Yes	No
New York	No	Yes	No
North Carolina	Yes	No	No
North Dakota	Yes	Yes	No
Ohio	Yes	Yes	No
Oklahoma	Yes	Yes	No
Oregon	Yes	Yes	No
Pennsylvania	Yes	No	No
Rhode Island	No	No	No
South Carolina	Yes	Yes	No
South Dakota	Yes	Yes	No
Tennessee	Yes	Yes	No
Texas	Yes	No	No
Utah	Yes	Yes	Yes
Vermont	Yes	Yes	No
Virginia	Yes	No	No
Washington	Yes	Yes	No
West Virginia	Yes	Yes	No
Wisconsin	Yes	Yes	No
Wyoming	Yes	Yes	Yes
TOTAL "YES"	**43**	**37**	**11**

All 50 of the United States and Washington, D.C., are at-will employment states. However, some states have exceptions.

Public Policy Exception: This exemption operates on the ideal that an employer should not fire an employee if it would violate the public policy doctrine of the state or a state or federal statute. As such, termination in such a situation would be improper. An example of this would be retaliation by an employer against an employee who performs an action that complies with public policy or, alternatively, an employee who refuses to perform an act that would be a violation of public policy. It should be noted that this is one of the more widely applied exceptions.

Implied Contract Exception: This exception applies in states where employers have employees sign at-will employment contracts, but include in the contract or other employee material (such as in the employee handbook) the statement that employment will only be terminated for "just cause" or other similar language. The effect of this "just cause" language is to create an implied contract such that an employee can't be fired when an implied contract is formed between the employee and the employer. This exception is typically difficult to prove, and the burden lies on the individual whose employment was terminated. A total of 36 states plus Washington, D.C., have implied contract exceptions.

Covenant of Good Faith Exception: The covenant of good faith exception is one of the broadest exceptions in the protections it offers. The exception essentially requires that employers only terminate employees for just cause, even if the employee handbook or employment contracts say nothing about that requirement or contain no such language. It is the narrowest exception, but it is the broadest in its application within the states that do recognize it.

APPENDIX D

Sample Mediation and Arbitration Clause

SAMPLE ARBITRATION AND MEDIATION CONTRACT CLAUSE

ARBITRATION RULES AND PROCEDURES

Article 1. Individuals Covered

This contract applies, as of the Effective Date provided in Article 4, to the following individuals, provided that they are not covered by a collective bargaining agreement with Employer:

a. Newly Hired Associates
b. All Store Associates hired by Employer with a first day of employment on or after January 1, 2019.

All Associates are automatically covered by all 4 steps of the program by taking or continuing a job with Employer. That means that all Associates agree, as a condition of employment, to arbitrate any and all disputes, including statutory and other claims, not resolved at Step 3.

However, arbitration is a voluntary condition of employment. Associates are given the option of excluding themselves from Step 4 arbitration within a prescribed time frame. Issues at Step 4 are decided by a professional from the American Arbitration Association in an arbitration process, rather than in a court process. Arbitration thus replaces any right you might have to go to court and try your claims before a jury. You are covered by Step 4 unless and until you exercise the option to exclude yourself from arbitration. Whether you choose to remain covered by arbitration or to exclude yourself has no negative effect on your employment.

Any Associate who experiences a break in service with Employer of sixty (60) days or less, remains covered by arbitration, unless the Associate previously requested to be excluded during the prescribed time period. If the Associate becomes re-employed with the Employer following a break in service greater than sixty (60) days, the Associate is treated as a new hire and is given the opportunity to elect to be excluded from arbitration during the prescribed time period.

Article 2. Claims Subject to or Excluded from Arbitration

Except as otherwise limited, all employment-related legal disputes, controversies, or claims arising out of, or relating to, employment or cessation of employment, whether arising under federal, state, or local decisional or statutory law ("Employment-Related Claims"), shall be settled exclusively by final and binding arbitration. Arbitration is administered by the American Arbitration Association ("AAA") under these Early Dispute Resolution Rules and Procedures and the employment arbitration portion of the AAA's Employment Arbitration Rules and Mediation Procedures. Arbitration is held before a neutral, third-party Arbitrator. The Arbitrator is selected in accordance with these Early Dispute Resolution Rules and Procedures. If there are any differences between the Early Dispute Resolution Rules and Procedures and the employment arbitration portion of the AAA's Employment Arbitration Rules and Mediation Procedures, the Early Dispute Resolution Rules and Procedures shall apply.

Arbitration shall apply to any and all such disputes, controversies, or claims whether asserted by the Associate against the Employer and/or against any employee, officer, director, or alleged agent of the Company. Arbitration shall also apply to any and all such civil disputes, controversies, or claims asserted by the Employer against the Associate.

All unasserted employment-related claims as of January 1, 2021 arising under federal, state, or local statutory or common law shall be subject to arbitration. Merely by way of example, Employment-Related Claims include, but are not limited to, claims arising under the Age Discrimination in Employment Act (ADEA), Title VII of the Civil Rights Act of 1964, the Americans with Disabilities Act (ADA), the Family and Medical Leave Act (FMLA), the Fair Labor Standards Act (FLSA), 42 U.S.C. § 1981, including amendments to all the foregoing statutes, the Employee Polygraph Protection Act, state discrimination statutes, state statutes, and/or common law regulating employment termination, misappropriation, breach of the duty of loyalty, the law of contract or the law of tort; including, but not limited to, claims for malicious prosecution, wrongful discharge, wrongful arrest/wrongful imprisonment, intentional/negligent infliction of emotional distress, or defamation.

Claims by Associates that are required to be processed under a different procedure pursuant to the terms of an employee pension plan or employee benefit plan shall not be subject to arbitration under Step 4. Claims by Associates for state employment insurance (e.g., unemployment compensation, workers' compensation, worker disability compensation) or under the National Labor Relations Act are also not subject to Arbitration under Step 4. Statutory or common-law claims made outside of the state employment insurance system alleging that the Company retaliated or discriminated against an Associate for filing a state employment insurance claim, however, shall be subject to arbitration.

Nothing in these Early Dispute Resolution Rules and Procedures prohibits an Associate from filing, at any time, a charge or complaint with a government agency such as the EEOC. However, upon receipt of a right to sue letter or similar administrative determination, the Associate's claim becomes subject to arbitration as defined herein.

Article 3. Dismissal/Stay of Court Proceeding

By agreeing to arbitration, the Associate and the Employer agree to resolve through arbitration all claims described in or contemplated by Article 2 above. This means that neither the Associate nor the Employer can file a civil lawsuit in court against the other party relating to such claims.

If a party files a lawsuit in court to resolve claims subject to arbitration, both agree that the court shall dismiss the lawsuit and require the claim to be resolved through the arbitration proceedings.

If a party files a lawsuit in court involving claims that are, and other claims that are not, subject to arbitration under Step 4, such party shall request the court to stay litigation of the nonarbitrable claims and require that arbitration take place with respect to those claims subject to arbitration, assuming the earlier steps have been exhausted. The Arbitrator's decision on the arbitrable claims, including any determinations as to disputed factual or legal issues, shall be entitled to full force and effect in any later court lawsuit on any nonarbitrable claims.

Article 4. Effective Date

As to any Individuals Covered (as defined in Article 1), the program is effective January 1, 2021.

Article 5. Time Limit to Initiate Arbitration

Arbitration must be initiated in accordance with the time limits contained in the applicable law's statute of limitations. The period of time elapsed during which the Associate pursued his or her claims under Steps 1–3 of this Program is added on to the applicable limitations period.

Article 6. Commencement of Arbitration

To initiate arbitration, the Associate or Employer must give written notice to the other party and/or person who is alleged to be liable in the dispute ("Claimant"). Notice to the Employer must be given to the Human Relations Department.

Notice to the Associate must be given by mailing to the Associate's last known home address.

The notice shall include a statement of the nature of the claim together with a brief description of the relevant facts, the remedies including any amount of damages being sought, and the address which the Claimant will use for the purpose of the arbitration.

Within thirty (30) days after notice of a dispute is given, the other party shall give its response ("Respondent"). The response shall state all available defenses, a brief description of relevant facts and any related counterclaims then known.

Within thirty (30) days after such counterclaims are given, the Claimant shall give Respondent a brief statement of the claimant's defenses to and relevant facts relating to the counterclaims.

Claims and counterclaims may be amended before selection of the arbitrator and thereafter with the arbitrator's consent. Notices of defenses or replies to amended claims or counterclaims shall be delivered to the other party within the thirty (30) days after the amendment.

Article 7. Selection of an Arbitrator

Both the Employer and the Associate shall participate equally in the selection of an Arbitrator to decide the arbitration. After receiving and/or filing an Arbitration Request Form, the Human Relations Department Manager shall ask the American Arbitration Association to provide the Company and the Associate a panel of seven (7) neutral arbitrators with experience deciding employment disputes.

The Employer and the Associate then shall have the opportunity to review the background of the arbitrators by examining the materials provided by the American Arbitration Association. Within seven (7) calendar days after the panel composition is received, the Associate and the Employer shall take turns striking unacceptable arbitrators from the panel until only one remains. The Associate and the Employer will inform the American Arbitration Association of the remaining arbitrator who will decide the dispute. However, if both parties agree that the remaining arbitrator is unacceptable, a second panel will be requested from the American Arbitration Association and the selection process will begin again. If both parties agree no one on the second panel is acceptable, either party may request the American Arbitration Association to simply appoint an Arbitrator who was not on either panel.

Article 8. Time and Place of Arbitration

The arbitration hearing shall be held at a location within fifty (50) miles of the Employer, unless the parties agree otherwise. The Parties and the Arbitrator shall make every effort to see that the arbitration is completed, and a decision rendered, as soon as possible. There shall be no extensions of time or delays of an arbitration hearing except in cases where both Parties consent to the extension or delay, or where the Arbitrator finds such a delay or extension necessary to resolve a discovery dispute or other matter relevant to the arbitration.

Article 9. Right to Representation

Both the Associate and the Employer shall have the right to be represented by an attorney. If the Associate elects not to be represented by an attorney during the arbitration proceedings, the Employer will not have an attorney present during the arbitration proceedings.

Article 10. Discovery

1. **Initial Disclosure**

   Within fourteen (14) calendar days following the appointment of an Arbitrator, the Parties shall provide each other with copies of all documents upon which they rely in support of their claims or defenses. However, the parties need not provide privileged documents that are protected from disclosure because they involve attorney-client, doctor-patient, or other legally privileged or protected communications or materials. Throughout the discovery phase, each party shall provide the other party with any and all such documents relevant to any claim or defense.

Upon written request, the Associate shall be entitled to a copy of all documents (except privileged documents as described above) in the Associate's "PERSONNEL FILE."

2. **Other Discovery**

   a. **Interrogatories/Document Requests**

      Each party may propound one (1) set of twenty (20) interrogatories (including subparts) to the other party. Interrogatories are written questions asked by one party to the other; the recipient must answer under oath. Such interrogatories may include a request for all documents upon which the responding party relies in support of its answers to the interrogatories. Answers to interrogatories must be served within twenty-one (21) calendar days of receipt of the interrogatories.

b. **Depositions**

A deposition is a statement under oath that is given by one party in response to specific questions from the other party. It is usually recorded or transcribed by a court reporter. Each party shall be entitled to take the deposition of up to three (3) relevant individuals of the party's choosing. The party taking the deposition shall be responsible for all associated costs, such as the cost of a court reporter and the cost of a transcript.

c. **Additional Discovery**

Upon the request of any party and a showing of appropriate justification, the Arbitrator may permit additional relevant discovery, if the Arbitrator finds that such additional discovery is not overly burdensome, and will not unduly delay the conclusion of the arbitration.

3. **Discovery Disputes**

The Arbitrator shall decide all disputes related to discovery. Such decisions shall be final and binding on the parties. In ruling on discovery disputes, the Arbitrator need not follow but may consult the discovery rules contained in the Federal Rules of Civil Procedure.

4. **Time for Completion of Discovery**

All discovery must be completed within ninety (90) calendar days after the selection of the Arbitrator, except for good cause shown as determined by the Arbitrator. In order to expedite the arbitration, the parties may initiate discovery prior to the appointment of the Arbitrator.

Article 11. Hearing Procedure

1. **Witnesses**

Witnesses shall testify under oath, and the Arbitrator shall afford each party a sufficient opportunity to examine its own witnesses and cross-examine witnesses of the other party. Either party may issue subpoenas compelling the attendance of any other person necessary for the issuing party to prove its case.

a. **Subpoenas**

A subpoena is a command to an individual to appear at a certain place and time and give testimony. A subpoena also may require that the individual bring documents when they give testimony. To the extent authorized by law, the Arbitrator shall have the authority to enforce and/or cancel such subpoenas. Subpoenas must be issued no less than ten (10) calendar days before the beginning of an arbitration hearing or deposition.

The party issuing the subpoena shall be responsible for the fees and expenses associated with the issuance and enforcement of the subpoena, and with the attendance of the subpoenaed witness at the arbitration hearing.

b. **Sequestration**

The Arbitrator shall ensure that all witnesses who testify at the arbitration are not influenced by the testimony of other witnesses. Accordingly, unless the Arbitrator finds cause to proceed in a different fashion, the Arbitrator shall sequester all witnesses who will testify at the arbitration; however, the Arbitrator shall permit the Associate involved in the arbitration and the Employer's designated representative to remain throughout the arbitration, even though they may or may not testify at the hearing.

2. **Evidence**

The parties may offer evidence that is relevant and material to the dispute and shall produce any and all non-privileged evidence that the Arbitrator deems necessary to a determination of the dispute. The Arbitrator need not specifically follow the Federal Rules of Evidence, although they may be consulted to resolve questions regarding the admissibility of particular matters.

3. **Burden of Proof**

Unless the applicable law provides otherwise, the party requesting arbitration or the party filing a counterclaim has the burden of proving a claim or claims by a preponderance of the evidence. To prevail, the party bringing the arbitration must prove that the other's conduct was a violation of applicable law.

4. **Briefing**

Each party shall have the opportunity to submit one (1) dispositive motion, one (1) pre-hearing brief, and one (1) post-hearing brief, which is a written statement of facts and law, in support of its position. Submission of such briefs is not required; however, briefs shall be typed and shall be limited in length to twenty (20) double-spaced pages.

5. **Transcription**

The parties may arrange for transcription of the arbitration by a certified reporter. The party requesting transcription shall pay for the cost of transcription.

6. **Consolidation**

a. **Claims**

The Arbitrator shall have the power to hear as many claims as a Claimant may have consistent with Article 2 of these Early Dispute Resolution Rules and Procedures.

The Arbitrator may hear additional claims that were not mentioned in the Arbitration Request Form. To add claims, the Claimant must notify the other party at least thirty (30) calendar days prior to a scheduled arbitration. The additional claims must be timely, under the applicable law, as of the date on which they are added. The other party must not be prejudiced in its defense by such addition.

b. Parties

The Arbitrator shall not consolidate claims of different Associates into one (1) proceeding. Nor shall the Arbitrator have the power to hear an arbitration as a class or collective action. (A class or collective action involves representative members of a large group, who claim to share a common interest, seeking relief on behalf of the group.)

7. Confidentiality

All aspects of an arbitration pursuant to these Early Dispute Resolution Rules and Procedures, including the hearing and recording of the proceeding, shall be confidential and shall not be open to the public. The only exceptions are: (i) to the extent both parties agree otherwise in writing; (ii) as may be appropriate in any subsequent proceeding between the parties; or (iii) as may otherwise be appropriate in response to a governmental agency, legal process, or as required by law.

All settlement negotiations, mediations, and any results shall be confidential.

Article 12. Substantive Choice of Law

The Arbitrator shall apply the substantive law, including the conflicts of law, of the state in which the Associate is or was employed. For claims or defenses arising under or governed by federal law, the Arbitrator shall follow the substantive law as set forth by the United States Supreme Court. If there is no controlling United States Supreme Court authority, the Arbitrator shall follow the substantive law that would be applied by the United States Court of Appeals and the United States District Court for the District in which the Associate is or was employed.

Article 13. Arbitrator Authority

The Arbitrator shall conduct the arbitration. The arbitrator shall have the authority to render a decision in accordance with these Early Dispute Resolution Rules and Procedures, and in a manner designed to promote rapid and fair resolution of disputes.

The Arbitrator's authority shall be limited to deciding the case submitted by the party bringing the arbitration. Therefore, no decision by any Arbitrator shall serve as precedent in other arbitrations.

The arbitration procedure contained herein does not alter the Associate's employment status. The status remains alterable at the discretion of the Employer and/or terminable at any time, at the will of either the Associate or the Employer, with or without cause or prior notice. Accordingly, the Arbitrator shall have no authority to alter the Associate's employment status by, for example, requiring that the Employer have "cause" to discipline or discharge an Associate. Nor may the arbitrator otherwise change the terms and conditions of employment of an Associate unless required by federal, state, or local law, or as a remedy for a violation of applicable law by the Employer with respect to the Associate.

The Arbitrator shall have the power to award sanctions against a party for such party's failure to comply with these Early Dispute Resolution Rules and Procedures or with an order of the Arbitrator. These sanctions may include assessment of costs or prohibitions of evidence. If justified by a party's wanton or willful disregard of these Early Dispute Resolution Rules and Procedures, the Arbitrator may award the sanction of an adverse ruling in the arbitration against the party who has failed to comply.

Article 14. Award

Within thirty (30) calendar days after the later of the close of the hearing or the receipt of post-hearing briefs, if any, the Arbitrator shall mail to the parties a written decision. The decision shall specify appropriate remedies, if any, if a violation of law is found. If the Associate's claim arises under federal or state statutory law, the award should include findings of fact and conclusions of law; otherwise, the inclusion of such findings and conclusion is at the Arbitrator's discretion. The parties to an arbitration shall be provided with a copy of the Arbitrator's award.

Article 15. Fees and Expenses

1. Costs Other Than Attorney Fees

i. Definitions

Costs of an arbitration include the daily or hourly fees and expenses (including travel) of the Arbitrator who decides the case, filing or administrative fees charged by the AAA, the cost of a reporter who transcribes the proceeding, and expenses of renting a room in which the arbitration is held. Incidental costs include such items as photocopying or the costs of producing witnesses or proof.

ii. Filing Fee/Costs of Arbitration

An Associate initiating arbitration shall pay the cost of arbitration up to a maximum of the least of one (1) day's base pay or One Hundred Twenty-Five Dollars ($125), whichever is less. Upon filing the request for arbitration, the Associate shall remit such fee. The Employer shall pay the remainder of the costs of the arbitration. The Employer shall pay the entire filing fee should it initiate arbitration. Except as provided below, each party shall pay its own incidental costs, including attorneys' fees.

The AAA has developed guidelines for waiving administrative fees. This Plan is subject to those guidelines.

2. Reimbursement for Legal Fees or Costs

The program does not infringe on either party's right to consult with an attorney at any time. In fact, the Employer will reimburse an Associate for this legal consultation and/or representation during Step 4 of the program, at a maximum benefit of Two Thousand Dollars ($2,000) per Associate in a rolling twelve (12) month period. If the Associate is not represented by counsel, the Gallery will reimburse an Associate for incidental costs up to a maximum of Two Hundred Fifty Dollars ($250) per Associate in a rolling twelve (12) month period. The Associate will not be entitled to such reimbursement by the Employer if the Arbitrator determines the arbitration claim by the Associate was frivolously filed. Any reimbursement to the Associate will occur following the conclusion of the proceedings upon submission of the Associate's bills for costs of legal services or incidental costs.

3. **Shifting of Costs**
   If the Associate prevails in arbitration, whether or not monetary damages or remedies are awarded, the filing fee shall be refunded to the Associate. The Arbitrator may (based on the facts and circumstances) also require that the Employer pay the Associate's share of the costs of arbitration and incidental costs.

Article 16. Remedies and Damages

Upon a finding that a party has sustained its burden of persuasion in establishing a violation of applicable law, the Arbitrator shall have the same power and authority as would a judge to grant any relief, including costs and attorneys' fees, that a court could grant, in conformance with applicable principles of common, decisional, and statutory law in the relevant jurisdiction.

Article 17. Settlement

The parties may settle their dispute at any time without involvement of the Arbitrator.

Article 18. Enforceability

The arbitration agreement, the arbitration proceedings, and any award rendered pursuant to them shall be interpreted under, enforceable in accordance with, and subject to the Federal Arbitration Act, 9 U.S.C. § 1, et seq. regardless of the state in which the arbitration is held or the substantive law applied in the arbitration. If for any reason the Federal Arbitration Act is inapplicable to enforce this agreement, the Parties agree it will be enforced under the governing state arbitration statute(s).

Article 19. Appeal Rights

The decision rendered by the Arbitrator shall be final and binding as to both the Associate and the Employer. Either party may appeal the Arbitrator's decision to a court in accordance with the provisions of the Federal Arbitration Act, 9 U.S.C. § 1, et seq.

Article 20. Severability/Conflict with Law

In the event that any of these Early Dispute Resolution Rules and Procedures are held to be unlawful or unenforceable, the conflicting rule or procedure shall be modified automatically to comply with applicable law.

In the event of an automatic modification with respect to a particular rule or procedure, the remainder of these rules and procedures shall not be affected. An automatic modification of one of these rules or procedures shall apply only in regard to the particular jurisdiction and dispute in which the rule or procedure was determined to be in conflict with applicable law. In all other jurisdictions and disputes, these Early Dispute Resolution Rules and Procedures shall apply in full force and effect.

Article 21. Cancellation or Modification of Dispute Resolution Rules and Procedures or Program

The Gallery may alter these Early Dispute Resolution Rules and Procedures or cancel the program in its entirety upon giving thirty (30) days' written notice to Associates. If such notice is not provided to an Associate, the Early Dispute Resolution Rules and Procedures that covered the Associate prior to the modification or cancellation shall govern.

Glossary

A

Acceptance is a term used in contract law to describe an element of a contract, which occurs after an offer has been made. See *contract, offer.*

Accountant is a trained professional who provides accounting services such as setting up and maintaining a company's books and tax preparation. See *certified public accountant.*

Action, sometimes referred to as "cause of action," is the legal claim or right that one has against another. It is frequently written in the form of a legal document known as a complaint, which is filed in court and used to begin a lawsuit.

Addendum is a document attached at the end of another document and is customarily intended to supplement the terms of the document to which it is attached. See *contract.*

Administrator is the person or organization named by the court to represent a probated estate when there is no will or the will did not name an executor. A female administrator may be called an administratrix. Also called a *personal representative.*

Agency is the relationship between one person, known as the *principal*, and another, known as the *agent*. Customarily, the agent works for or on behalf of the principal and is subject to the principal's control or right of control. Typically, the agent owes a duty to the principal. See also *principal.*

Agreement is an arrangement, written or oral, whereby two or more parties reach an understanding. When conforming to the requirements of contract law, it is known as a *contract*. If one or more of the requirements for a legal contract are missing, the agreement may be subject to certain legal defenses and, thus, not enforceable. See also *contract.*

Amendment is the term used to when an agreement is modified, as when a contract is changed. See also *contract.*

Americans with Disabilities Act of 1990 (ADA) is a federal statute enacted by Congress for the purpose of providing individuals with defined disabilities the opportunity to obtain fair treatment in employment, housing, transportation, and the like. The courts have been wrestling with the definition of "disability" for purposes of interpreting the statute and with the amount of "reasonable accommodation" required to be provided under the act.

Antidilution is a term used in trademark law to describe one of the forms of protection available to trademark owners under the law. It prohibits another from weakening, tarnishing, disparaging, or otherwise undermining the strength and credibility of the protected trademark. See also *trademark.*

Apparent Authority is a legal term used to define the authority an agent appears to have when dealing with third persons. This is intended to protect the third person's reasonable expectations when dealing with the agent and is available for third-person protection even when contrary to the express instructions of the principal. See also *agency, principal.*

"Articles of Incorporation" is a legal document filed with the state in which a company desires to do business as a corporation and is the "charter" or creating instrument for the corporation. It defines the authority granted by the state for the company to be conducted in the corporate form and is analogous to a constitution. All business corporations are created under the law of the state in which they are incorporated and may do business in other states by filing the appropriate document(s) in those states as a "foreign" (corporation chartered in another state) corporation doing business in that state. The only entities incorporated under federal law are federally chartered banks and certain federal mandated organizations, such as the Smithsonian Institution and the Postal Service. See also *articles of organization, bylaws, corporation, partnership.*

"Articles of Organization" is a legal document filed with the state in which a business desires to do business as a limited liability company (LLC) and is the "charter" or creating instrument for the LLC. It defines the authority granted by the state for the company to be conducted as an LLC and is analogous to a constitution. All LLCs are created under the law of the state in which they are created and may do business in other states by filing the appropriate document(s) in those states as a "foreign" (LLC chartered in another state) LLC doing business in that state. See also *articles of incorporation*, *bylaws*, *limited liability company*, *partnership*.

Authority is the power granted by law or by a principal to a person to perform a prescribed act or combination of acts. The act or combination of acts, when performed, will be legally binding. See also *agency*, *attorney-in-fact*, *principal*.

B

Bankruptcy is the legal term defining the consequences of insolvency. In other words, when liabilities are greater than assets or when bills cannot be paid in the ordinary course of one's business, one is technically insolvent or bankrupt. Laws have been enacted that provide relief for those who are insolvent, as well as for their creditors. See also *Chapter 7*, *Chapter 11*, *Chapter 13*, *receiver*, *trustee*.

Board of Directors is the governing board of a business entity charged by statute with responsibility for administering the business and affairs of that entity. It is frequently used in the context of corporate boards of directors, though it can refer to the administrative board of other types of entities, such as nonprofit corporations, limited liability companies, or the like. See also *corporation*, *limited liability company*, *partnership*.

"Branding" is the term used to describe the identification and reputation of a product or service. This modern concept has been used by businesses to describe the process of identifying the qualities, unique characteristics, reputation, market awareness, and the like of specific products or services. One of the most famous "brands" in the world today is Coca-Cola.

Business Plan is a document used to describe the process of developing a new or existing business.

Buy-Sell Agreement is a document customarily used by business organizations for the purpose of establishing a formal arrangement whereby the ownership interest in the business may be sold or transferred only in accordance with the terms of the agreement. These agreements typically impose restrictions on sale or transfer to "outsiders" and establish methods for valuing the interest when the owner desires to transfer the interest, dies, or becomes incapacitated. These agreements are frequently used in closely held businesses, as distinguished from those that are publicly traded.

Bylaws are formal documents adopted by corporations for administering the internal affairs of the company. They typically cover the rules and regulations for calling meetings, defining key positions, and the like. Bylaws may not be broader in scope than the company's articles of incorporation. Articles of incorporation are analogous to a constitution and define the boundaries of a company's power and authority. The bylaws are analogous to laws and statutes and are the rules and regulations for implementing the powers and authority. Bylaws are not filed with any governmental agency but are kept in the corporation's minute book. See *articles of incorporation*, *corporation*.

C

Certified Public Accountant (CPA) is a professional who has passed the examinations required by the appropriate state agency to provide kinds of accounting services. These services include, for example, setting up and maintaining a company's books and tax preparation. One of the services unique to CPAs is providing audited financial statements. See *accountant*, *audit*.

Closely Held Business is a business owned by a small number of people or other business, rather than one that is publicly held or traded on the stock markets. It is frequently a business arrangement between one or more family groups or groups of friends, though the term could describe a larger group of owners, so long as the group is small enough to avoid the necessity of complying with the technical requirements set forth in the state and federal securities laws for publicly held businesses. See also *corporation*, *limited liability company*, *partnership*.

Common Law is the legal system based on English common law and follows past practice or legal precedent, known as *stare decisis*. In this process, rules established in court cases become binding and are followed until modified, extended, or reversed. This should be distinguished from civil law, which is based upon the Napoleonic Code and is limited to statutory pronouncements. See *civil law.*

Common Stock is the form of stock issued by a corporation that has unrestricted voting rights, dividend rights, and ownership in the corporation. It is the kind of stock every corporation must have, and is distinguished from "preferred stock," which must, by definition, must have some form of "preference" in either dividends, or distribution on dissolution, or both. See also *preferred stock.*

Confirming Memorandum is a written document sent by one party to another for the purpose of confirming the terms of an oral arrangement.

Consideration is a contract element, which requires the giving or receiving of something of value by one party in exchange for something of comparable value from the other party. Consideration can be in the form of money, property, services, or an agreement to refrain from some action. Historically, consideration did not have to be comparable, as when "token" consideration was used for transactions, such as the classic use of "a single peppercorn." Today, the law tends to require the parties to give or receive things of comparable potential value in order for the "consideration" to be deemed valid.

Contract is a legal concept whereby one offers consideration to another in exchange for the other's providing comparable consideration. To be legally valid, all contracts require an offer, acceptance, and consideration. They may be oral or written. The are other legal requirements for certain types of contract; for example, contracts for the sale of real property (land) and contracts for personal property worth $500 or more must be in writing. See *acceptance, consideration, offer.*

Copyright is the right whereby any original work of "authorship" that is put in a tangible form is protected by law. In the United States, the copyright laws have been enacted pursuant to the enabling provision set forth in Article I of the United States Constitution. The most recent copyright statute was enacted in 1976 and became effective January 1, 1978. This law continues to evolve and has been amended a number of times. It is known as "the Copyright Revision Act of 1976, as amended." There are numerous treaties throughout the world dealing with copyright on a multinational level.

Corporate Shield and **Corporate Veil** are the terms used to define the limited liability available for those who conduct business through corporate or other business entities. It is said that shareholders in corporations and owners of limited liability companies are "shielded" by the limitation of liability available to them when they properly conduct business through these entities. Creditors cannot "pierce the corporate veil" or "penetrate the corporate shield" without establishing a valid legal reason to do so, and the reasons available are very limited.

Corporate Trustee is an institution, generally a bank or trust company, that specializes in managing trusts.

D

Damages is the compensation sought or awarded for legal injury sustained.

Defined Benefit Plan is a retirement plan that pays a specific amount after the employee retires. This payment stream is used to determine the method and amount necessary to fund the plan. See also *defined contribution plan.*

Defined Contribution Plan is a retirement plan that establishes the amount to be paid into the plan, and the benefits then flow from the preretirement contribution. See also *defined benefit plan.*

Discharge is the legal concept whereby a debtor in bankruptcy is permitted to extinguish all pre-bankruptcy debts when the legal requirements of the bankruptcy law are followed. See *bankruptcy, creditor, debtor.*

E

Electronic Signature is the electronic communication adopted by a party for purposes of taking advantage of the E-Sign statute and consummating contracts through "e-commerce." See *e-commerce, Electronic Signature in Global and National Commerce Act (E-Sign).*

Electronic Signature in Global and National Commerce Act (E-Sign) is a federal statute that prescribes a method whereby an "electronic signature" may be used for purposes of validating contracts in cyberspace, which contracts are binding in the same manner as they would be if entered into through traditional means.

Employee Stock Option Plan (ESOP) is a plan established by a business entity using the company's stock for purposes of funding an employee retirement plan.

F

Federal Trade Commission (FTC) is the federal agency charged by Congress with responsibility for policing interstate commerce and trade within the United States and at its borders. It has also assumed responsibility for policing activities on the World Wide Web when those activities affect commerce in the United States.

Franchising is a process whereby a successful business pattern is licensed by the originator (franchisor) so that a licensee (franchisee) can create comparable businesses. In order for a franchising arrangement to be legal, the franchisor must comply with federal and state requirements and provide potential franchisees with the disclosures, known as a franchising disclosure document, required by those laws. Classic examples of successful franchises include McDonald's, Burger King, KFC, and other purveyors of fine foods.

I

Implied Contract is a contract created by the law for the purpose of preventing injustice. It is a contract that the parties may or may not have expressly agreed to. For example, when a merchant sells a product without an appropriate disclaimer, the law implies a contract whereby the purchaser may expect the product to be "merchantable," even though merchantability was never specifically bargained for. See also *contract*.

Independent Contractor is a person who engages in their own independent business and provides goods or services to another. An independent contractor must be distinguished from an employee, who is employed by another for purpose of providing goods or services. The legal distinction between these two categories is that an employer has the right of control over the conduct of an employee's activities, whereas the employer does not have a right of control over the conduct of an independent contractor's activities; rather, the employer contracts for the results. For example, an in-house bookkeeper who provides bookkeeping services for only the employer and is subject to the employer's direction and control is an employee, whereas a bookkeeper who provides similar services for several businesses and is not subject to the employer's control is likely an independent contractor.

Individual Retirement Account (IRA) is a form of pension account created by Congress for individuals.

Intellectual Property is the body of law that deals with "products of the mind." It includes patent law, copyright law, trademark law, trade secret law, and other forms of protection for creative works. See *copyright, patent, trade dress, trade secret, trademark*; see also Chapter 10.

K

Key-Person Insurance is a type of insurance procured on the life of a person key to a business. It is typically obtained by the business entity to compensate it for the loss it will sustain when the key person dies.

L

License is a permitted use. In business, licensing is typically used to permit one to use the intellectual property of another. For example, a copyright owner may license the use of a copyright. Licensing may also refer to other permitted uses; for example, states issue driver's licenses and municipalities issue business licenses.

Limited Liability Company (LLC) is a business form that allows those who conduct business through it to enjoy the benefits of limited personal liability while electing the method by which the entity is to be treated for tax purposes.

It was created to overcome the restrictions imposed on small businesses that could qualify for so-called "S-corporation" status.

Limited Liability Partnership (LLP) is similar to a limited liability company except that it was created for the purpose of allowing partners in partnerships to have a personal liability shield similar to those who conduct business through corporations.

Limited Partner is a person or entity who owns an interest in a limited partnership but who is a passive investor and who enjoys limited liability.

Limited Partnership is a partnership having one or more general partners with full personal liability and one or more limited partners who may enjoy limited liability but may not play an active role in conducting the business of the limited partnership. It is created by statute and the partnership must comply with the limited partnership statute of the jurisdiction in which it is created.

Liquidation is the process of converting assets to cash and distributing the cash. It should be distinguished from "dissolution," which refers merely to the legal relationship between those who are conducting the business. For example, when a general partner in a general partnership dies, there is a dissolution by virtue of the death of a partner. The remaining partners may, if their agreement permits, continue the partnership or, if the agreement does not or they do not wish to, they may then liquidate the partnership by converting its assets to cash and properly distributing the cash.

Litigation is the term used to describe filing and prosecuting a lawsuit.

M

Magnuson-Moss Warranty Act is a federal statute that imposes requirements for warranties when products are sold in interstate commerce.

Merger and Acquisition are the terms used to define corporate and other business entity arrangements whereby two or more entities are formally combined, or one entity is acquired by another. A merger is a situation where two or more business entities are combined together and the combined entity emerges as a single entity. Acquisitions are when one business entity acquires another business entity or only the assets of another entity. Both mergers and acquisitions are regulated by statute. That is, the business organization statutes regulate the process and the federal, as well as state, securities laws also impose requirements on entities covered by them.

Minutes. State statutes governing corporations, LLCs, and other business entities typically require those entities to have annual meetings and permit those entities to have periodic meetings. Written records of these meetings are known as "minutes" and are customarily kept in the organization's "minute book."

Multilevel Marketing (MLM) is a form of doing business whereby a product or service is distributed through a multitiered structure. The structure is referred to as a "down line" and, customarily, each person in the line receives some compensation for "down line" sales. It is referred to "multilevel marketing," because" since each person is able to both sell product or service and enlist "down line" distributors, who can establish their own sales and distribution networks as well. The consumer who pays for the product or service is actually providing a revenue stream that flows up through all distribution levels. Classic examples of successful multilevel marketing are Amway and Mary Kay Cosmetics.

O

Offer is an element of contract whereby one party, known as the "offeror," presents an opportunity, known as the "offer," to another party, known as the "offeree." If the offer is accepted, a contract is made. See *contract*, *counteroffer*.

Operating Agreement is the document that defines the internal workings of a limited liability company. By statute, the agreement can be extremely flexible, and the law provides the parties creating the agreement the ability to determine whether the organization will be run by its owners, a panel of owners, or a single manager, and whether the organization will be taxed as an "entity" or not. In fact, the law makes it clear that the drafters have extraordinary flexibility in creating the organizational arrangement they desire, so long as the limited legal requirements of the law are adhered to. This document is not filed with any governmental agency, but is kept in the organization's minute book.

P

Partner. See *limited partnership.*

Partnership. See *limited partnership.*

Partnership Agreement is the agreement between two or more persons who desire to conduct business in a partnership form. A partnership agreement can be expressed, when the parties work out the arrangements between themselves; implied, when they merely conduct their business as a partnership; oral or written. When the parties do not work out the details of a formal partnership agreement, the law imposes certain terms on the relationship.

Patent or **Letters Patent** is legal document issued by the government to those who comply with the strict and technical requirements of the patent law. It is a form of intellectual property.

Pension Plan is a plan adopted for the purpose of providing a pension for individuals who retire so they can augment the Social Security payments obtained from the government.

Per Stirpes is a way of distributing an estate so that all of the surviving descendants will receive only what their immediate ancestor would have received if that person had been living at the time of death.

Principal is the term used to define the person on whose behalf an agent acts and who controls or has the right to control the conduct of the agent. This term also refers, in a financial context, to the amount upon which interest is calculated. It may also be used to describe the job held by a school administrator.

Product Liability is the legal doctrine that applies to situations where a defective product results in injury to person or property. The defect can be a design defect or a manufacturing defect.

Profit-Sharing Plans are plans whereby business owners agree to share business profits with participants in the plan. These plans are very technical and require specialists to assist in their formation and administration.

R

Reorganization is the process whereby a business may be restructured for the purpose of satisfying its creditors when it is unable to pay them in the regular course of business. Reorganizations can involve use of the business entity's stock or ownership interest as vehicles for payment. Non-insolvency reorganizations can occur when businesses are restructured for the purpose of accomplishing other goals; for example, a business may reorganize in order to change its business form, add or delete new product lines, or the like.

S

S-Corporations are corporations that comply with the requirements set forth in the Internal Revenue Code and elect to be treated, for tax purposes, as if they were still run as sole proprietorships or partnerships.

Simplified Employee Pension Plan (SEPP) is a type of pension plan permitted by statute for employees.

Sole Proprietorship is the term used to define a business owned by a single individual.

Statute of Frauds is a law that was first enacted in England for the purpose of preventing fraud and perjury. It recognized the fact that certain transactions are so touched with the public interest that they should not be permitted enforcement over the objection of a party unless they were evidenced by a writing signed by that party, though parties could voluntarily perform the transactions if they wished. Because the English feudal system was a governmental process based on landownership, one of the first transactions covered by the law was real estate transfers. The law was later extended to cover transactions in goods in excess of a certain value. The law also prohibited oral wills, because it would be too easy for unscrupulous individuals to misstate the wishes of a dead person. These laws have been refined and adopted in the United States.

Stock refers to the ownership interest in a corporation and, traditionally, was evidenced by a stock or share certificate. The stock can be common or preferred. In addition, both common and preferred stock may be issued in different "classes," typically identified by alphabetical designations.

Stock or **Share Certificate** is the document used to evidence stock ownership in a corporation. Historically, it was a steel-engraved form, though some companies created unique and distinctive versions of their certificates. For example, Playboy Enterprises used stock certificates with "Playmates" depicted on them. Today, many stock transactions are electronic, and no physical certificates are issued.

Stock Option is a method by which an individual or business may acquire the right to obtain corporate stock at a defined price for a limited period. Options themselves are tradable and, in fact, there is an option exchange. Those who deal in options are said to "trade on equity," because their exchanges are for the appreciation in the value of the underlying stock, rather than trading in the stock itself.

T

Tax is the term used to define a government's right to extract payment from its citizens. In the United States, the federal income tax was initially declared unconstitutional, as "confiscatory," and voided. Unfortunately for the taxpayer, the Constitution was amended to permit an income tax.

Trade Dress is a form of intellectual property law that was initially developed through cases for the purpose of protecting the unique and nonfunctional characteristics of product packaging. It was later extended, by case law, to cover everything from product design to the "look and feel" of businesses. It has even been used to protect the distinctive characteristics or "look and feel" of an artist's distinctive style.

Trademark is any words, phrases, name, symbol, logo, or combination of them, when used to identify a product or service. When used in connection with services, they are referred to as *service marks*.

U

Uniform Commercial Code (UCC) is a body of commercial law, adopted in every state of the United States, though its periodic modifications may not have been universally accepted.

V

Vesting is the process whereby an individual's interest in a retirement or pension plan is secured. For example, many pension plans provide that plan participants are "vested" 20 percent per year for five years; thus, an employee who leaves the company after three years will be 60 percent vested and entitled to receive only 60 percent of the amount that would otherwise have been available to a fully vested participant.

W

Winding Up is the process whereby a business completes its activities and prepares to end its operations. This can be a technical dissolution and liquidation.

About the Authors

Leonard D. DuBoff is an internationally recognized expert who has lectured on legal issues throughout the world. He began his legal career in New York, then relocated to Palo Alto, California, where he started teaching at the Stanford Law School. Subsequently, he moved to Portland, Oregon, where he taught law at Lewis & Clark Law School. DuBoff spent almost a quarter of a century teaching business law, including employment and intellectual property law.

While a full-time law professor, DuBoff was also Of Counsel to law firms and maintained that relationship until 1994 when he left full-time teaching to found his own law firm that specializes in business, employment, and intellectual property law. DuBoff has received academic awards from President Lyndon Johnson and New York Governor Nelson Rockefeller, and, in 1990, he received the Governor's Arts Award from Oregon Governor Neil Goldschmidt.

In addition to practicing law, DuBoff has also been involved in its creation. In the late 1980s, he testified in support of the Visual Artists Rights Act of 1990 and assisted in drafting that law at the request of Senator Edward Kennedy of Massachusetts. He has also provided Congress with testimony related to several cultural and intellectual property treaties and has worked with state legislatures on their legislation as well.

A prolific author, DuBoff has written numerous articles for scholarly journals, practical articles for lawyers' bar publications, and articles for nonlawyers as well. He has regular columns in several publications. He is coauthor of the law school text *Cases and Materials on Art Law.* He has also written more than 30 other books including: *in Plain English)® for Writers, The Law (in Plain English)® for Publishers, The Law (in Plain English)® for Photographers, ® for Nonprofit Organizations, The Law (in Plain English)® for Collectors, The Law (in Plain English)® for Galleries*, and *Estate Planning (in Plain English).*

DuBoff continues to serve as an educator by presenting continuing legal education programs for attorneys and seminars for nonlawyers. He has lectured all over the world including a recent keynote speech in Beijing, China.

Christopher Perea graduated from Cornell University, where he majored in English Literature and History. He then became a substitute teacher in California and ultimately went to Willamette Law School. While attending law school he worked in both the Deschutes County General Counsel's office and the Marion County District Attorney's office. Chris has assisted his father, a prominent labor arbitrator, with employment arbitrations for a significant amount of time. He has firsthand knowledge of much of the material in this book. Chris is a coauthor of *The Law (in Plain English)® for Galleries* and now this book, *Employment Law (in Plain English)®*. In addition, Chris is a practicing attorney with the DuBoff Law Group P.C., where he handles cases of all kinds including many related to employment law.

Kenneth A. Perea served as an Intelligence Officer in the US Army from 1973–1974, following graduation from the University of San Francisco School of Law and admission to the State Bar of California. After active duty, Ken began practicing law in San Diego as in-house counsel for a large public entity, which included serving as management counsel in a number of labor-management disputes with its employees. Wishing to concentrate his practice to labor-management matters, Ken became in-house counsel for the largest public-sector labor organization in the State of California, headquartered in Sacramento, where he handled labor-management matters on behalf of public-sector workers.

In 1977, following creation of the California Public Employment Relations Board (PERB) with expansive jurisdiction over labor-management matters throughout the public sector, Ken began serving as an Administrative Law Judge (ALJ) in its Los Angeles offices. In his role as an ALJ, he focused on issuing orders concerning establishment of appropriate bargaining units, the conduct of representation elections and adjudication of the entire span of unfair labor practice cases from bad-faith bargaining to retaliation for the exercise of protected activities. While still serving as an ALJ, Ken was accepted as one of only twenty apprentices into the Labor Arbitrator Development Program at UCLA's Institute of Industrial Relations, sponsored by the American Arbitration Association, Federal Mediation and Conciliation Service, and the Los Angeles and Beverly Hills Bar Associations. After successful completion of the Program in 1980, Ken briefly heard cases part-time as a mutually selected Impartial Arbitrator in both the public and private sectors.

In 1981, Ken left PERB, returned to San Diego, and began service as a full-time Impartial Arbitrator of traditional labor-management disputes throughout Southern California. As binding arbitration gained acceptance for the resolution of employment law disputes generally, Ken, through the American Arbitration Association, expanded his arbitration practice to include cases involving the rights of employees not represented by labor organizations such as corporate officers, managers, and other non-represented workers.

In 1986, Ken was admitted to the National Academy of Arbitrators, where he was recently recognized as a thirty-year member. Ken has also served in various leadership capacities, including its Board of Governors, Membership Committee, and Committee on Professional Responsibility and Grievances.

During his over thirty-eight years' service as a full-time Impartial Arbitrator of labor management disputes, Ken has authored several thousand binding arbitration awards in every imaginable industry in America, including entertainment, professional sports, horse racing, manufacturing, shipping, telecommunications, trucking and storage, hotels and restaurants, and the US Postal Service. His awards have involved all levels of the public sector throughout the Western United States, including Hawaii, the Pacific Northwest, and Nevada. Ken is also a coauthor of *Absenteeism in the Workplace*, CCH and Chapter Editor of *Discipline and Discharge*, First Edition, BNA.

In his free time, Ken enjoys spending time with his family and friends, home gardening projects, collecting antique clocks, and fine wine tasting in California's Central Coast and Oregon's Willamette Valley.

Lauren Barnes is an attorney in Portland, Oregon, where her practice focuses on personal injury law. She graduated from Colorado State University in 2013 with a B.A. in International Studies and Political Science. Barnes graduated from Willamette University College of Law in 2017, where she was a Student Assistant for Legal Research and Writing, Vice President of the Moot Court Board, and an Executive Editor for the Willamette Journal of International Law and Dispute Resolution.

Index